# THE GLOBAL ECONOMIC CRISIS

# THE GLOBAL ECONOMIC CRISIS

## A CHRONOLOGY

Larry Allen

REAKTION BOOKS

*This book is dedicated to my teachers*

Published by Reaktion Books Ltd
33 Great Sutton Street
London EC1V 0DX, UK

www.reaktionbooks.co.uk

First published 2013

Printed and bound in Great Britain
by TJ International, Padstow, Cornwall

British Library Cataloguing in Publication Data
Allen, Larry, 1949–
The global economic crisis : a chronology.
1. Global Financial Crisis, 2008–2009. 2. Economic
history – 1990– 3. Comparative economics.
I. Title
330.9'0511-DC23

ISBN 978 1 78023 092 4

# Contents

# Preface

This book aims at a scholarly treatment of global economic history since 2000. It aspires to treat the subject at a level that holds the interest of other economists, but also at a level that is intelligible to general readers. It may be a bit early to undertake such a scholarly endeavor. Economic events arouse emotions. These emotions narrow our focus, choose facts for us, and pin down our thoughts to the pressing problems we face. A later time, after recently aroused emotions have died down, might furnish a better vantage point for a wholly dispassionate and disinterested treatment of the subject.

Therefore interpreting and analyzing recent economic events poses some risks, but it is not too early to advance some suggestive generalizations about the crisis. Events are still fresh in our minds and we can always keep in mind that in economics exceptions disturb every generalization. Besides, it is a study that could wait except the first decade of the new millennium is not just any decade, not in economics terms anyway. The most revealing economic events come about when economies are going through turning points, transitioning from expansion to contraction, or vice versa. Prosperous times are not that revealing to study because the economy is only going in one direction and that is up. Over a long time frame we expect the economy to continue growing, given growth in knowledge. That is not to say that prosperity does not have a way of moving around geographically. The first decade of the new millennium, however, is not a story of a steadily expanding economy that hit a few air pockets while climbing. On the contrary, it saw a major economic turning point on a whipsawing scale not seen since the 1930s.

Moreover the turning points involving a transition from expansion to contraction are by far the most fascinating and thought-stirring. The downturn is much sharper and quicker than the upturn that occurs when an economy transitions from contraction to expansion. The sharp downturn often wears the aspect of a 'crisis' whereas nothing so dramatic happens on the upside. These crises vary in intensity. The one that occurred in 2008 was unusually brutal. Not often in economies do crises on this historic scale play out. If we measure a crisis by the length and depth of its aftershock, then the crisis of 2008 belongs in a species of crisis that only happens once or twice in a century. At least that has been past experience.

Another reason for fast-forwarding the scholarly study of recent economic history has to do with the science of economics itself. Economics has assimilated a vast amount of empirical research and theoretical development since the last global meltdown of this magnitude occurred in the 1930s. The development of economic knowledge and theory has multiplied the angles from which a major economic event can be studied. It is almost as if accumulated knowledge in economics has been waiting for a crisis of this magnitude to pounce upon, dissect, and interpret using new knowledge and analysis learned since the last major crisis.

A last reason for rushing the scholarly study of recent economic history has to do with the methodology of economics as a science. Economics cannot conduct isolated laboratory experiments. The best that can be done is to pore over actual events as they unfold. An economist who wants to study major crises has to wait for one to happen. When one comes to pass, no one wants to wait any longer. It needs to be studied promptly while it is least likely that any data will be lost. This book takes up where my previous book, *The Global Economic System Since 1945* (2004), left off. That book took a broad sweep in which it was possible to explore how economic events shaped political developments. This book focuses on a crisis in which things happen too fast for the political system to react in a large way. It therefore focuses on the mechanics and logic behind the makings of the crisis.

# ONE

# Overview

## Speculation Trumps Globalization as Culprit

The central theme of this book revolves around how the growing strength of speculative forces deepened the global financial crisis that began unfolding toward the end of 2007. The theme embraces how widely a spirit of speculation and risk-taking spread into the nooks and crannies of the global economic and financial system. A global economic system developed in which family homes become instruments of speculation and worker retirement plans ride the tossing waves of financial markets where speculation runs hottest. The book leaves the reader to judge whether the passion for speculation reflects a distorted cultural development toward an incautious striving for quick wealth.

Growth in speculation on a global scale comes under fire partly because it is a byproduct of globalization proper. Yet very few of the criticisms lodged against globalization find space in this book. In a sense the growth of foreign trade aids and abets global speculation. It clears the path for investors in one country to undertake speculative activities in others. On the subject of foreign trade, however, the verdict of history seems unmistakable. Countries welcoming foreign trade have outlasted countries that shunned it. Chapter Ten on the weakening of the labor market in developed countries agrees that there has been weakening, but lays no guilt on foreign trade. In general this book brings no knowledge or insights to light suggesting the process of globalization should be reversed or slowed.

Even before the global financial crisis flared up, various critics and interested parties rained fire and brimstone upon globalization on several counts. Globalization hampered efforts to shield the environment and lift the living standards of workers. In developed countries cheap foreign imports seemingly turned domestic workers out of doors. Armies of protestors took to the streets when the World Trade Organization met.

It is worth noting that the wisest sages of the past who have drawn up plans for ideal and utopian societies have rarely put in a kind word for foreign trade. According to Plato (427?–347 BCE), "The sea [meaning foreign trade] fills a country with merchandise and money-making and bargaining; it breeds in men's minds habits of financial greed and faithlessness, alike in its internal and in its foreign relations."[1] Without Plato dropping this intriguing hint, who would have guessed that some of the economic problems of today can lay claim to a long history? In the same vein we would never have known of the fabled sunken continent of Atlantis if Plato had not brought it up in one of his dialogues.

A thinker much more modern in outlook, Sir Francis Bacon (1561–1626) resurrected Plato's myth of Atlantis to blueprint his own utopia in *The New Atlantis*. In Bacon's utopia the islanders consume what they produce and produce what they consume, but they also engage in a foreign trade of sorts. This utopian society sends out 'merchants of light' to live among the peoples of every quarter of the civilized globe. Their mission is to learn the languages, sciences, industries and literatures of other peoples and bring them home to Atlantis:

> But thus you see we maintain a trade, not for gold, silver, or jewels, nor for silks, nor for spices, nor for any other commodity or matter, but only for God's first creature, which was light; to have light, I say, of the growth of all parts of the world.[2]

Aside from the distant views of Plato and Bacon, among the wealthiest and supremely sophisticated economies today stands one that held out almost to the last against the allurements of foreign trade. Japan uncompromisingly shunned foreign trade until U.S. Commodore Perry in 1854 employed military menaces to secure Japan's signature on a trade treaty.

Nevertheless, the world historical process boasted a mind and impartial dialectic of its own. The world went in for foreign trade, and in countless ways the outcome deserved a standing ovation. The wonders of the world multiplied. Advances in communication and transportation seemingly gave the world no choice. Many of these advances originated in parts of the world heavily engaged in foreign trade, proclaiming these areas wellsprings of innovation.

Today we call the world economy a global economy because acceleration in goods and investment crossing borders has intricately woven various national economies into one global economy. Intercountry flows in goods, services and capital play a large part in what is now called globalization.

## Methods of Economic History

The center stage in this book is the global economy during the first decade of the twenty-first century. The book's approach can be viewed as a synthesis between a philosophy of history and an economy history. Philosophy of history is meant in the Hegelian sense; economic history is assumed to unfold according to a rational process, and is able to accommodate Francis Bacon's famous quote: "He that will not apply new remedies must expect new evils, for time is the greatest innovator."[3] It extends beyond mere economics in that it draws in the social and political corollaries of underlying economic events and developments. What people are saying and thinking becomes part of the record. Philosophy of history allows for the innovating and resourceful processes of growth while economic theory often simplifies economic behavior to a syllogism in logic.

It turns out that in the case of macroeconomics, reducing economic behavior to a principle in logic does go a long way toward explaining the courses of economic events. One vital principle of logic oozing from every page of this book is that what is true for the part is not necessarily true for the whole. One individual can choose to save more, spend less, and thus accumulate wealth at a faster rate. If everyone in society simultaneously embraces the same idea, and in chorus all slash individual spending at once, the economy is likely to nose over. Before it is over, society's accumulated savings go down rather than up. Again, one small government can close a budget deficit by raising taxes and slashing spending. However, all governments acting simultaneously to close budget deficits are unlikely to meet with success

As stated above, the main theme of the book is how growth in speculation set up the global economy for a big fall. The exact trigger of the financial crisis, this book argues, lies with the combined effects of speculation and the logical principle that what is true for the part is not necessarily true for the whole. Henry Simons was a depression-era economist who wrote widely on the subject of money. One similarity between the years leading up to the 1930s and those leading up to the global financial crisis of 2008 was a banking system that became more dependent upon short-term borrowing. In the 1960s Milton Friedman, later to become a recipient of the Nobel Prize for economics, wrote an article, "The Monetary Theory and Policy of Henry Simons." This article discusses Simons's theories and quotes widely from his works. According to Simons's argument shifts in confidence cause changes in the desire for liquidity (cash). In the following excerpts the phrases in quotes are Friedman quoting Simons. A combination of Simons's and Freidman's wording puts it succinctly:

> It[a change in desire for liquidity] reflected rather a change in "the speculative temper of the community." Such changes, he [Simons] argued produce changes in velocity that can develop into "catastrophic disturbances as soon as short-term borrowing develops on a large scale . . . Short-term obligations provide abundant money substitutes during booms, thus releasing money from cash reserves [that is raising velocity] . . . Widespread borrowing on short-term in order to finance long-term obligations is the key to instability because, in Simons' view, it makes the economy vulnerable to changes in confidence and hence to the desire for liquidity. *Each individual separately may be in a position to convert his assets into cash but the economy as a whole is not.*[4]

The last sentence sums up the problem. The nemesis of the macroeconomic system lies in the simple logical principle that what is true for the part is not necessarily true for the whole. There is not enough circulating cash for all short-term obligations to be converted into cash on a given day. One individual can convert assets into cash, but not all. If all individuals holding assets try on the same day to convert all assets into cash, they break the financial system. Short-term debt involves short-term commitments from the lenders. They can pull out quickly at any time. The economy builds in extra instability when higher long-term interest rates fail to lure lenders into longer-term debt. We will discover later how in the build-up to the crisis of 2008 banks became more dependent upon short-term borrowing and less dependent upon deposits. Banks established off-balance sheet, offshore, structured investment vehicles, virtual banks, in regulatory havens such as the Cayman Islands. These virtual banks borrowed short-term and lent long-term.

As the above quotes of Plato and Francis Bacon show, the words of the wisest sages do not always give the clearest signal of where the world is heading. Nevertheless these words provide a record of what some of the wisest individuals are thinking at a particular point in history. Who would say that a point in history can be thoroughly comprehended without taking into consideration what contemporary thinkers of this caliber were thinking? The same principle applies to an analysis of recent economic history. In the course of an unfolding economic debacle, the evolving economic expectations and interpretations become a proper unit of study themselves.

It may seem unfair to knowingly pluck a quote from the *Wall Street Journal* in which a leading policy-maker shares an interpretation of current events that subsequent history shreds into nonsense. Economic fluctuations have a way of wringing from the minds of the most rational and seasoned individuals sentences that voice thoughts bearing the stamp of immediate circumstances and events. These things are mostly transparent in hindsight. It is unfair to assume that other individuals would have uttered wiser thoughts. Economic events themselves can induce the thoughts of economists and policy-makers who are reacting to them.

More specifically this study assumes that the contemporary thoughts and interpretations are as much a product of a stream of natural causation as the actual economic events themselves. If the world economy goes ten years without a downturn, a few economists may declare the business cycle obsolete. After twenty years without a downturn most economists would leap to the conclusion that the business cycle is obsolete. After 75 years virtually all economists would share the same mind and likely cite innumerable compelling reasons for a vanishing business cycle. These seemingly airtight reasons, however, never carry the certainty of reasons in physics or astronomy. Unpredictable economic events bestow a new mind upon financial investors every day. To a lesser extent the same holds true for economists and policy-makers.

Parallel to the psychological history runs the material and physical history of economic activity. Booms and crashes come measured in statistics, such as house price inflation, oil price inflation, home foreclosure rates, unemployment rates, and so on. This is the area where this book brings forward specialized studies that throw light on the behavior of housing markets, labor markets, and commodity markets. In these areas the book does not originate new knowledge but weaves into one narrative the work of specialists across several fields.

## The Spur of Falling Interest Rates

This book zeroes in on the global economy during a time when it was far from displaying its sunniest side. It focuses on economic history and developments leading up to the global financial crisis that began in the latter part of 2007. It then traces an aftershock through sovereign debt crises that rocked the eurozone in 2011 and are still ruthlessly unfolding as this book goes to print.

Speculation owed two trends, one economic and one social and political, for its freshly won exalted place in the global economic system. Firstly, interest rates had been trending down for over two decades. This was the economic trend. Global economic growth brought in its wake a glut of savings, particularly given China's high savings rates. Falling interest rates forced asset managers and holders of financial capital to bear greater and greater risks to earn an accustomed or desired rate of return. Shouldering greater risks furnished one way of shoring up rates of return, keeping them from falling in the face of sinking interest rates. Secondly, hand in hand with growth of speculation and falling interest rates went an immoderate idealization of free markets. This was the social and political trend. If markets settled all issues most efficiently, then government policy was left with the very secondary and inert task of staying out of the way. Government regulators and even credit rating agencies could pay less attention to what was happening. Markets had everything under control and guaranteed every asset remained properly valued. Regulators and credit rating agencies contented themselves in the knowledge that the market was always right. Just as riskier investments met with warmer acceptance from banks and private investors, government oversight slackened its oversight guard. These two trends, falling interest rates and riskier investments on the one hand and slacker regulation on the other, made for highly incompatible trends. Regulation grew less vigilant just when riskier financial practices called for stronger vigilance.

The softening of regulation grows more critical amid the multiplying artificialities and complexities of novel financial instruments and strategies. The proliferation of these new financial instruments and speculative tools belongs with the other offspring of low interest rates. Even at very low interest rates some investors can capture above average rates of return if they possess information and techniques that outsmart those of average investors. Informed investors can still sweeten rates of return at the expense of uninformed investors. A race breaks out between the fast learners and the slow learners, and the fast learners are sponsoring the race. Geographically this means that some investors are constantly searching for hidden opportunities in some distant corner of the world. By getting there first, they stand to win handsome profits. These same inducements give rise to a widening and deepening range of synthetic and intricate financial instruments and investment strategies. They also discourage the engineering of newer and sharper regulatory tools to match newer financial instruments. On the contrary, outwitting regulation is part of the motivation for developing new financial instruments. It is another way of winning higher rates of return.

## The Balancing Wheels of Economic Policy Sit Neutralized

The book has a secondary theme that has to do with government efforts to stabilize and revitalize slumping economies. There are times when economic ailments readily and vigorously respond to policy initiatives aimed at kick-starting sputtering economies. As an example, take an economy where short-term interest rates stand around 4 percent and inflation registers in the 3 percent range. In these circumstances monetary officials have the option of pushing short-term interest rates well below the inflation rate, leaving inflation-adjusted interest rates negative. If inflation-adjusted interest rates sink deeply into negative territory, the economy will incontestably receive a boost from added borrowing. It just happens that this last crisis occurs at a time when interest rates and inflation sit fairly low. Maneuvering room to enliven the economy by slashing interest rates remains narrow.

The same low interest rates that disable monetary policy make it easier, less costly, for governments to run public deficits. These deficits can go to finance everything from economically strategic tax cuts to public works and economic development projects. Either incentive-improving tax cuts or a range of economic development projects, or even more generous social benefits, can prime the economic pump and jump-start a faltering economy, putting it on a sound path of protracted growth.

It came about, however, that in 2008 governments had long been indulging in sizeable government deficits. Japan, the second largest economy in the world when the crisis broke, had been wrestling with the aftershock of a pricked bubble for nearly two decades. It had piled up a mountain of public debt in the process. The u.s., the largest economy in the world, had been heaping up public debt since the dot-com bubble burst in 2000. The u.s. government finished 2007 in happier shape than Japan on this score, but it stood sufficiently deep in debt to inhibit the government's stimulus response. In some eurozone countries public debts reached lofty heights that rattled edgy government bond holders. Increasing deficits in these countries invited bond holders to push government bond interest rates above affordable levels. Countries that most needed deficit spending could least afford it. In a summarizing nutshell, the crisis hit at a time when government stabilization policies were least ready to act.

If an unwanted and damaging economic event was foreseen, but could not be averted, then it bore the mark of inevitability. It was likelier born of an irreversible and unstoppable inner economic logic. The global financial crisis and economic aftershock did not sneak up without policy-makers spotting dark clouds in the economic sky. Monetary authorities were looking ahead, and studying the global economy to divine where it was headed. In the early 2000s, monetary officials in the u.s. and Europe were very alive to the possibility of deflation. They caught its scent and regarded it as a rock of danger. Given the difficulties of forecasting the future, a forecast of deflation makes the cut as a sensible forecast of the kind of economic difficulties that lay ahead. Deflation puts debtors in a squeeze because falling prices depress incomes without reducing payments owed on debt. Monetary officials warn that the fallout from deflation included bank failures and high loan default rates. In many respects it remains a rare feat of forecasting.

The depth of the global economic recession showed that monetary authorities were right on target in suspecting the peril of deflation. Central banks succeeded in dodging the deflation bullet. If they erred it lay in assuming that if deflation could be sidestepped, the economic crisis could be sidestepped. The economy was spared deflation but it did not succeed in eluding the byproducts of deflation, the wave of bank failures and loan defaults. Without a doubt the global slump would have happened much sooner and ended much deeper if the deflation hazard had not been neutralized.

## A Kind Word for Regulation

This book takes the view that a large part of stability in any sphere of life has to do with planning ahead, which includes having regulations in place even when they appear unnecessary. Therefore, the reader should occasionally expect a kind word for economic regulation. No doubt the very word regulation carries an unholy ring in the ears of those whose hopes rest with today's world of free market global capitalism. This level of regulation will not involve anything as thorough and detailed as price floors and ceilings. It falls far short of the regimented planning that went on in communist countries such as the Soviet Union or even the less pervasive planning in Western European countries such as France.

Another side of planning ahead has to do with governments using information available about the future needs of the economy. Mainstream economists and monetary officials warned as much as four years in advance that deflation and all the ills it entails was becoming a reasonable scenario. No one in government, however, connected the dots: if the economy ran risks of exploding bank failures and defaults, regulatory strategies called for tightening, not loosening. Likewise, it was no secret that global economies had wandered into economic terrain where monetary and fiscal policies could not be counted on for economic stabilization in the way they had been in the past. Again it was not the time to be loosening the regulatory grip.

The book should persuade the reader that any type of economic policy and regulation must be global in scope. It must reflect a cooperative initiative of the world's governments. Globalization has undercut and diluted the national economic impact of individual policies originating from governments acting solo.

The last chapter of the book will discuss what the road back to prosperity will look like, whether it will be rocky or smooth, and how winding and hilly. One can always hope that a bursting financial bubble triggers a catharsis that opens paths for clearer and fresher thinking on economic issues and policies. The main themes of the last chapter are the roles booming commodity prices and high East Asian saving rates play in retarding a rapid rebound from economic depression.

## TWO

# Twilight of the Japanese Miracle

### The Making of the Japanese Miracle

The way Japan catapulted itself from feudalism to capitalism in the late nineteenth century caught the trained eye of one famous observer. In 1889 Japan adopted a new constitution patterned after that of Prussia. Professor Woodrow Wilson, later President of the U.S., observed:

> Her choice of it [the Prussian Constitution] as a model is but another proof of the singular sagacity, the singular power to see and learn, which is Japan's best constitution and promise of success.[1]

In the decades preceding the First World War, Japan intentionally studied Western institutions in various Western countries. It borrowed what it thought was best. In the 1880s the U.S. lived without a central bank. In 1881 Japan's minister of finance visited European countries and studied the operations of various central banking systems. He concluded that the National Bank of Belgium ran the most advanced central bank in operation. In 1882 Japan launched the Bank of Japan, patterned after the National Bank of Belgium. The U.S. shelved the establishment of a central bank until the Federal Reserve Act of 1913.

This country with "singular sagacity, the singular power to see and learn" would not always make the wisest choices. In the twentieth century it made adversaries of two countries destined to become dominant political powers of the twentieth century, Russia and the

U.S. These fateful choices might easily have entailed dire consequences had Russia and the U.S. remained allies after the Second
World War. Nevertheless Japan deserves no small credit for being
the first non-Western country to purposely remold and redirect its
economy into a developed capitalist system. As the two superpowers
concentrated on waging a subterranean war against each other, post-
war Japan pulled itself together and finished the twentieth century
with an advanced, high-tech economy second only to the U.S.

During the years immediately following the Second World War,
Japan's model of capitalism underwent further mutations. Occupation authorities sought to remake Japan's economy in the image of
the U.S. model of capitalism. Japan's constitution underwent major
revisions. Occupation authorities dissolved the zaibatsu, mammoth
financial combines that had emerged in nineteenth-century Japan,
lording over the advanced sectors of the Japanese economy. They
were Japan's version of the monopolizing trusts that the U.S. had
outlawed with the Sherman Antitrust Act of 1890. Japan's Anti-
Monopoly Act of 1947 aimed to ban monopolizing behavior.

Following the Second World War Japan gravitated toward the U.S.
model of laissez-faire capitalism. The philosophy of free markets did
not make itself felt in Japan's financial sector until the later 1970s and
'80s. During Japan's phase of miracle growth in the 1950s and '60s its
financial system lay thickly overgrown with government regulations.
It would be hard to argue that this highly regulated and protected
system did not work, given Japan's record of spectacular growth during the decades following the Second World War. A growing economy soon outgrows a constricting mesh of regulation. Japanese
financial reform invariably displaced regulatory determination with
free market outcomes.

One pivotal area of regulatory control has to do with capital flows.
When residents purchase foreign assets, capital flows out. When
foreigners purchase domestic assets, capital flows in. Japanese regulations severely restricted these types of transactions until the early
1970s. During the 1970s the Japanese government periodically eased
or tightened these regulations. In 1980 the Japanese government put
into force the Foreign Exchange and Foreign Trade Control Law. This
law permanently lifts bans on Japanese residents holding interest-

bearing foreign bank accounts in other currencies, or foreign residents holding yen bank accounts in Japan. This law also widens the rights of foreigners to own stakes in Japanese companies. Reporting requirements slightly subtract from the attractiveness of these transactions, but the trend moves toward fully unleashing cross-border financial flows.

The 1980 law left in place restrictions on institutional ownership of foreign assets, but over the decade these restrictions also evaporated from the scene. By the close of the 1980s Japanese life insurance companies held as much as 34 percent of portfolio investment in the form of foreign securities.[2] Regulations in the Netherlands and the UK placed no restrictions on life insurance companies in the area of foreign investment. Nevertheless, insurance companies in these two countries reported smaller percentages of foreign investment than the Japanese companies. In the U.S. regulations kept the foreign investment portion in the 3 percent to 6 percent range for life insurance companies.

Financial liberalization smoothed the path for multiplying the size and diversity of short-term money markets in Japan, making Japanese companies less dependent upon bank financing. Japan kept a close-knit web of interest rate controls that fixed not only interest rates but also slopes of yield curves. A yield curve charts the relationship between interest rate and time period of financial instruments. It makes easy a comparison between the interest rate on a 90-day government bond with the interest rate on a 30-year government bond. The Japanese government allowed new financial instruments paying unregulated and market-driven interest rates. November 1987 saw the first activity in a Japanese commercial paper market. Deregulation of interest rates raised the cost of funds to banks. Bank profitability suffered just as bank profitability in the U.S. suffered in the years preceding the subprime crisis of 2008.

Other reforms strengthened the deregulating trend.[3] In May 1982 the government gave Japanese banks permission to extend long-term yen loans to foreign borrowers. Starting in 1985 the withholding tax no longer applied to yen bonds sold in Europe to non-Japanese citizens. In 1987 Japanese banks, securities houses and insurance companies won permission to trade in the overseas financial futures markets. Short sales in bonds also became legal in 1987. The same year saw the Osaka Stock Exchange launch the Osaka Stock Futures 50, a composite of 50 stocks, marking the end of a ban on futures trading imposed in 1945. In 1988 the government enacted a futures law that permitted financial markets to open share-indexed futures markets. That same year Japanese banks won permission to securitize mortgages. In the U.S. securitization of mortgages set the stage for the U.S.'s subprime crisis of 2008. Japan's Tax Reform Act of 1988 largely scaled back a tax on stock and bond transactions. That high tax had acted against incentives for short-term trading. June 1989 saw the Tokyo International Financial Futures Exchange open for business. By October of that year the Tokyo, Osaka and Nagoya stock exchanges had opened trading in share price options.

From the beginning Japan clocked galloping growth rates. Its secret lay in combining its own strengths with what it selectively incorporated from the West. A literate, resourceful, and energetic population inhabited the feudal and traditional society that Commodore Perry had burst upon in 1853. The people of Japan stood more than competent and ready to quickly access and soak up the accumulated backlog of Western technologies, and welcome the stream of new technologies usable in their industries. Between 1885 and 1914 per capita output in Japan sprinted at a growth rate over twice that of the UK for the same time frame.[4] Like Britain, Japan launched industrialization with the production and export of textiles, but unlike Britain it added silk production to its list of export industries. Japan also resembled Britain in the large role shipbuilding played in its early phase of industrialization.

## The Tide at Full

It was only in the post-Second World War era that people began to talk of the "Japanese Miracle." Following the war the U.S. government provided aid to Japan for combating high unemployment, inflation and shortages. U.S. officials saw economic development and democracy as the best vaccination against communism and militarism. Then the Korean War broke out and U.S. military procurement spending ignited Japan's economic growth. The U.S. overrode British opposition to gain Japan's membership in GATT (General Agreement on Tariffs and Trade) as a temporary member. The end of the Korean War saw economic growth in Japan sputter a bit, but not for long. In 1957 Japan posted an annual output growth rate of 11.5 percent. Between 1960 and 1973, Japan posted output growth averaging a lively 9.8 percent annually, more than double the rate of most developed countries. Output growth slowed in some years, but for the years 1960 and 1961 output grew at annual rates above 15 percent. For the years 1967 and 1968 output grew at annual rates above 13 percent. Between 1973 and 1980, annual economic growth in Japan cooled to an average of 3.9 percent, still an enviable growth rate for that time frame. The u.s. reported an average of 2.1 percent growth for the same time frame. Nearly all countries saw much smaller growth rates between 1973 and 1980. Between 1980 and 1988 Japan's growth converged closer to the norm of other developed countries, averaging annual growth of 3.6 percent. The u.s. averaged growth of 3.3 percent for the same years.

The growth and success of Japanese corporations sent many Western corporations and management experts scurrying to find the secret recipe behind the Japanese Miracle. Instead of Japan digesting and applying Western methods and technology, American and European companies threw Japanese corporations under the microscope desperately looking for the holy grail of productivity. An influential book of the era was entitled *Theory Z: How American Business Can Meet the Japanese Challenge* (1981). The author, Dr William Ouchi, argued that Japan's secret lay not in advanced technology but in management style. He saw participatory management and consensus decision-making at center stage in Japan's management style. He also felt that corporate culture, long-range staff development and company philosophy shared in the singular success of Japanese corporations. Ouchi argued that a more effective management style led to less turnover, higher job commitment, and unmatched worker productivity.

Just as Western countries eagerly turned to Japan for ideas, events in the global economic system unfolded that would not be good news for the Japanese Miracle. In 1985 there was international concern that a strong dollar created strong headwinds for the ailing u.s.

economy, fueling a hefty excess of imports over exports. A strong dollar, making imports less costly, was seen as helpful in the early 1980s when the U.S. regarded inflation as public enemy number one. Once inflation subsided, the strong dollar became a major hurdle for the U.S. economy. At least that was the view in official circles. A depreciation of the dollar was aided with the help of an international agreement. On 22 September 1985 five governments agreed to jointly undertake a depreciation of the dollar against the Japanese yen and German Deutschmark. The five governments were France, West Germany, Japan, the United States, and the United Kingdom. This agreement was called the Plaza Accord, named after the Plaza Hotel in New York City where it was signed. The agreement committed the central banks of these countries to buying and selling foreign currencies aimed at depreciating the dollar's value. A similar drama would be replayed in the mid-2000s when China came under pressure to raise the value of its currency.

Japan took steps to protect its growing economy from a weaker dollar. Between July 1985 and February 1987 the number of yen it took to buy a U.S. dollar fell from 241 yen to 153 yen.[5] Put differently, a dollar did not buy as many yen. Depreciation of the dollar put Japanese goods selling for higher prices in the U.S. The depreciation of the dollar relative to the yen equates to the appreciation of the yen relative to the dollar. In 1986 the appreciation of the yen began taking a bite out of Japan's exports. Japanese exports for the fourth quarter of 1986 stood 5 percent below the exports for the fourth quarter of 1985. Falling Japanese exports spelled falling demand for Japanese goods. The effect of falling demand in one sector radiates and ripples throughout the whole economy. For the first quarter of 1987 Japan's output growth sank to 1 percent, a painfully low number for Japan. Japanese officials sought to outflank the effect of falling exports by expansionary monetary policy. In theory the expansionary monetary policy would give a boost to business investment and other interest-sensitive expenditures. Expanding expenditures in these other areas was aimed at offsetting falling exports and holding the Japanese economy in the groove of racy economic growth.

It was not as if what was about to happen to Japan had never happened to any other country. Something similar happened in the spring of 1927 when European countries faced an outflow of gold largely to the u.s. This exodus of gold threatened the ability of these countries to maintain a gold standard. They could stop the gold outflow by raising domestic interest rates but that induced economic sluggishness at home. Another option lay in persuading the u.s. to lower its interest rates. At the time Montagu Norman headed the Bank of England. He and governors of other European central banks asked the Federal Reserve officials in the u.s. to lower the Federal Reserve discount rate. The officials of the Federal Reserve cooperated and lowered the discount rate from 4 percent to 3.5 percent. The reduced interest rate sweetened the incentive to buy corporate stocks on margin (buying stock partly on borrowed funds and applying the stock certificates as collateral). The interest rate reduction helped fuel a speculative bubble in u.s. stocks. The bubble burst in October 1929 after the Federal Reserve backtracked and pushed up interest rates in a bid to cool a heated speculative frenzy. Not until 1955 would the Dow Jones Industrial Average stock index overleap the height it reached in 1929.

What was about to happen in Japan is analogous to the u.s. in 1929. In 1987 the u.s., unlike European countries of 1927, did not face a gold outflow. The u.s. was not even on a gold standard. Instead the value of the u.s. dollar was declining in value against other currencies. It was taking more dollars to buy Japanese yen and German marks, leaving goods from Germany and Japan costlier in the u.s. Perhaps the Plaza Accord worked too well since it required another accord, the Louvre Accord, to stabilize the depreciation of the dollar. The remedy sounded a familiar note. To strengthen the dollar other countries needed to keep interest rates low, just as the u.s. lowered interest rates in 1927 to strengthen the gold position of European countries. To achieve the objective of a stronger dollar, six countries (France, West Germany, Japan, Canada, the u.s., and the uk) signed the Louvre Accord on 22 February 1987. These countries were then labeled the G6. The agreement required the u.s. and France to reduce deficit spending, and West Germany and the uk to reduce public expenditure and cut taxes. Japan agreed to cut interest rates more than it had already cut them, and trim its trade surplus. Japan committed itself to continue monetary expansion.

A look at the Bank of Japan's discount rate policy in the second half of the 1980s succinctly tells the story. This discount rate is the rate of interest that the Bank of Japan charges to commercial banks. It wields a strong influence on short-term interest rates. Between October 1983 and December 1985 this interest rate stood at 5 percent. Through 1986 the Bank of Japan steadily cut this interest rate, putting it at 3 percent in January 1987. In February, the month the Louvre Accord was signed, the Bank of Japan cut this interest rate to 2.5 percent.

At first the strategy bore fruit. Falling interest rates touched off a speculative fever in Japan. In September 1985 the Tokyo's Nikkei Index, ^N225, traded in the mid-12,000 range. The Tokyo stock market sprinted upward, reaching a level of 26,367 for the week of 12 October 1987. By the first quarter of 1988, Japan's GDP had grown 9 percent above the fourth-quarter level of 1987. Japan's trade surplus also narrowed. In the third quarter of 1985 the trade surplus equaled ¥10,514.7 billion. By the third quarter of 1987 that number had dropped to ¥5,656.9 billion. Signs of an overheating economy and rising asset prices, however, clearly loomed on Japan's economic horizon. The Bank of Japan was poised to belatedly start monetary tightening, when Wall Street's Black Monday shifted Japanese expectations from fear of inflation to fear of recession. From a high of 2,722 the Wall Street's Dow Jones Industrial Average on 25 August 1987 tumbled. In the financial world Black Monday refers to Monday, 19 October 1987. On that day the Dow Jones industrial average fell 508 points, the largest one-day percentage decline in the Dow ever. The Dow finished that day at 1,738. The wave of crashes began in Hong Kong, swamped Europe, and climaxed in the U.S.

The downdraft of crashing stock markets ricocheting around the world certainly whacked Japan's stock market, but it did not stay down for long. By the week of 28 December 1987 the Nikkei Index had fallen to 21,564, a loss of nearly 500 points. It was a stunning loss but did not rival the jolt that whipsawed the U.S. stock market.

The biggest difference appeared in the hasty rebound. As an antidote against the global stock market crash and economic deceleration, the Bank of Japan hurriedly cast aside its plan to tighten monetary policy. Instead it gladly clung to a path of easy money. It kept its discount rate at 2.5 percent through April 1989. Between 1983 and 1984 Japan's money supply growth rates, measured by M2, registered in the 7 percent range. In August 1987 money supply growth touched the 11 percent range for the first time, remaining there until July 1988, except for two months when it entered 12 percent territory. Japan may likely have received some foreign encouragement for its expansionary policies. After the u.s. stock market debacle of 1987, healthy growth in Japan and Germany offset deceleration in the u.s. and Britain, and acted to hold the global economy afloat.

By the week of 4 April 1988 the Japanese market was exuberantly recording new highs. Hong Kong's stock market waited until mid-1991 before bouncing back and setting new highs. The Australian stock market clawed back only to post new highs in 1994. The Dow Jones put off setting new highs until the latter part of 1989. The Tokyo stock market finished 1988 in the 30,000 range, well above its high in 1987. It reached a dizzy peak in December 1989, right at 39,000.

The bubble in stock prices told only part of the story. By the 1980s the myth that property prices only go up had sunk deep roots in Japan, as well as the u.s. and Britain. In Japan the attachment to land went deeper. Not that long ago Japan had been a feudal society where land was the primary form of wealth. Financial wealth still passed as a relatively new innovation in Japan. It is also possible, however, that multiplication of financial instruments overshadowed the role of land in economic analysis more than was justified.

Going back to economic theories of the nineteenth century throws light on Japan's property bubble. The ideas of American economist Henry George (1839–1897) received scant attention from observers and interpreters of the economic debacle of 2008. George earned fame mainly for his ideas on the single tax. He wrote *Progress and Poverty* (1879), a book not now widely read by economists, but still occupying a revered place in the lore of economic thinking. His book treats the subject of inequality and the origins of cycles in industrialized economies. It also proposes a single tax on land value as a possible remedy. A single tax on land values is a way of shifting taxes away from current production. The supply of land remains fixed and unaffected by taxation.

George's theory of business cycles hinges on the role of land as a key resource and commodity. Human beings need living space. Businesses need land as an irreplaceable factor of production like labor or any other resource. Land, however, is not a product of current production and its supply is fixed. While current productivity can supply other goods and services, it cannot enlarge the fixed supply of land. Therefore, as economic development unfolds, the price of land goes up faster than other prices. If advances in technology assure steady growth in production of everything but land, land prices can be counted on to move up. Seemingly unstoppable growth in property prices soon invites speculators. The belief takes hold that property prices can only go one way and that is up. Speculators feel free to employ all their favorite tools, such as buying speculative assets with borrowed money. Speculators drive up property prices beyond levels that make sense to businesses wanting to buy property for practical use in a commercial activity. Once stratospheric property values interfere with the profitable production of goods and services, economic expansion slows and the curtain closes on the boom. The demand for property falls, but not necessarily the prices. The expectation that property prices will go higher in the future acts to keep property prices propped up. With regard to economic depression, George makes the following observation:

That land speculation is the true cause of industrial depression is, in the United States, clearly evident. In each period of industrial activity land values have steadily risen, culminating in speculation which carried them up in great jumps. This has been invariably followed by a partial cessation of production, and its correlative, a cessation of effective demand (dull trade), generally accompanied by a commercial crash; and then has succeeded a period of comparative stagnation, during which the equilibrium has been again slowly established, and the same round been run again. This relation is observable throughout the civilized world. Periods of industrial activity always culminate in a speculative advance of land values, followed by symptoms of checked production, generally shown at first by cessation of demand from the newer countries, where the advance in land values has been greatest.[6]

Japan comes to mind when George argues that the "cessation of demand" begins in the newer countries "where the advance in land values has been greatest." George's theory never enjoyed warm acceptance among academic economists. The u.s. where he wrote may have been too much of a land-abundant country to see land as a limiting factor in production. Japan was a different story. It was not land-abundant and its efforts to expand through colonization had been thwarted. George's logic seemed to unfold with cold merciless precision in Japan where a population 41 percent the size of the u.s. population fed and supported itself on a land area 4 percent the size of the u.s. land area. While in square miles Japan was only $1/25$ the size of the u.s., by 1990 it was four times bigger than the u.s. in the value of its property.[7] In theory Japan could have sold off the metropolitan district of Tokyo and reinvested the proceeds to buy the whole of the u.s.

The easy money policies that fueled the Japanese stock market boom also sparked a boom in Japanese real estate. Between 1984 and 1990 land prices doubled in Japan. Loans for construction and property management broke into the 20 percent range between 1985 and 1989.[8] According to a piece in the *New York Times*, 11 October 1987, central Tokyo saw real estate prices leap "85 percent in the last year alone."[9] The same article states that the previous three years had seen land prices quadruple in Minto, Chioda, and Chuo, the three central wards of the city. Typical payback periods extended beyond 100 years for office buildings in Tokyo. In 1989 land prices rose 50 percent in Osaka as speculators strove to match property values in Tokyo.[10] Rising house prices aroused fears in potential home buyers that home-ownership would soon be financially out of reach, forever unaffordable. Rather than risk never owning a home Japanese couples mortgaged six- to tenfold annual incomes. Not expecting to repay these mortgages in one lifetime, these couples negotiated mortgages with the understanding that their children would finish repayment. Mortgage amortization ranged between 50 and 90 years. One lender offered 100-year contracts.[11] These financing arrangements were called "two generational" mortgages. Amidst escalating housing costs, married couples in areas such as Tokyo settled for smaller apartments. With curious children and parents only a rice-paper sliding door away, couples retreated to love hotels, which became a new booming business.

With financial deregulation Japanese property owners mortgaged property to purchase everything from Impressionist art to corporate stock. Because of the high status accorded land in Japanese culture, a borrower could not furnish better collateral than land. Japanese banks applied a loan to value ratio of virtually 100 percent for real estate loans. The absence of a capital gains tax enriched the makings for a fast run-up in real estate prices. As real estate prices headed skyward, property owners borrowed more money on mortgaged property, turning capital gains into collateral for further borrowing. The borrowed funds often went to buy stock, and then the stocks served as collateral to purchase more stock on credit.

The Japanese pattern of corporate stock ownership plays its part in inflating the asset bubble. During the years of Japan's economic miracle its largest corporations were once again organized into financial combines along lines similar to what existed before the Second World War. These new combines are called "keiretsu." The member corporations of a keiretsu own each other's stock. At the center of the keiretsu stands a bank that is a major source of credit to the member corporations. This bank also holds equity shares in the member corporations. The member corporations are linked as suppliers, customers, and creditors. Mitsubishi, Mitsui, and Sumitomo number among the larger and better known keiretsu. In 1990 it is estimated that 70 percent of the value of the Tokyo Stock Exchange First Section is held by corporations.[12] The Tokyo Stock Exchange First Section lists Japan's major corporations.

It was a circle spiraling up without end. Skyrocketing land prices churned out capital gains that served as collateral for low-interest loans to purchase more property or stock. With climbing property prices, the corporations who owned property saw their net worth going up. Also as stock prices climbed, the net worth of corporations went up since much of the corporate stock was owned by corporations owning each other's stock. Capital gains in property and stock handed over more collateral to corporations. With more collateral they borrowed more funds to purchase more property or stock, further fueling the escalation of property and stock prices.

With this monster money engine puffing up an asset bubble at home, Japanese investors went shopping for overseas investment opportunities. Tokyo money poured into Wall Street, contributing to a u.s. stock market boom that crashed in October 1987. Mitsubishi Estate Company of Tokyo became one of the world's biggest real estate developers. In October 1989 it purchased controlling interest in The Rockefeller Group, the owner of Rockefeller Center, Radio City Music Hall and other mid-Manhattan office buildings. In September 1989 Sony Corporation purchased Columbia Pictures. In 1992 Hiroshi Yamauchi, president of Nintendo Co. Ltd, head-quartered in Kyoto, led a group of investors wanting to purchase the Seattle Mariners. After overcoming opposition within the baseball community, the purchase went ahead. Nintendo of America is the u.s. division of Nintendo Co. Ltd. Yamauchi ranked by far the largest investor within the group of investors angling for the Seattle Mariners. To win permission to purchase the baseball team, he had to enlist some local investors.

Backed by exploding real estate collateral and cash-stuffed banks, the Japanese became the newest international players at the art auctions in New York and Paris. In 1987 Yasuda Fire and Marine Insurance Co., the second largest casualty and property insurance firm in Japan, left the art world stunned when it paid a staggering $39.9 million for Vincent van Gogh's *Sunflowers*.[13] One Japanese collector, Yasumichi Morishita, is ranked among the most notorious art collectors in the world. He is described as a Tokyo financier with ten homes, a criminal record and one who socializes equally with all gangster groups. In November 1989 he purchased 100 Impressionist and post-Impressionist paintings for $100 million dollars in New York. He claimed to have invested $900 million altogether, and his self-proclaimed goal was to invest $1 billion in art. Some Tokyo art dealers heaped scorn on him as the worst of the "new real estate money." They laid the blame for soaring art prices at his feet, citing his bulk purchases of second-rate Impressionist works. Old elites in New York and London mourned the sight of Western civilization's most beloved paintings migrating to Japan. One of Picasso's most haunting and valued paintings, *Pierrette's Wedding*, went to an auto-racing theme park in the mountains of southern Japan. Nippon Autopolis Co. paid $57.1 million for it, planning to feature it as the main attraction at its theme park museum. In November 1989 Japanese buyers purchased 43 percent of the paintings sold at Sotheby's and Christie's, New York's two leading auction houses. American buyers accounted for 38 percent of the sales and European investors 19 percent.[14] One Japanese buyer, Shigeki Kameyama, paid $20.6 million for Willem de Kooning's *Interchange*, the highest price ever paid for a painting by a living artist. Tokyo collectors and dealers portrayed Kameyama as an elusive former used-car sales-man blessed with a shrewd eye, vast real-estate holdings, and un-limited funds. When Americans sneered at Japanese art purchases as mere speculative ventures by a crass nouveau riche, the Japanese retorted that they were from a much older culture than the Ameri-cans. Besides, they were not doing anything the Americans had not done at the close of the nineteenth century when American art buyers emptied out the aristocratic houses and palaces in Europe, not to mention Japan.

The Bank of Japan kept its discount rate at the low level of 2.5 percent from February 1987 through April 1989. In May of 1989 the Bank of Japan, hoping to cool speculative fever, pushed its discount rate up to 3.25 percent. The Nikkei finished May in the 34,000 range. The Japanese stock market shrugged off the rate hike, and willfully chalked up new highs. The Nikkei began October in the 35,000 range. In that month the Bank nudged up its discount rate to 3.75 percent, but the stock market barely took notice. It finished Novem-ber in the 37,000 range. The Bank of Japan raised its discount rate again in December, this time to 4.25 percent. The market finished December at a heart-thumping peak just short of 39,000. Then the upward spiral ominously sputtered.

The Japanese stock market never exactly crashed, but prices trended downward. By April 1990 the market had given up roughly 25 percent of its peak value. It remained flat until August when it slipped again. By the end of December 1990 the market sat roughly 40 percent below its peak. Over the next decade the Nikkei retreated gradually, despite occasional adventures above the 20,000 range. In March 2000 it touched 20,000 for the last time. It finished the next decade, on 30 December 2010, at 10,228.92. Over that decade it had briefly traded above 18,000 a couple of times. Probably some manipulation behind the scenes, perhaps with government help, avoided a severe crash.

The Bank of Japan went on raising interest rates in the face of a tumbling stock market, an action that in hindsight raises some questions, but Japan had had too long a period of prosperity for anyone to believe it was ending. In March 1990 the Bank of Japan raised its discount rate again, this time a full point, from 4.25 percent to 5.25 percent. In August 1990 the discount rate was raised again, this time to 6 percent, where it was kept through June 1991. Then the Bank of Japan began gradually cutting its discount rate. By February 1993 it was back to 2.5 percent, where it had stood in 1987 when the stock and real estate markets took flight and rocketed upwards. After the Bank of Japan had lowered its discount rate to 2.5 percent in February 1987, the stock market had roughly doubled in less than four years. Nothing nearly of that order was on the cards now.

### The Floundering Miracle

Stock markets fluctuate daily, but real estate markets experience longer swings. Toward the end of 1990 Japan had yet to see much fall in real estate prices, but talk in the air said it was imminent. Real estate prices quietly and ominously stood still. The market saw a fall in the number of condominiums sold the first month after being put in the market. Rumors spread that Shuwa Group wanted to sell some of its American holdings. It was one of those Japanese property companies that graduated to stock market speculator, and then to the loftier status of high-flying investor in American property.[15] By December a stock market index of property shares had skidded 56 percent. The *Economist* in its 3 November 1990 issue carried an article on property markets. A sub-title read, "Japan at the cliffs edge?"[16] The same magazine carried an article the next month specifically about the Japanese property market. Its first sub-title read, "The property market hangs on the brink."[17] The Governor of the

Bank of Japan, hoping to dodge a crash later on, called for a gradual downward adjustment of 20 percent in land prices. He kept monetary policy tight despite a gasping stock market. He also directed banks to scale back real estate lending. The government talked of removing tax breaks on mortgage-interest payments and urban farm land, and raising taxes on land ownership.

It is characteristic of forecasters to rarely forecast sudden changes. More often they forecast that things will remain the same with modest adjustments. A 20 percent decline in Japanese real estate prices became the consensus number in both Japan and the West. It was a safe number since many Japanese banks claimed to only finance 80 percent of real estate value. Proponents of a modest decline cited reasons why Japan's property market enjoyed immunity to wide cyclical swings observed in other property markets. It was said that Tokyo enforced tight zoning and building regulations that foreordained a land "shortage." It was mentioned that the effective land holding tax stood much lower in Tokyo than in the u.s. Another factor weighing against a sudden drop in property values was a tax system that severely punished pocketing short-term capital gains. Besides, no one would sell their property anyway. Japan was an immobile society. Since people rarely moved, paper losses on a house were beside the point. If someone had to sell property, they sold it to a relative; if a company had to sell property, they sold it to a parent company. It never hit the market.

Early in 1991 property prices toppled over. By December 1991 prices of second-hand condominiums in Osaka slumped 50 percent.[18] In Tokyo residential land prices sat 20 percent to 30 percent below 1989 levels. Despite rising vacancy rates, cranes still blemished the Tokyo horizon well into 1992. New buildings were still going up, though at slower rates. In 1987, the Japanese price index of urban land values stood at 99.2.[19] This price index peaked in 1991 at 147.8. In 1992 it sagged to a modest 145.2. A price index of commercial property in six larger urban areas betrayed a scarier picture of what was happening. In 1987 this index stood at 222.2. It peaked in 1991 at 519.4. The following year the index slid to 440.2. The psychology of a bursting bubble echoes in the voice of a salesman for Japan's largest condominium builder when he protested: "There is no point in telling people that the market has hit bottom because the [Japanese] media keep warning that prices might fall again."[20]

According to textbook supply and demand analysis, falling prices make a commodity affordable to a wider range of buyers. If prices overshoot a reasonable market price, a glut emerges. Sellers slash prices until demand catches up with supply. Prices adjust until the scales of supply and demand rest in balance again. When a speculative bubble pops, a crazy psychology invades this rational process. Slipping prices father the expectation that prices will fall even lower. New buyers do not rush in to buy commodities previously unaffordable to them. Instead, they wait to see how low prices will fall before they step in as buyers. Once prices drop below what anyone ever expected was possible, no one wants to buy anything. They are afraid of being caught in a crunch and left unable to sell. Once this psychology takes over, the money supply cannot grow fast enough to spark a turnaround.

By February 1993 the Bank of Japan had already cut its discount rate to 2.5 percent, the same rate that had previously seen the stock market double in less than four years. Now a 2.5 percent interest rate was far from low enough. By December the bank had cut its discount rate to 1.75 percent. That also proved inadequate. Land prices kept sinking. The price index of urban land hit 126.1 in 1995. The commercial land price index for the six largest urban areas posted 210.8 for 1995. That index was now off its high by 308.6 points, a hand-wringing drop of nearly 60 percent. The bank kept slashing its discount rate until it reached the historically low level of 0.5 percent in September 1995. It stayed at 0.5 percent until the new millennium when the bank shaved off more points.

## Japan in the Economic Doldrums

Between 1991 and 1996 Japan underwent a financial crisis that unfolded at speed. Borrowers were unable to repay bank loans and banks were stuck holding real estate collateral worth much less than loan values. Land prices continued to fall as bankers kept alive the hope that prices would turn up again. What bankers needed was for land prices to re-inflate to the point that borrowers could resell real estate and pay off loans. The extent of bad loans held by banks loomed greater than they could disclose without facing a bank-run. Hiding bad loans involved falsifying financial statements, a legal violation that brought stiff criminal penalties. Both the Ministry and Finance and the Bank of Japan, however, favored hushing up the raw facts. The specter of several large financial institutions either insolvent or undercapitalized was not a pretty sight politically. Resolving the problem required taxpayers bailing out the banks. Top officials in the Ministry of Finance rotate out every few years. It was much easier to wait for the next person to address the crisis. Keeping the troubles of Japanese banks a tightly held secret, nevertheless, proved an impossible task. By 1992 credit ratings of Japanese banks had sunk to the bottom among banks of major countries.

By 1997 investors' confidence in Japan's accounting and auditing system lay shattered. Three Japanese financial institutions failed that year – Sanyo Securities, Hokkaido Takushoku Bank, and Yamaichi Securities. After bankruptcy, auditors laid bare 260 billion yen in losses that Yamaichi Securities had keep hidden from bank auditors and inspectors. The Hokkaido Takushoku Bank was posting profits and paying dividends as it bellied up. Bank inspectors unearthed about 1.5 trillion yen in window-dressing on its financial statement. Instead of having equity of 0.3 trillion yen as reported in its financial statements, it had negative equity of 1.2 trillion yen.

Japan had a type of bank known as long-term credit banks. These banks held deposits but also sold bank debentures to raise capital. Debentures resemble a bond, pay higher interest rates than deposit accounts, but go uncovered by deposit insurance. These credit banks began to see accelerated redemption of deposits. The premium Japanese banks paid for overseas credit increased. More banks sought credit from the Bank of Japan. Borrowers faced a credit crunch that squeezed corporate investment, hiring, household consumption, housing, and boosted bankruptcies. The economic contraction in Japan deepened. Since the crises began in 1992 GDP growth numbers limped along barely inside positive territory. GDP growth turned negative in 1998.[21]

Toward the end of 1997 the Japanese government put together a 13 trillion yen bailout package for banks and bank depositors. Only a small fraction of the money was actually put to work. The plan was generally a failure, particularly since it did not lead to a comprehensive examination and clean-up of bank balance sheets. In 1998 the government enacted a more aggressive plan to bail out its banking sector, this time handing over 60 trillion yen, about 12 percent of GDP. One part of this plan, the Financial Revitalization Act, nationalized the Long-term Credit Bank and the Nippon Credit Bank. This effort succeeded in calming worries about the Japanese banking system.

Life insurance companies stood second only to banking as a major financial industry in Japan. These companies also sprang serious leaks. Seven failed between 1999 and 2001. In October 2000 Chiyoda Life and Kyoei Life filed for bankruptcy. Later AIG, a u.s. company, rescued Chiyoda, and Prudential, another u.s. company, rescued Kyoei Life. The real estate bubble saw more deflation. By 2000 the price index of urban land values, which peaked in 1991 at 147.8, had fallen to a sobering 100. The price index for commercial property in the six largest urban areas painted a crueler story for banks holding property as collateral. Recall that the index had peaked in 1991 at 519.4. By 2000 it had sunk to 100, a staggering 80 percent drop. By 2010 the commercial index had sunk to 75, and the urban land index to 58.5. Japan now boasted nearly twenty years of proof that land prices do not always go up.

The year 1998 marked the nadir of Japan's financial crisis. Japanese banks would struggle with lousy profits, bad loans, and low capital for a decade and longer. Despite lackluster profits, Japanese banks still ranked among the larger banks in the world. Japan's three largest banks, Mitsubishi UFJ, Sumitomo Mitsui, and Mizuho, ranked in 2011 among the world's 30 largest banks in terms of assets.[22] The internal ailments of Japanese banks helped them dodge the worst pitfalls of the u.s. subprime fiasco. Growth in China also brought opportunities to their doors. Japanese banks had recovered enough to turn the financial crisis of 2008 to some advantage. Mitsubishi UFJ bought a stake in Morgan Stanley and snatched control of an American retail bank. The operations in Europe and Asia of Wall Street's failed Lehman Brothers went to Nomura, Japan's sixth-largest firm.

The Bank of Japan went on frantically trying to resuscitate Japan's dying economic miracle by cutting interest rates. By the end of 2000 the Bank of Japan's discount rate stood at a record low of 0.5 percent. That same year prices overall fell 0.077 percent. Since interest rates cannot fall below zero, the Bank of Japan ran out of space to maneuver. The bank cut its discount rate to 0.35 percent in February 2001, then to 0.25 percent in March 2001, and to 0.1 percent in September 2001. It kept its discount rate at 0.1 percent until July 2006, when it raised it to 0.4 percent. Later it was raised to 0.75 percent before being cut back after the subprime crisis of 2008. In August 2011 it stood at 0.3 percent.

The government of Japan turned to budgetary policy to augment expansionary monetary policies. Japan's public debt as a percent of GDP rose from 68.3 percent in 1989 to 220 percent in 2010. The public debt in the u.s. for the same timeframe rose from 62 percent to 92 percent.[23]

The Japanese economy never regained its footing. In 1989 Japan's GDP in purchasing power parity dollars equated to roughly 39 percent of u.s. GDP.[24] If Japan could have returned to the 10 percent GDP growth that it enjoyed in 1950s and '60s its GDP would have exceeded u.s. GDP by 2011. Instead, for two decades Japan labored against sputtering growth, falling far behind the u.s. By 2010 Japan's GDP in purchasing power parity dollars stood at roughly 29 percent of u.s. GDP. In the 1990s the speed of Japan's economic growth went from a stampede to a crawl, averaging less than 1 percent annual growth between 1992 and 2002. Between 2002 and 2010 Japan's average annual GDP growth flickered under 1 percent per year. Inflation gradually decelerated until it swung over to deflation in 1995. Prices did not fall every year, but between 1995 and 2010 the annual rate of inflation averaged -0.07 percent. Minus inflation equates to deflation.

Thus was the end of the Japanese Miracle. It has to be remembered that Japan's strident growth was not going to continue endlessly under any circumstances. Sooner or later Japan's growth was bound to converge to more normal rates. Most economists think that long-term average growth of the order of 3 percent is sustainable.

## Japan as an Omen

Japan's experience highlights several factors that are relevant to the major themes of this book. Firstly, we saw Japan deregulating a rapidly growing and innovating financial sector. Japan's banks grew to become among the largest in the world. Secondly, we saw Japan create a bubble at home to shake off the effects of recessionary forces abroad. Thirdly, we saw Japan develop a real estate bubble fed by innovative mortgage practices and the myth that land prices only go up. In the next chapter we will see Japan persisting with financial deregulation in the face of deflation and unprecedented low interest rates. Deflation invariably brings higher bankruptcies and low interest rates persuade investors to bear higher risks in the search for higher returns. Put differently, low interest rates drive investors to migrate toward the speculative end of the financial spectrum. A growing appetite for risks does not mix well with loosening regulation. These forces become more destabilizing by the tendency to create speculative bubbles at home to offset depressing economic conditions abroad. Japan was the first country to push its policy interest rate to zero. Its interest rates still rank among the lowest in the world.

# THREE

# Financial Revolution

## The Coming of Deregulation and Free Markets

The cultural idealization of markets rarely weathers a deflationary unwinding in prices. Deflation means that regardless of what a household or business buys, it should count on selling it at a loss, at less than its purchase price. When markets turn against people, people turn against markets. Markets come to be seen as a treacherous mechanism that favors middlemen who have discovered the secret art of buying cheap and selling dear. Therefore it is not surprising that one legacy of the deflationary 1930s lies in closer regulation of markets. In the financial sphere particularly, tighter regulation seems exactly what the doctor orders. After all, the worst economic damage seems to fan out from stock market crashes and bank failures.

One depression-era piece of legislation enacted in the u.s. was the Glass-Steagall Banking Act of 1933. This Act for the first time in the u.s. insured customer deposits at commercial banks. It also banned interest-bearing checking accounts. The Act gave the Federal Reserve System authority to regulate interest rates on savings and time deposits. The Act also barred deposit banks from providing investment banking services. The u.s. government later repealed these prohibitions. Investment banks find buyers for newly issued corporate stock and securities and earn a profit by selling stocks and securities for more than they paid for them. Before Glass-Steagall, a person's broker and banker could easily be one and the same. Investing depositors' money in the stock market greatly widens the risk exposure of both the bank and the depositor.

Another piece of Depression-era U.S. legislation targeted abuses and fraudulent practices in the stock market. The Securities and Exchange Act of 1934 provided for the creation of the Securities and Exchange Commission. It also mandated federal regulation of buying stocks on margin, on borrowed money that is. Then as now the lender held the stock as collateral.

Just as deflation corrodes confidence in free markets, inflation inspires fresh confidence in free markets. Under inflation sellers find it easier to sell things for more than they paid for them. Under widespread inflation, sellers worry less about middlemen and more about rigid government controls that can unjustly deny them the market price of what they are selling. With inflation a market price is likely to beat a regulated price. The market price becomes the "fair market price." As a sweetener, inflation furnishes some very democratic opportunities for earning speculative profits. Under inflation all kinds of people buy land and houses on credit and sell for profit. No college degree or even high school diploma is needed. Blue-collar workers entering the stock market may be taken as a sign that the market is overheated. That is not the case when inflation is lifting the prices of land, houses, antique cars, boats, and what have you. Under these conditions households and businesses come to idealize the market as the best and fairest measure of value. As speculative profits from real estate and the like pour into the political sphere, politicians awaken to the virtues of free markets. Politicians who most eloquently defend free markets are catapulted to the forefront. To bolster these arguments inflation furnished countless instances of market forces, pushed out the door, coming back in through the window.

The idealization of the free markets echoes in a new gospel called deregulation. As one observer in 2006 confidently put it regarding London's financial deregulation, "Over-zealous and risk-averse regulators are prone to the laws of unintended consequences. Continual assessment of the value of regulations is essential to make sure that they are not driving business away, or reducing competition, or dampening innovation."[1] Businesses often bemoan an unlevel playing field thanks to tighter regulation at home than abroad.

A wave of inflation engulfed most of the world during the decades following the Second World War. Among developed countries it reached a crescendo in the late 1970s. Inflation once again infused confidence in free markets. Government regulation became a hindrance to market forces trying to efficiently and optimally guide the allocation of resources. Therefore, it was natural to see governments move toward deregulation of markets. Toward the end of the 1970s the move toward deregulation quickly acquired momentum.

Inflation was only one factor laying seeds for a creed of free, unregulated markets. The other factor was the prestige and success of the u.s. economy. The global economy was increasingly becoming the mirror image of an economy shaped by one of the most individualistic cultures in history. The u.s. inherited an English philosophical tradition that underscored the importance of individual liberty. John Locke, David Hume (1711–1776), Adam Smith (1723–1790), and John Stuart Mill (1806–1873) ranked among the more famous political philosophers and economists in this tradition. They argued that an individual over his own mind and body should remain sovereign so long as other members of society go unharmed. These ideas laid the philosophical underpinning for a high level of individualism. In Britain these ideas could only develop so far. After all, Britain was a country with powerful enemies nearby. The threat of external dangers helped maintain unity and solidarity, which acted to hold individualism in check despite strong philosophical arguments. The u.s. was another matter. Here was a country separated from potential enemies by two large oceans. It was also too large for conquest anyway. The philosophical seeds planted by the British philosophers could hardly have fallen on more fertile soil. A philosophy of individualism was free to develop without fear of external dangers. Perhaps never in history was there a society where the philosophy of individual liberty was able to flower and bloom so fully. Thus a high level of individualism became one of the distinctive characteristics of life in the u.s.

Individualism stresses the value of individual achievement of all kinds, including achievement in the arts and sciences. The challenges of harnessing a vast quantity of unused natural resources led the u.s. to favor business and entrepreneurial activity as the most prestigious form of achievement. It was a labor-short country—people were needed to work the land. The opportunity cost of attending school for too many years was unaffordable. The outcome was a culture not overly embarrassed with the dictum that "greed is good," particularly when greed involved earning a profit harnessing otherwise unused resources for society's benefit. As the threat of nuclear war and other attacks receded into the background, the u.s. went all out for laissez-faire capitalism, and the rest of the world gladly and innocently followed into the era of globalization.

In the political and economic spheres individualism equates to the maximization of political and economic freedoms. Economically speaking, individualism always prefers free markets over regulated markets, private property over publicly owned property, and private initiative over public initiative. The efficiency of unfettered markets is a thing of pure beauty to those who believe, with Thomas Jefferson, that the best government is the one that governs least. No institution better than free markets provided more watertight, unimpeachable evidence for vindicating Jefferson's political philosophy. The efficiency and social optimality of market prices could be mathematically proven with sunlit clarity.

In short, two factors account for the global economy's eagerness to cast its lot with free markets. One was the culture of expected inflation; the other was the infectious influence of perhaps the most individualistic society ever, the u.s. The result was an idealization and consecration of free markets that wore the aspect of religious zeal. Trust in markets numbered among the infallibilities of the time.

Exaltation of free markets ran wild in financial markets where there was even room to say a kind word about speculators. Speculators see value in products that others do not see. They buy and hold products when nobody else will, because they see their future value. Otherwise the products would lie neglected and waste away. Speculative opportunities give individuals an incentive to invest time collecting information about the economy's future needs. When better informed buyers bid up the price of an asset, they are making the price of the asset a better measure of its value to society. The higher price becomes a vehicle for passing this information to the less informed.

Scholars of finance developed a stock market theory called the Efficient Market Hypothesis. This hypothesis came in three different variants, each reflecting various levels of confidence in the stock market and stock prices. What was called the weak form of the Efficient Market Hypothesis argued that current stock prices reflect all the information that can be extracted from past price movements. Therefore charting past prices does not help predict future prices. Another form, called the semi-strong form of the Efficient Market Hypothesis, argued that current stock prices reflect all publicly available information. Therefore stock traders gained no advantage by poring over annual reports and other published data as that information was instantaneously incorporated into stock prices. The most extreme position, the strong form of the Efficient Market Hypothesis, argued that current stock prices reflect all pertinent information, both public and private. This version suggested that the market is a better gauge of a stock's value than company insiders. Scholarly studies were not lacking that found support for the weak, semi-strong, and strong forms of the Efficient Market Hypothesis, although the evidence for the strong form was not as convincing.

By 2009 market participants on the ground were doing some soul searching about the Efficient Market Hypothesis. In a *New York Times* story on 5 June 2009 Jeremy Grantham, a respected market strategist with a large global investment firm, is quoted from one of his recent newsletters:

In their desire for mathematical order and elegant models, the economic establishment played down the role of bad behavior [not to mention] flat-out bursts of irrationality . . . The incredibly inaccurate efficient market theory was believed in totality by many of our financial leaders, and believed in part by almost all. It left our economic and government establishment sitting by confidently, even as a lethally dangerous combination of asset bubbles, lax controls, pernicious incentives and wickedly complicated instruments led to our current plight. "Surely, none of this could be happening in a rational, efficient world," they seemed to be thinking. And the absolutely worst part of this belief set was that it led to a chronic underestimation of the dangers of asset bubbles breaking.[2]

Despite strong forces favoring deregulation, governments had reasons to balk at deregulation of financial markets. Financial markets were the one place where historically unregulated markets had furnished the scene of out-and-out disasters. The wild gyrations of these markets had destroyed people's life savings overnight. Sometimes out of despair individuals took their own lives. Crashes in key financial markets caused whole economies to crumble and lie lethargic for a decade while a generation of young workers went without meaningful job opportunities.

Governments did not balk. By the beginning of the new millennium they had already advanced a long way down the road of financial deregulation or, as many prefer, financial liberalization. The exact date when liberalization began might be hard to pinpoint, but one source claims that 1969 was a pivotal year for opening up stock markets to foreign investors. The list of countries who by that measure started down the path of financial liberalization that year include the u.s., the UK, Switzerland, Sweden, Singapore, the Netherlands, Luxembourg, Italy, Ireland, Hong Kong, France, Finland, Denmark, Canada, Belgium, Austria, and Australia.[3] Spain opened their market in 1978, Japan in 1980, New Zealand in 1984, and Portugal in 1986. Emerging markets took longer to embrace financial liberalization. Argentina liberalized its financial markets in 1989, Brazil in 1991, Chile in 1992, Columbia in 1991, Greece in 1987, India in 1992, Indonesia in 1989, Jordan in 1995, Malaysia in 1988, Mexico in 1989, Nigeria in 1995, Pakistan in 1991, Philippines in 1991, South Korea in 1992, Taiwan in 1992, Thailand in 1987, Turkey in 1989, Venezuela in 1990, and Zimbabwe in 1993. Japan was a bit late opening up its equity markets, considering the large size of its economy. Smaller, emerging countries worried about foreign speculators manipulating their smaller and less developed financial markets. Eventually the attraction of lower-cost foreign capital overrode fears of outside manipulation. By 1995 most countries had opened up financial markets to foreign speculators.

Steps toward financial liberalization had to accommodate the evolution of electronic trading platforms and world-shattering innovations in telecommunications and computer networking. The world's first electronic stock market made its debut in 1971. By 2010 the NASDAQ, as it was called, would be the third largest stock market in the world after the New York Stock Exchange and the Tokyo Stock Exchange. By 2000, money moved around like it had never moved before. Rapidly changing technology spawned new possibilities for competitive markets, but also new risk. Computerized program trading became a popular tool among stock investors in the 1980s. These programs were set to trigger automatically, without human intervention, when a predetermined relationship occurred between different asset prices. It appeared by the late 1980s that program trading added to stock market volatility. In 1990 the U.S. Congress enacted legislation empowering the Securities and Exchange Commission to suspend program trading when necessary to curb market volatility.

## Unveiling the Big Bangs

Nevertheless, governments cast their lots with deregulation. These same ground-breaking strides in technology enlarge the volume of international trading. Now traders can choose between London, Tokyo, and New York for the best place to transact business. Traders usually favor the least regulated market. Regulatory havens come to rival tax havens. Regulations are difficult to enforce across borders anyway. Competition between national markets helps drive the trend toward deregulation. In 1975 the New York Stock Exchange saw fixed commissions go by the wayside. Intense competition slashed commissions for both institutional and retail investors, leading to a multiplication of mutual funds and helping inspire a shareholder culture.

A wave of deregulation surged across Europe from Amsterdam to Paris, to Frankfurt, to Milan. Exchanges deregulated membership and other rules, improved trading floors, and added state-of-art communications facilities.

The London Stock Exchange saw its business usurped by rising foreign competition. Several reforms to reinvigorate the London stock market went into effect on 27 October 1986. The reforms were billed as the "Big Bang." They scrapped fixed commissions, opened up membership to foreign companies, and set up an electronic trading platform patterned after the NASDAQ.[4] The Big Bang removed the barriers between order-taking brokers and big market-makers. A year later the volume of foreign equities in London matched domestic equities. London stock broking and market-making firms sold for lofty sums to new players wanting to buy goodwill. Foreign banks, including American banks like Citicorp, were well represented among the new players.[5] It was a bid to make London an international center of finance at a time when both New York and London were still focused on domestic markets. By the day of the 'Big Bang' nearly half the dealers in British bonds were owned by foreign financial institutions. Most of the 33 market-makers in equities were domestic firms formed from mergers of brokerages, so-called jobbers, and commercial and domestic banks.[6] On 3 April 1987 the *Wall Street Journal* carried a page one story entitled: "London Foreign-Share trading Booms as Exchange Lures Overseas Business."

Seeing what the Big Bang had done for the London market, Japanese officials laid plans for opening Japanese markets, hoping to make Japan an international financial center of the order of London and New York. The bursting of the Tokyo Bubble in 1989 chilled Japan's eagerness at first. Authorities on the Tokyo Stock Exchange felt that sales of stock index futures hastened the decline in stock prices after the Tokyo bubble burst. Stock index futures allow investors to bet on broad movements in the whole index instead of individual stocks. Tokyo authorities took measures to discourage sales of index futures. In 1993 Eisuke Sakakibara, a senior official in Japan's International Finance Bureau, is quoted in the *New York Times* as saying:

In my personal opinion the age of laissez-faire policy is over. In the mid-1980s this Reagan–Thatcher deregulatory movement was in full swing and this affected the mentality of the authorities here as well. We did not want the Tokyo markets to lag behind other markets.[7]

Despite Japan's initial reluctance, u.s. officials pressed the country to open up its financial system. They saw Japanese manufactures raising capital at rates much lower than u.s. manufacturers could get in the u.s. Cheap capital gave the Japanese firms an advantage. Opening up Japan's financial system became a crusade for a level playing field.

Growing competition from less regulated financial markets in Hong Kong and Singapore stock markets helped Japanese officials see the light. In 1991 the Tokyo Stock Exchange listed 125 foreign companies, a number that would be cut in half by 1998. Tokyo was the only large financial center that saw its share of global foreign exchange trading shrink between 1992 and 1995.[8] One-third of the trade in Japanese stock index futures had migrated to Singapore. The specter of the coming euro threatened to undercut the status of the yen as an international currency and Japanese banks still staggered under a mountain of bad debt. New financial products had to be approved by the Japanese Ministry of Finance. Many financial products were banned in Japan though commonplace in foreign markets.

In 1996 Japan's prime minister committed the government to a plan of financial deregulation. It was billed as a plan comparable to London's Big Bang and became Japan's "Big Bang." It involved a more ambitious agenda than London's, partly because Japan's financial system was more antiquated. Rather than put it all into effect on one day, however, the government unveiled a plan of rolling financial deregulation stretched out over three to four years.

Japan's Big Bang officially kicked off on 1April 1998. On that day the government deregulated brokerage commissions on large stock trades. A year later fixed commissions were abolished altogether. It also opened foreign exchange transactions to all businesses. This action cut costs for multinational corporations and allowed Japanese savers to invest abroad with less hassle. Banks received authorization to sell Japan's version of mutual funds, giving savers a wider choice and improving efficient allocation of savings.

Prior to the Big Bang, Japan had progressed toward financial deregulation. Japan had its own version of the u.s. Glass-Steagall Act (the depression-era u.s. act that prohibited commercial deposit banks from investing in the stock market). American occupation authorities grafted a version of Glass-Steagall on Japan's financial regulations. The u.s. repealed Glass-Steagall in 1999. In 1993 Japan began allowing banks and securities firms to enter into other businesses through their subsidiaries. Nevertheless it kept a tight firewall separating the two types of financial operations. Its aim was to reduce conflicts of interest and abuse of dominant bargaining positions. In

2009 these firewalls were lowered to allow company executives to act as senior management of both deposit and investment banking. Deregulation also allowed banking and brokerage units of a financial company to share client information. Despite an ailing economy, strong internal opposition, and a weak banking system, Japan bravely opted for the medicine of deregulation. In 2000 for the first time Japanese authorities allowed the sale of a Japanese bank to a u.s.-based company.

From 1978 until the subprime crisis of 2008, the u.s. steadily dialed back regulation of its financial system. Until 1978 many states enforced usury laws that put a ceiling on interest rates but a Supreme Court decision in 1978 led to the removal of those ceilings. In 1980 Congress enacted the Depository Institution Deregulation and Monetary Control Act. This Act deregulated deposit interest rates and enabled banks to pay interest on checking accounts. It also opened the door for thrift institutions to make consumer loans. In 1982 Congress with strong bipartisan support enacted the Garn-St Germain Depository Institution Act. This Act gave thrifts complete freedom to make commercial loans and offer higher money market accounts. These new accounts could compete with money market mutual fund accounts offered by other institutions.

The failure of large numbers of thrifts in the late 1980s kept u.s. deregulation in a holding pattern until 1994. That year Congress, with bipartisan support, enacted the Riegle-Neal Interstate Banking and Branching Efficiency Act. This Act dismantled restrictions on interstate banking and branching. In 1996, the Federal Reserve System went back to the depression-era Glass-Steagall Act several times for reinterpretation. It decided bank holding companies could earn up to 25 percent of their revenue from investment banking without violating Glass-Steagall. Three years later Congress enacted the Financial Services Modernization Act of 1999. Enactment of this legislation freed u.s. deposit-holding commercial banks to form financial holding companies able to offer a full range of financial services, including holding deposits, extending personal and commercial loans, underwriting and brokering securities, and selling insurance. This legislation superseded prior legislation that forbade deposit banks from providing the services of a securities firm or insurance company.

Under Glass-Steagall a securities firm could neither conduct deposit banking nor sell insurance. Likewise, insurance companies had to remain separate. New legislation eased these prohibitions.

## Founts and Forms of Speculation

Favorable social attitudes toward financial liberalization only shared in driving the winds of change reshaping the financial world. Other factors straightened the path. By 2000 old financial habits, processes, institutions, and mechanisms were crumbling under the brisk growth of new technology and speculative instruments. Future financial legislation was needed to address concerns about legal hurdles to the sale of some new and off-the-rack speculative instruments. The UK had already addressed the issue by 2000, and the U.S. was about to do so. This legislative attention betrays the growing importance of these financial instruments. A new word circulated— "derivatives." Derivatives were not new, but the word was new, symbolizing a significant acceleration in the speed, complexity, and variety of change in finance and speculation.

Some derivatives are traded in public exchanges similar to stock market exchanges, but most are private transactions consummated in over-the-counter markets. The name "derivative" comes from the fact that the profit or loss a derivative earns is "derived" from that of other financial instruments. Financial performance is "derived" from the financial performance of other instruments. Among the oldest derivatives are options. An option is a contract between a buyer and seller. The buyer of the option has the right, but not the obligation, to buy or sell something at a future date. The exact date and price is specified in the option. An option to buy something is termed a "call"; an option to sell something is termed a "put." Puts and calls made their first documented appearance during the seventeenth century amidst Holland's famed "Tulip Mania" (a speculative frenzy over tulip bulbs). At that time these speculative tools went by the name "windhandel," meaning trading in air. New derivatives marked a milestone in the evolution of "trading in air."

The last three decades witnessed a multiplication in the range and variety of underlying assets that support derivatives markets. Nowadays the underlying asset might be the weather, which is not exactly an asset. Weather derivatives are a good example of how companies and individuals can for a price shift an unwanted risk to another party. The other party is either willing to assume the risk or has other risks that act counter to the risk in question. Farmers buy weather derivatives to insure against drought- or frost-related losses. Theme parks and sports events make use of weather derivatives to hedge against rainy days. Utility companies can use contracts for "heating degree days" and "cooling degree days." These contracts help utility companies smooth out fluctuations in earnings caused by unpredictable weather. Weather derivatives give some hint of the ingenuity that goes into the development of new financial products. The underlying "something" behind a derivative may be a non-asset random thing such as weather, or it could be another derivative, such as a futures contract or an option.

The year 1997 saw the first over-the-counter trading in weather derivatives, and the market for these products grew. In 1999 the Chicago Mercantile Exchange started exchange trading in weather futures contracts, and options on those contracts. By 2008 weather derivatives traded for eighteen u.s. cities, nine European cities, six Canadian cities, and two Japanese cities. Weather derivatives caught the attention of hedge funds which treated them as a separate investment class. From the angle of an investment strategy, weather derivatives were unlikely to be correlated with other investments. Therefore they reduced volatility in an investment portfolio.

The multiplication and popularity of derivatives hatched a whole new business education curriculum called "financial engineering." The new field devoted itself to designing new financial instruments, usually exotic options and derivatives involving interest rates. Specialists in this field had to be proficient in differential equations, statistics, finance, and computer modeling. They usually held phds in mathematics or computer science. Prestigious universities launched degree programs in financial engineering. Columbia University boasted a degree leading to Master of Science in Financial Engineering. According to their website: "Students take courses in stochastic processes, optimization, numerical techniques, Monte Carlo simulation, and data analysis. They also study portfolio theory, derivatives valuation, and financial risk analysis, making use of the methods they have learned."[9] MIT's Sloan School of Management opened a "Laboratory for Financial Engineering."

University programs only mirror the growing role derivatives are playing in the financial world. The Bank of International Settlements has been gathering data on over-the-counter derivative contracts since 1998. At the end of that year these contracts covered underling assets measuring over $80 trillion dollars. For comparison keep in mind that U.S. GDP, calculated in 2005 selling prices, stood at $13.2 trillion in 2011. By the end of 2001, over-the-counter derivative contracts covered underling assets measuring over $111 trillion. By the end of 2004 that number had more than doubled with underlying assets measuring over $258 trillion. This pace of exploding growth lasted through the end of 2007 when the value of underlying assets totaled over $585 trillion. After 2007 the growth rate slowed. At the end of 2010 these underlying assets measured over $601 trillion and from the end of 2000 to the end of 2010 the value of underlying assets grew roughly 20 percent per year.[10]

Derivatives are traded on organized exchanges, but here the numbers are not nearly as large. At the end of 2000 the value of underlying assets for derivatives traded on organized exchanges stood a bit over $8 trillion. By the end of 2010 that number stood slightly above $22 trillion. Three fundamental financial instruments form the basis of most derivatives. One is options, which are discussed above as one of the oldest derivatives. Then there are forward contracts in which a buyer and a seller commit themselves to buying and selling something at a later date, but at a price that is decided on the day the agreement is made. Forward contracts evolve to another contract called a futures contract. Unlike forward contracts, futures contracts are traded on organized exchanges and may exchange ownership several times during the life of the contract. Futures contracts are usually closed out before maturity, therefore actual delivery of a commodity never happens. Otherwise futures contracts resemble forward contracts. Combinations and variations of these basic instruments have multiplied the range of mutations in derivatives. One type of derivative that has become common is the "swap." A swap is a contract in which two parties agree to "swap" cash-flow streams. Perhaps one party is receiving a cash flow in dollars and needs one in yen, while the other party is receiving a cash flow in yen and needs one in dollars.

The derivative that gained the widest media coverage during the 2008 financial crisis was the credit default swap. Despite being called a swap it more closely resembles an insurance policy. Like all derivatives, it is a financial tool for managing risks. The purchaser of a credit default swap could be the owner of a bond or loan. This purchaser gives a series of payments to another party. Should a default or credit downgrade occur on the bond or loan, the recipient of the payments makes a payoff to the bond or loan owner in compensation for the loss. That part is not much different than a traditional insurance policy but the difference lies in the fact that purchasers of credit default swaps do not have to own the bonds or loans in question. They do not have to own any bonds or loans, but can be pure speculators. They have no insurable interest. Anyone can purchase a credit default swap for a bond or loan, and make a series of payments to the seller. If the bond or loan, which belongs to another party, defaults, the purchaser of the credit default swap receives a payoff. In 2001 credit default swaps covered assets totaling $918.9 billion. By 2007 that number had exploded exponentially, growing to $62.2 trillion. The value of the underlying assets for these contracts had multiplied over 62-fold. By 2009 it has sunk back to $30.4 trillion.[11]

Swift changes in technology and methods give fast learners advantages over slow ones. The outcome is greater income inequality. In 2008 Byron Wien was a 40–year stock market veteran and chief investment strategist at one of the largest hedge funds. With regard to the ability of people running Wall Street firms to understand these new financial products he observed:

These are ordinary folks who know a spreadsheet, but they are not steeped in the sophistication of these kinds of models. You put a lot of equations in front of them with little Greek letters on their sides, and they won't know what they're looking at.[12]

It is quite possible that in 2008 the Wall Street players did not care about equations with Greek letters. By then "the market" was sacrosanct. In marshaling, and in intelligently and fairly using information, it endured no peer. The value it placed on an investment was the only thing that mattered. The market price defined the fair and efficient value.

By 2001 indexes had sprouted up for the credit default swap market, serving the same purpose in that market as the Dow Jones Industrial Index or any other stock market index serves in the stock market. In 2004 the various credit default swap indices merged into the CDX (Credit Default Swap Index) in North America and the iTraxx in Europe and Asia. Like the stock market indices, the market for credit default swaps offers speculators all the tools they love. Options can be purchased for individual credit default swaps or for indices for the whole market, the CDX and the iTraxx. Credit default swaps sold to buyers who do not own the underlying loan or bond are called "naked" credit default swaps. The buyers of these are in it purely for the speculation. What they do can be compared to a person who sees a fire risk at a neighbor's house and, instead of sharing the knowledge with the neighbor, they buy fire insurance on the neighbor's house and wait for it to burn. They are insuring something they do not own. According to estimates of Eric Dinallo, the former superintendent of the New York State Insurance Department, naked credit default swaps accounted for about 80 percent of all credit default swaps in 2008.[13] Credit default swaps are enough to tantalize the best of the Dutch speculators who boasted of trading in air during the seventeenth-century "Tulip Mania."

Operational bottlenecks plague the exploding growth of credit default swaps. On 15 September 2005 the New York Federal Reserve Bank summoned to its offices representatives from fourteen banks. The Federal Reserve wanted the record-keeping cleaned up. Every day saw billions of dollars traded in credit default swaps, but the record kept lags behind two weeks, creating severe risk management issues. The UK faced the same problem.

The wild growth and mathematical sophistication of these new financial products (derivatives) made understandable the findings of one scholar, James B. Ang, who concluded: "There is also evidence supporting the hypothesis that financial liberalization relocates talent from the innovative sector to the financial system, thus retarding technological deepening."[14]

The growth of financial derivatives raised new regulatory issues. The concern by now was not for putting new regulations in place, but for sheltering new innovations from antiquated regulations. Regulations conceived in a simpler time risked hindering the growth of vital and newer innovative practices. Some of the new financial derivatives bore more than a faint resemblance to gambling. Rather than risk inhibiting the growth of a socially useful industry, governments acted to overtly let derivatives off the legal hook of anti-gambling statutes. In 1986 the UK's parliament enacted the Financial Services Act of 1986, providing for some government regulation, but also making use of self-regulation. The Act specifically exempted financial derivatives from the Gaming Act of 1845. This declared a wager was an unenforceable contract and its purpose was to discourage betting. It could, however, be interpreted to outlaw the new financial derivatives. To protect these new derivatives, the UK's Financial Services Act of 1986 defined the condition where gaming contracts were enforceable. The condition was that at least one of the parties had to enter into the contract for legitimate business purposes. The UK's Financial Services and Markets Act of 2000 superseded the act of 1986. It also specifically exempted derivatives from earlier statutes against enforcing gaming contracts. It did, however, embrace provisions against insider trading and issuing false information to mislead markets and investors.

## Financial Regulation in Retreat

How far the passion for markets and deregulation had swept public debate can be gathered from discussions leading up to the enactment of the U.S.'s Commodity Futures Modernization Act of 2000. The Futures Trading Practices Act of 1992 enabled the Commodity Futures Trading Commission to exempt swap derivatives from state laws, including gaming laws. There was some question, however, whether credit default swaps were exempted. Others argued that credit default swaps should be subject to state laws regulating insurance. Brooksley Born, chair of the Commodity Futures Trading Commission, made unforgivable waves when in May 1998 she issued a "concept release," publicly arguing that the unregulated market for derivatives posed latent risk. Alarms sounded in the Clinton administration that a loose-lipped bureaucrat wanted to hobble new innovations in the financial markets. Three heavyweights rushed into panicky action to checkmate any such inconvenient development. They were Robert Rubin, secretary of Treasury, Lawrence Summers, who would succeed Rubin, and Alan Greenspan, chair of the Board of Governors of the Federal Reserve System. On the very day of the "concept release," Alan Greenspan, Robert Rubin, and Arthur Levitt (chair of the Securities and Exchange Commission) expressed in a joint statement grave concerns. They expressed fears that regulations could dampen financial activity and drive traders to overseas markets, and they recommended legislation to clarify ambiguities in the law and to specifically exempt many kinds of derivatives from federal oversight. Senator Phil Gramm stood even more sternly hawkish on the need to curb regulatory oversight. He would not stand for either the Commodity Futures Trading Commission or the Security Exchange Commission sticking their noses into the derivatives market. His wife had preceded Ms Born as chair of the Commodity Futures Trading Commission. While she was chair, the commission had issued rules exempting some swaps and derivatives from regulation.

After Lawrence Summers became secretary of Treasury, he and the chairs of the Commodity Futures Trading Commission and the Securities and Exchange Commission brokered a compromise with Gramm. Without debate or review, Congress enacted the Commodity Futures Modernization Act of 2000 amid a chorus of bipartisan support. It was appended as rider to an 11,000-page spending bill. The Act included a special exemption for energy derivative trading that later earned notoriety as the "Enron loophole." The bill continued the preemption of state gaming laws and other laws that could be invoked to challenge the legality of derivative contracts. It also repealed previous legislation that banned the sale of futures for single stocks or narrow indexes of stocks. The bill helped fuel the 62-fold jump between 2001 and 2007 in derivative trading cited earlier.

Ms Born did not stay in her position long enough to help negotiate the final bill. In June 1998, a month after the "concept release," she held her ground in Congress, refusing to consider halting the study about the need for new regulations governing the over-the-counter derivatives market. Greenspan, Rubin, and Levitt met privately with Born, hoping to dissuade her from pursuing the matter. According to a *Wall Street Journal* account, "An exasperated Mr. Rubin lectured her that he and his fellow regulators had a lot of experience in markets."[15] Born was coldly turned out of doors politically over her position. She announced in January 1999 that she would be leaving her position when her term expired in August. According to a piece in the *New York Times*:

> Administration officials say there was little expectation that she would have been reappointed because Ms. Born openly broke ranks with some of the Administration's top economic advisors . . . The issue was her edging toward tighter regulation of over-the-counter derivatives.[16]

Mark Brickell, a board member of the International Swaps and Derivatives Association, gave the commission under Ms Born some credit for educating Congress about the importance of derivatives, but with regard to suggestions that tighter regulation might be helpful, he sternly warned: "Regulations that make it harder to manage risk raise widespread concerns."[17] The Clinton administration replaced Ms Born with William Rainer. In October the *Wall Street Journal* carried an article about the new chairman entitled: "CFTC Chairman Seeks to Deregulate Trading." This article paraphrased Mr Rainer's first major address as saying that,

> under changes supported by a majority of the five-member commission, the CFTC would give the exchanges free rein to introduce financial-futures contracts and would let exchanges make their own rules without agency interference.

At a Chicago news conference in October 1999, the new chairman was quoted in the same article as saying:

> These markets are simply too important to the nation's economy to ignore the potential damage from disparate regulatory

structures. The government must not inadvertently pick winners and losers as we attempt to reshape the regulatory landscape for all financial markets.[18]

The Securities and Exchange Commission also began to march in lock step with the philosophy of a light regulatory touch. In 2004 William D. Donaldson chaired the Securities and Exchange. He would be replaced in 2005 because Republicans thought he sided with Democrats too often. On 28 April 2004, however, the five members of the Commission voted unanimously to relax a rule that affected the ability of investment banks to remain solvent. The rule dated back to 1975 and was concerned with the amount of liquid assets brokerage units held relative to the securities they owned. A broker-dealer had to compute the liquidation value of its assets by a certain rule. The rule aimed at making sure broker-dealers always held an adequate cushion of liquid assets, ensuring that they could pay obligations owed to customers. The investment banks pled with the commission members that the rule went too far. These banks wanted to get by while holding a smaller reserve cushion. Relaxing the rule set free billions of dollars held in reserves against potential losses on investments. These were funds that could be redirected to other purposes. The parent companies of broker units were in a hurry to usurp a larger slice of the mushrooming market of mortgage-backed securities and other exotic financial products. They needed these funds that were held as reserves. Senior executives from the five investment banks wrote letters whining about excessive regulation and oversight. One of the five pleading for easing the rule was Goldman Sachs, headed then by Henry M. Paulson Jr, before he became secretary of Treasury. None of the major media outlets covered the meeting, including the *New York Times*.

The staff at the Securities and Exchange Commission favored relaxing the rule for the largest banks. Annette L. Nazareth, head of market regulation, spoke to gloss over issues that might disturb commission members. She highlighted that under the new rules the Securities and Exchange Commission could limit excessively risky activity by these firms. She later became a commissioner herself. Part of the agreement was that the Securities and Exchange Commission could monitor the riskiness of investments at these investment banks. The commission, however, elected not to exercise this oversight option and, in a step toward laxer regulation, opted to rely on the banks' own computer models, in effect letting the banks monitor themselves.

The parent company oversight program went by the bureaucratic title of "consolidated supervised entities." The agreement behind this program permitted the Securities and Exchange Commission to monitor parent companies when technically its oversight responsibilities were limited to the companies' brokerage firm components. The investment banks eagerly embraced this concession because it exempted them from stiffer European regulation. European Union authorities vowed to subject foreign subsidiaries of American investment banks to European oversight unless these companies could show they were subject to oversight at home. Thus the American investment banks killed two regulatory birds with one lobbying stone. They went away with lower reserve requirements at home and sidestepped the threat of European regulation abroad.

In a 2008 *New York Times* article, Professor James D. Cox is quoted as saying:

We foolishly believed that the firms had a strong culture of self-preservation and responsibility and would have the discipline not to be excessively borrowing. Letting the firms police themselves made sense to me because I didn't think the sec had the staff and wherewithal to impose its own standards and I foolishly thought the market would impose its own self-discipline. We've all learned a terrible lesson.[19]

The only dissent came from a software consultant and risk management expert in Indiana. He sent a two-page letter to the Commission warning against relaxing the rule, making the point that computer models used by investment banks to determine investment risks could not foresee incidents of extreme volatility.[20] The Commission never bothered to get back to him.

Despite some relaxation of the rules, the chair of the Securities and Exchange Commission was seen as way too heavy-handed by the two Republican members of the Commission. In July 2005 he was replaced by Chris Cox who favored looser regulations. Time in the trenches may have given him second thoughts. On 26 September he was quoted in the *New York Times* as saying: "The last six months have made it abundantly clear that voluntary regulation does not work."[21]

Subsequent events suggested that the financial services industry is not a fertile field for finding evidence favoring deregulation. They more likely proved the hypothesis that too often the people who cry the loudest for hands-off government and light-touch regulation are the very ones who most need supervision.

## Macroeconomic Corollaries

This chapter hardly exhausted the full width and depth of the movement toward financial deregulation and innovation. As we will see later, just the change in the home mortgage industry alone amounted to a revolution. Then there were the banks setting up offshore operations to escape banking regulations at home. While governments dismantled financial regulation, financial instruments grew in complexity and artificiality. Hopes raised by financial deregulation and innovation helped fuel speculative fevers. Soon individuals could conveniently invest retirement funds in commodities markets where riskier speculation was business as usual. Falling interest rates left the most grounded investors happier to experiment with newer and wilder investments. Governments added an extra layer of complexity by turning to bubble-building monetary policies when foreign recessions threatened to make economic waves at home. All these factors led to national economies less able to intelligently and resiliently assimilate external shocks.

# FOUR

# Euphoria in the Housing Market

## Understanding the Housing Market

The distinction between tradable and non-tradable goods holds the key to a post mortem on the housing bubble. The ease with which a good can be traded numbers among those market characteristics that widely vary between goods. A ton of wheat typifies a highly tradable good. It can be hauled overland in a truck, loaded onto a ship, and sent anywhere in the world. Its shelf life outlasts the time spent in transport. Transportation costs add little percentage-wise to total costs. A McDonald's Big Mac enjoys less tradability. It must be prepared close to where it is consumed. The same is not necessarily true of some of its ingredients. Therefore a Big Mac belongs in the somewhat tradable category. It is not nearly as tradable as one of its ingredients, wheat. The upshot is that the price of wheat is similar everywhere, but varies owing to transportation costs. The price of a Big Mac varies more. In July 2011 the price of a Big Mac in U.S. dollars ranged from $1.89 in India, to $4.07 in the U.S., to $8.06 in Switzerland.[1] The Big Mac exemplifies many goods that lie between two extremes. At one extreme lie the perfectly tradable goods, at the other the perfectly non-tradable goods. In proportion as a good is tradable, its price at various points around the world converges to one price. Market forces coax prices around the world into alignment. In the case of the perfectly non-tradable good, prices at various points differ wildly. No market forces hammer prices at various geographical locations into alignment.

If the domestic demand for a tradable good gets a boost, the price does not automatically go up. Global market forces hold the price roughly level against prices of the same good abroad. Instead of the price going up, domestic producers supply more of the good, or the domestic market imports more of the good from foreign producers. If the domestic demand for a non-tradable good strengthens, the price is free to move up. No added supplies from foreign producers pour into the market and hold prices down.

Real estate belongs on the non-tradable end of the scale. No global market forces squeeze house prices in London, Shanghai, or Houston toward convergence. Countless u.s. home-owners in Oklahoma would love to haul their houses to California and sell them. At least that holds true until the u.s. housing bubble fell apart. During the bubble house prices in California stood free to soar without shiploads of imported houses disembarking from China, or even Canada.

In a summarizing nutshell, manufactured goods, such as automobiles, exhibit high tradability. Houses exhibit no tradability. Therefore automobiles sell for about the same price in all regions, whereas house prices vary markedly between regions. In the decade of 2000–2010, foreign competition held the prices of tradable manufactured goods in check while house prices ran free to rocket.

The distinction between tradable and non-tradable goods holds a valuable clue for diagnosing the makings of a housing boom. One must dig deeper, however, to unearth the full story. The time between 2001 and 2007 saw housing markets come wildly alive in response to government economic stimulus policies. These policies included faster money supply growth and bargain interest rates. Other sectors heard the call of easier credit, but they sat on their hands. Most if not all forces of stimulation went straight to the housing market. It greedily usurped them.

The housing market owes part of its frenzied dash uphill to the special place home-ownership holds in family life. Homes often equate with family life, but the family angle masks the speculative role that houses play. Houses have acquired characteristics that make the mouths of speculators water. The housing market allows purchasers to acquire assets with small down payments, much smaller than the margin requirements in the stock market. Capital gains from home-ownership easily become in the u.s. and other countries collateral for home equity loans. Credit from home equity loans becomes available to finance riskier ventures. As an added carrot in the u.s. at least, housing is perhaps the least taxed investment to be owned. Interest paid on mortgages enjoys full deductibility for income taxes. In 1997 President Clinton signed tax legislation that allowed couples to earn up to $500,000 dollars in tax-free capital gains on any house they lived in for two years before selling. Within these criteria the capital gains tax sat at zero.

## The Changing Home Mortgage Industry

As the housing market gained momentum, financial engineers raced to the drawing boards and busied themselves designing new financial products based upon the housing market. In April 2006 Standard & Poor's launched eleven indices of house prices. This is the same Standard & Poor's that owns and maintains the Standard & Poor's 500 which, after the Dow Jones Industrial Average, is the most widely followed index of stock prices in the u.s. These new indices provided the basis for futures and options contracts traded on the Chicago Mercantile Exchange. Futures and options rank among the most beloved in the speculators' toolboxes. (The futures and options contracts on housing indices were intended to provide the same tools for risk management and investment that similar products provided to agriculture and finance.)

For investors expecting a housing bubble to pop, they could now bet not only on when the bubble would pop, but also on where. One index was a composite index reflecting house prices all across the u.s. In addition ten regional indices reflected house prices in selected cities: Boston, Chicago, Denver, Las Vegas, Los Angeles, Miami, New York, San Diego, San Francisco, and Washington DC. Later indices for ten more large cities became available. David Blitzer of Standard & Poor's touted the new index: "Obviously all the talk about housing bubbles is going to enhance interest in the product."[2]

Scholarly research has scrutinized the possibility that financial liberalization affects the housing market. One study collected data from three countries, Finland, Sweden, and the UK. It measured the degree of financial liberalization in each country and estimated the impact that money supply growth exerted on house prices for each.

It found that countries exhibiting greater financial liberalization saw higher correlation between money supply growth and house prices. Not only was the magnitude of the initial response to monetary shocks larger in financially liberalized countries, but the persistence and length of the response received a boost. This same study also reported that financial liberalization tended to elevate house prices absolutely in addition to increasing the sensitivity of the housing market to monetary policy.[3]

Most advanced countries saw some degree of financial liberalization after 1970. It usually began with lifting interest rate ceilings. Liberalization as a rule widened household access to mortgage financing and lengthened the payout period. The UK by the 1980s boasted the most deregulated system of housing finance in Europe or North America. In the 1980s, 66 percent of home-owners in the south of England withdrew some equity from home mortgages. The average amount was 10,000 pounds.[4] Financial liberalization for housing, however, can vary substantially. By 2003 the U.S., the UK, Denmark, and Australia had readily available mortgage equity withdrawal loans of some variety. France, Italy, and Portugal forbade equity withdrawal loans. Germany and Spain had a few of these loans. France even limited the availability of second mortgages. Mortgages for rental units were readily available in virtually all advanced countries. The Netherlands, the UK, and the U.S. offered interest-only loans. France and Germany offered interest-only loans, but the loan to value ratio in those countries stood relatively low at 67 percent. Only one Organization for Economic Cooperation and Development (OECD) country, Italy, reported a lower loan to value ratio at 55 percent. The Netherlands boasted the highest loan to value ratio at 90 percent. Belgium, Denmark, Japan, and Portugal reported loan to value ratios in the 80 percent range. Canada, Finland, Greece, Spain, Sweden, and the U.S. reported loan to value ratios in the 70 percent range.

Virtually all countries saw mortgage debt as a percent of GDP climb between 1992 and 2002. For the U.S. it increased relatively modestly from 45.3 percent to 58 percent. The UK also reported a modest increase of comparable magnitude. Australia's mortgage debt as a percent of GDP jumped from 24.2 percent to 50.8 percent and

Spain's from 11.9 percent to 32.3 percent. Portugal's mortgage debt ballooned from 12.8 percent to 49.3 percent of GDP.[5]

In December 2006 France reformed its mortgage law to allow home equity loans and reverse mortgages. France had been mulling over mortgage reform since 2004 when OECD research reported a correlation between consumer spending growth and mortgage finance.[6] The *Economist* ran a story in its 11 December 2004 issue in which the first sub-title read: "The best way for the euro zone to boost demand is to deregulate the mortgage markets."[7] Economies in the U.S., UK, and Australia felt a much stronger shot in the arm from rising house prices than did economies of countries without ready access to home equity loans and easy refinancing. Germany, France, and Italy numbered among the latter group. House prices in euro countries, excepting Germany, were rising as they were in the U.S. and Australia, but strong domestic housing markets were not translating into faster economy-wide growth. In the U.S. lower interest rates afforded home-owners an opportunity to refinance and slash monthly house payments. The savings on house notes went into higher consumer spending, strengthening the demand for all kinds of goods. As low interest rates boosted house prices, U.S. home-owners easily negotiated home equity loans. These loans further inflated consumer spending. Home-owners enjoyed similar advantages in the UK, Australia, and smaller euro countries such as the Netherlands. In the U.S. mortgages with 10 percent down and a 30-year payout were regular fare. In France and Belgium the transaction costs of buying and selling houses amounted to 15 percent of house value. These types of transaction fees thwarted the use of houses as liquid assets.

An OECD study singled out the U.S. for its system of mortgage financing that tightened the link between money supply growth and economic growth. This linkage holds a large place because money stock growth can be regulated by public policy. Faster money stock growth leads to cheaper interest rates and easier credit. The stock market furnishes one obvious channel connecting money stock growth and the economy. Lower interest rates at first put the rate of return for bonds below the rate of return for stocks. Stock prices spike as a consequence, putting profits on the table for investors to pocket if they held the stock before the price hike. These profits at least partly go to higher consumer spending.

By the early 2000s many an investor had grown weary of the stock market. In countries like Australia, the UK, and U.S. the housing market turned into a conduit for monetary policy. Lower interest rates boosted house prices. Home-owners accessed capital gains from home-ownership and stepped up consumption expenditures. Changes in house prices now packed a much greater punch on demand for goods in general. When house prices went up, the production of goods went up. Mortgage equity withdrawal and refinancing happened more frequently in the U.S. and smaller euro countries. Because of sophisticated and fully developed systems of mortgage financing, these economies stood ready and equipped to ride the wave of faster money supply growth. At least that was the way it looked in 2004. The OECD study particularly cited regulations on maximum loan to value ratios, stamp duties, and capital gains taxes as examples of European regulations that loosened the linkage between faster money stock growth and faster economic growth.[8]

The *Wall Street Journal* (20 October 2004) carried a story, "Greenspan Again Plays Down Fear of Housing Bubble." According to the article that mostly paraphrased a speech that Greenspan, at the time the chair of the Federal Reserve System, gave to a bankers' group:

> Houses aren't as prone to bubbles as stocks because high transaction costs and a seller's need of shelter are "significant impediments to speculative trading," the Fed chief said. While some buyers have bid through offering prices, they have "contributed only modestly to overall house price speculation," he added . . . Mr. Greenspan, in a speech to a banking group here, also said U.S. households shouldn't have any trouble handling record debt levels, though he acknowledged that worries over such debt "cannot be readily dismissed." . . . "Many of those who purchased their residences more than a year ago have equity buffers in their homes adequate to withstand any price decline other than a very deep one."

Greenspan's verdict was not unanimous. The same article quoted a Goldman Sachs economist as saying: "home buyers seem to have developed a speculative mindset."[9]

## The Building of a Global Bubble

The beginnings of a bubble first come to light in the market for starter homes and mid-priced homes. This slice of the market profits from low interest rates that turn renters into buyers and lure home-owners into trading up. The market for upper-end luxury homes counts more on the stock market than interest rates. Until 2004 houses priced above $1 million were not moving. Then the high-end market perked up. That is when Los Angeles real estate agents started calling former clients, asking if they would like to sell and clear a couple of million in profits.

Housing markets in individual countries often seem to have a life of their own. Houses are non-tradable goods. Wide variations in house prices between regions in a large country such as the u.s. suggest that the housing market is a collection of walled and moated-in markets. The housing boom that took wing in 2004 bears one new feature that is hard to miss: it is a global boom. By the beginning of the new century, house-price inflation among individual countries largely marched in step. Most advanced countries saw house-price inflation accelerate between 2002 and 2006. Notable exceptions bear mentioning. Germany saw house prices remain stable between 1996 and 2006. In Japan house price deflation lasted through 2001, turning to a microscopic flicker of inflation from the beginning of 2002. Japan missed out on the global housing boom even though it probably boasts the highest population density of advanced countries. Germany and Japan are found at the low end of the house inflation scale. These findings come from a study using Bank of International Settlements data.[10] Comparisons of house inflation between countries can be tricky. Each country has its own underlying inflation rates that affect prices across the board. The numbers have to be adjusted for inflation in each country.

The study using Bank of International Settlements data (www. bis.org) puts the u.s. toward the lower end of the scale for house price inflation. It reports u.s. house prices climbing around 60 percent between 1995 and 2006, rather a low number compared to the Standard & Poor's index of u.s. house prices, which indicates that they rose 134 percent between 1996 and 2006. Therefore the inflation-adjusted house price numbers bear only a blurred resemblance with what was observed in each country. Nevertheless the relative ranking of house-price inflation even with inflation-adjusted data should corroborate with experience. The study using the inflation-adjusted data puts Ireland and Spain at the top of the house-price inflation scale. By this data house prices in these two countries skyrocketed above 180 percent between 1995 and 2006. House prices in the UK stampeded upwards over 150 percent during the same interval. Australia, Belgium, Denmark, Greece, New Zealand, and Norway saw house-price inflation in the 100 percent range or slightly above. France and Canada came in slightly below the u.s. and Finland, the Netherlands, and Sweden slightly above. Japan was the only country to see house prices significantly fall from 1995 to 2006. Korea suffered a slight drop in house prices. House prices remained roughly even in Germany and Austria and rose on the order of a 30 percent range in Portugal.

After 2000 countries in Central and Eastern Europe saw house prices start to rise, crossing into double-digit growth territory. In East and Southeast Asia housing remained relatively tame. In these areas house prices in 2006 stood below levels reached prior to the 1997 East Asian Financial Crisis. Emerging economies such as Russia, China, Brazil, and India also saw housing booms in major cities. In these countries housing markets remain highly segmented between large cities and rural areas.

The growing synchronization of regional housing markets stems from the broad trend toward globalization. The greater integration of national economies leads to business cycles that bear the stamp of a global phenomenon. House prices rising worldwide mirrors income rising in every quarter of the world. Financial liberalization and integration compels interest rates and credit availability to move in sync across countries. In 2004, interest rates sat low everywhere. There was talk of a global saving glut. Banks and mortgage lenders stood flush with capital, more competitive and aggressive than ever. No one could remember when houses could be financed for so long, at such low interest rates, and with such low down payments. Nomadic capital was enjoying freedom to migrate to the juiciest rate of return. With interest rates low at home and stock market prices low and volatile, enthusiastic investors shone a roving spotlight into every nook and cranny of the global economy, hunting for opportunities that promised to beat stocks and bonds.

Nomadic capital was not the only guilty party. People were also more mobile. According to one report of what was going on:

> Americans are searching out castles in Umbria. Londoners are gobbling up beachfront property on the shores of Bulgaria. Europeans are finding dream homes on the Indian Ocean near Durban. And in Bangkok, eight years after the city's property market collapsed, Golden Land is seeking buyers from Thailand and abroad with a sales pitch that promises "an environment so opulent, only in your dreams could it be imagined."[11]

One New York investor bought a castle in Italy with plans to carve it into twenty units and sell them to Londoners as second homes. He remarked:

> One thing you hear a lot is that the Italian economy stinks. But it does not really matter to us what is happening in the Italian economy. It's much more important to us what is happening 1000 miles away in Britain.[12]

As the u.s. housing market took off, "flipping" became a household word. It referred to the practice of purchasing a house and then quickly reselling it for a tidy profit. In the beginning most flipping involved buying a house that perhaps needed some repairs. The buyer completed the repairs and resold the house for a better price. As the housing boom gained speed, speculative buyers purchased new houses and in less than a year turned them for a profit. The National Association of Realtors reported in 2004 that investment purchases accounted for 23 percent of u.s. house sales. Second homes accounted for another 13 percent.[13] By 2005 "flippers" were buying and selling houses even before they were built. Perhaps half of the new apartments in Miami were quickly resold by the original buyers. Properties regularly changed hands two or three times before an owner actually occupied it.

Home builders cooked up ways to channel sales away from speculative buyers. Developers found it harder to sell a new house if neighboring houses had for-sale signs popping up in yards. For condominiums and townhouses, builders limited the number of units sold to a single buyer. Sales contracts began to include clauses prohibiting resale of the property within a specified period of time, often a year. This practice began in the condominium markets where speculation ran hottest. Then it spread to single-family homes. In the eyes of builders the problems caused by flipping outweighed the added profits from speculators bidding up the price of houses. Rampant flipping made it harder to sell a neighborhood as a family-friendly and stable community. Contracts allowed builders to nullify sales contracts and keep deposits if they caught buyers flipping property before closing the sale. In many states a builder could sue for damages if a buyer resold the house after closing the sale but before the contract's no resale date.[14]

In an affluent society such as the u.s., households no longer thought about saving up a down payment and buying a home to raise their children in and live out their retirement years. Instead they looked for a "starter home." As they became more affluent, they planned to move into a grander house. The capital gains they earned on their starter home became a stepping stone to the next house. As house prices hurried skywards, first-time buyers found affordable starter homes scarcer. Mortgage lenders in the u.s. rushed to the rescue with new mortgage options to help these buyers get into homes. A 40-year mortgage furnished one remedy. Monthly payments ran less even though the interest rate stood a quarter of a point above the rate on a 30-year mortgage. Since buyers did not plan to live in the house 30 years, much less 40, a longer payout mattered not at all.

Mortgage innovation graduated to the next level with negative amortization mortgages. Here was an exotic version of an interest-only mortgage. The difference lay in the option that let home-owners make monthly payments less than the full amount of interest owed. The difference between the amount paid and the interest owed backed up in the loan balance. It was supposedly designed to meet the needs of home-owners whose monthly income fluctuated sharply over the year, perhaps because of commissions and bonuses. Home-owners yielded ground in principal during the low-income months, and won it back during the high-income months.

Then there was the flexible version of adjustable-rate mortgages. This mortgage gave the borrower four payment options each month. One option was interest only, another was negative amortization, another was 30-year fixed-rate payment, and lastly, a 20-year fixed rate payment. The lender sent the borrower each month a payment coupon with the four options. Every month the bank recalculated the remaining balance under each of the four options.

For borrowers without down payments, there was the piggyback option. This offered a way around costly mortgage insurance for buyers with less than 20 percent down payment. It involved two mortgages: one covered 80 percent of a property's value, the other the remaining 20 percent. The smaller mortgage charged a higher interest rate. It was recommended for home buyers with high salaries but low savings.

Some borrowers qualified for the 103 and 107 mortgages. These mortgages were engineered for borrowers who had large cash reserves but were unwilling to tie up funds in real estate. These borrowers mortgaged between 3 and 7 percent above what the house was worth. They might invest the extra proceeds from the loan in the stock market.

Some mutations of the adjustable-rate mortgages offered low "teaser" rates to attract borrowers. The teaser rate might be as low as 1 percent and lasted from one to three months. Beyond the teaser-rate period, the interest rate fluctuated monthly with a benchmark short-term interest rate. Interest charges could fluctuate widely, but provisions for negative amortization sheltered home-owners against sharp increases in monthly payments. These mortgages became available at a time when adjustable-rate mortgages charged a lower interest rate than 30-year fixed-rate mortgages. Said Robert Moulton, president of Americana Mortgage Group Inc. about these mortgages, "You could really put a borrower into a buying category which they could not traditionally qualify."[15]

The negative amortization options entailed a minimum payment that was recalculated each year. A cap limited the amount the minimum payment went up each year. The minimum payment option was removed once the loan balance rose above a target level, usually between 110 percent and 125 percent of the original amount borrowed.

Late in 2005 U.S. federal regulators proposed tighter standards for borrowers seeking interest only and adjustable-rate mortgages. Complaints poured into Washington from the American Bankers Association and other groups representing mortgage lenders. Countrywide Financial Corp., one of the more aggressive mortgage lenders, responded icily to the proposals in a letter: "We do not believe that the risks associated with these particular loan products justify the specific and prescriptive guidance."[16]

Regulators worried that some borrowers might see monthly payments double. They wondered if borrowers understood these complex loans. With regard to suggestions that lenders screen borrowers for suitability of certain types of mortgages, one banker group, America's Community Bankers, indignantly responded, "We do not believe it is appropriate or possible for the lender to dictate the best mortgage products for individual consumers."[17]

Lenders supplemented the multiplication of custom-tailored mortgages by loosening standards that borrowers had to meet before qualifying for mortgages. They lowered the qualifying credit scores, raised the debt loads that borrowers could bear, and asked for less documentation. In 2005 Countrywide Financial Corp., the U.S.'s largest mortgage lender, shaved twenty points off the minimum credit score a borrower needed for some of its popular mortgage products. Chase Home Finance, a part of JPMorgan Chase & Co., started offering home-equity loans and lines of credit without income verification. To qualify the total mortgage could not exceed $1.5 million or 90 percent of the property's value. Wells Fargo & Co. held out interest-only mortgages to buyers of investment property. In some markets the allowable share of household income going to pay housing expenses went up from 38 percent to 45 percent. Home equity loans became available to borrowers buying condominiums as investments or second homes. Ninety percent financing became available for investment property and second homes. That was up from the 75 percent of the second home's value that qualified for financing before the change.

According to some creative lenders, loosened standards reflected progress owed to advances in the internet and computing technology. The ability to marshal and analyze databases had taken a leaping stride forward. Electronic databases allowed more data to be quickly analyzed and in greater depth. Lenders felt more confident in their ability to zero in on borrowers who were a good credit risk. First Horizon Home Loan Corp. scaled up loan-to-value ratios and scaled down credit scores on limited and no-documentation loans. Jerry Baker, its chief executive, was quoted in the *Wall Street Journal* as saying, "One of the things that is often missed is that we've become much better predictors of loan performance with automated underwriting systems and appraisal practices."[18]

First Horizon's reference to limited or no-documentation loans highlights another innovation in mortgage lending. These loans became more casually known as "low-doc" or "no-doc" loans. Lenders waived some or all of the usual requirements for verifying income and assets so that no wearisome unearthing of old tax returns, pay stubs, or bank statements inconvenienced borrowers. This convenience to the borrower came at the price of an extra 0.25 to 0.75 percentage points tacked onto the interest rate. Countrywide Financial Corp. billed its "low-doc" and "no-doc" loans as a "Fast & Easy" loan program. The website of another large mortgage lender touted loan options tailor-made for borrowers who faced difficulty verifying income through conventional methods, whether due to self-employment or other circumstances. Tax returns may hold misleading clues about a self-employed person's income. Lenders, however, flaunted these loans to a wider audience looking for convenience, or an opportunity to pad income. The loans caught on in a hurry. In 2000, fully documented loans accounted for 72 percent of the mortgages backing up securities sold by Wall Street firms. For the first eight months of 2005 that number stood a mere 54 percent.

One of the latter mortgage innovations arrived just in time to see the housing bubble peak. By 2006 rising short-term interest rates had robbed adjustable-rate mortgages of much of their charm and home-owners saw monthly payments ratcheting up. Lenders offered a new fixed-rate, interest-only mortgage. The borrower was locked in a fixed-interest rate for the life of the loan. Moreover, for the first ten to fifteen years, the borrower paid nothing down on the principal. These were long-term mortgages, 20-year, 30-year, and in some cases 40-year. Once the interest-only period expired, the borrower paid interest and principal. Then the monthly payment rose steeply enough to pay off the principal over the loan's term. Lenders hoped ten years of interest-only payments gave the borrower ample time to raise their income, or sell out before the loan's later years when both interest and principal had to be paid. Lenders added between one-eighth and three-eighths extra percentage points to interest rates for these loans. According to a *Wall Street Journal* piece, an online lender, Quicken Loans Inc., said that demand for its fixed-rate, interest-only mortgage had "absolutely exploded."[19]

Many of these exotic mortgages went to borrowers with dingy credit records. These were called 'subprime' loans. Lenders charged interest rates as much as 4 percent points higher to subprime borrowers than to more credit-worthy borrowers. Many of these mortgages were "securitized"—used to back bonds sold worldwide. A large credit default swaps market centered on these bonds. Some large winners and losers surfaced after the subprime market crumbled. In time it came to light that lenders steered into subprime mortgages borrowers who could have qualified for conventional mortgages with far better terms. The mortgage-originating companies earned higher fees for negotiating subprime mortgages. In 2007 the Bush administration asked Congress to attack the problem of "predatory lending."

By 2006 the u.s. housing bubble was hard to miss. The *Wall Street Journal* carried a piece quoting Michael Jocoby, managing director and shareholder of Phoenix Management:

In the minds of lenders, the housing bubble has moved from Loch Ness Monster myth status to an economic reality that could have a significant economic impact on the lives of many Americans.[20]

One telling piece of evidence was seen in the real estate agents themselves, the middlemen of the housing market. The neighborhood real estate agents joined the neighborhood doctors, lawyers, bankers, and stockbrokers in status and income. Like the newly rich of every age they engaged in conspicuous consumption in a bid to raise social status. They drove the finest cars, dined at ritzy restaurants, wore costly clothes, and gave the best dinner parties. With blossoming lifestyles and ballooning income they rubbed elbows with their wealthiest clients. Among real estate agents many were called and few were chosen. In 2004 roughly two-thirds of real estate agents earned incomes at or below the u.s. median household income of $43,000. But those at the top surpassed their wildest dreams, particularly in places like Beverly Hills and Manhattan. One of the Beverly Hills agents affiliated with Ginnel Real Estate, Mr Michael Neeley, liked automobiles, purchasing four Mercedes, two Jaguars, and two Range Rovers. He also spent well on theater tickets and Louis Vuitton belts and shoes. His 28 pairs of Alain Mikli eyeglasses were color coordinated with his wardrobe. Some Manhattan real estate agents in 2004 cleared above $2 million.[21] In hot real estate markets sellers were often also buyers. An agent often earned more than one commission from each client. In 2004 real estate brokers earned $61.1 billion in commissions. That was 43 percent above the $42.6 billion earned in 2000.

Like other newly rich, the wealthiest real estate agents wondered if anyone was so poor as to do them honor. A survey conducted for the National Association Realtors found that the public ranked real estate agents above lawyers. A Harris poll reached a different finding. It found real estate agents ranked lowest in prestige among professions, below accountants, stockbrokers, and journalists. Mr Neeley, mentioned above, voiced the feeling of a profession now erect with pride: "Real estate is to me a profession, whereas before it was just sales . . . look at how they [clients] spend their money, and I'm getting more ideas."[22]

Awareness of a housing bubble began to spice conversation in the uk. In a May 2004 article, "The Big Bad Bubble," The *Economist* quipped: "To an Englishman, his home is his castle. To less confident observers it is a castle in air."[23] A British financial analyst felt house prices had eclipsed the weather as the favorite topic of conversation. Every home-owner, home hunter and those in between metamorphosed into amateur meteorologist scanning the housing market sky for storm clouds. One lender estimated that UK housing prices had climbed 18 percent in one year. Roughly a year later The *Economist* in its 18 June 2005 issue ran an article with an innocent enough title: "In Come the waves." The sub-title was more ominous: "The worldwide rise in house prices is the biggest bubble in history. Prepare for the economic pain when it pops." The *Economist* collected its own data and concluded that residential property in developed countries had grown in value by $30 trillion in the last five years. This increase equated to the combined GDPs of developed countries. The magazine further estimated that the late '90s global stock market bubble equated to only 80 percent of the combined GDPs of developed countries, compared with only 55 percent of GDP reached by America's stock market of the late 1920s. Therefore the housing bubble ranked the biggest ever.[24]

By mid-2005 the global housing bubble was showing signs of losing steam. In the UK, house price growth subsided from 20 percent per year to 5.5 percent. The Royal Institution of Chartered Surveyors reported that prices had started to fall. Nearly half of surveyors reported falling prices for May 2005, something that only happened in severe housing slumps. Perhaps more revealing was that sales volume had slid one-third over the past year. Ireland, the Netherlands, and New Zealand also reported house-price inflation tapering off, and Australia showed signs of house prices hitting the skids. After growing at rates of 20 percent in 2003, Australian house prices for the first quarter grew at an annual rate of 0.4 percent. The Commonwealth Bank of Australia's own index showed house prices falling 7 percent. The once-sizzling Sydney market saw prices tumbling 16 percent.[25]

Nevertheless, house prices still sprinted higher in France (15 percent yearly) and Spain (15.5 percent yearly). In the U.S., California, Florida, Nevada, Hawaii, Maryland, and Washington DC saw house-price inflation soaring above 20 percent. The numbers were a little tamer in France, Italy, Belgium, Denmark, and Sweden where house-price inflation stood at 9 percent or more.[26]

Standard & Poor's house price index for the u.s. stood at 100 in 2000. It reached a peak in the second quarter of 2006 at 189.93. It had risen by nearly 90 percent since 2000. By the first quarter of 2010 that index had fallen to 132.12. The Bank for International Settlements' index for u.s. real house prices reported house-price escalation more on the order of 57 percent. It showed prices peaking in the first quarter of 2007 and steadily creeping downward roughly 20 percent from peak levels. The Bank for International Settlements' data reflected inflation-free prices. That is, these indices were based upon house prices adjusted for inflation.[27]

A Bank for International Settlements' index for the eight largest cities in Australia finished 2000 at 61.9. That index in the second quarter of 2010 stood at 149.8. The numbers for Sydney, the capital city, paint a slightly different picture. It shows an index peaking at 103.1 in the fourth quarter of 2007 and sinking to 95.6 by the first quarter of 2009. Then it takes off again, posting 116.5 for the second quarter of 2011. It has only modestly dropped since then, posting 147 for the second quarter in 2011. House prices in Switzerland remained bullish. The Bank of International Settlements' housing index for Switzerland finished 2000 at 287.01. By the second quarter of 2011 it had achieved a new high of 396.27. The all houses price index for Spain topped in the first quarter of 2008 at 2,101. By the second quarter of 2011 it had fallen to 1,752. That index had finished 2000 at 893. The house price index for France peaked in the third quarter of 2008 at 207.06. That was up from 100 at the end of 2000. After dropping through mid-2009, the French index turned up, and posted a value of 214.1 for the second quarter of 2011. The index for the uk peaked during the third quarter of 2007 at 183.6. It also rebounded after a dip. After sinking to 158.5, it climbed back to 175.2 by the end of 2010. The data for the Netherlands displays a similar pattern. After peaking in the latter part of 2008, the index bottomed out in 2009 and showed signs of turning upward. The house price index for Hong Kong finished 2000 at 81.06. It climbed to an interim peak of 126.6 in June of 2008. The Hong Kong price index sank during the remainder of 2008, finishing at 104.8 in December. Then it rebounded and reported 184.0 for July 2011.

A house price index for China is missing in the Bank of International Settlements' data set, but this data set does report a Chinese land price index, reflecting land prices for all of China. The land price index ended 2000 at 100.5. It sprinted upward, posting 116.5 for the first quarter of 2008, then it backtracked to 101.5 before turning upwards again, posting 122.1 for the second quarter of 2010. It dropped back to 114.8 before the year was out. Another source (www.globalpropertyguide.com) reports China's house price inflation at 40 percent annually around 2008, but dropping to almost zero. China's government enacted measures to cool its housing market.

## The Pricking of a Bubble

House prices skidded first in the United States. In 2003 the interest rate on three-month U.S. Treasury Bills dropped to below 1 percent point. By November 2006 that rate had climbed to over 5 percent points. Home-owners with adjustable-rate mortgages suffered brutal jumps in monthly payments. At first lenders relaxed credit standards, not wanting higher interest rates to repel new borrowers. As we have seen, a credit default swap was an insurance-like financial derivative. The holder of a loan bought a credit default swap from a seller. The swap obliged the seller to compensate the buyer in the event of loan default. Worry about the U.S. housing market first cropped up in this derivative market. Between August and October 2006 the price of these derivatives surged 16 percent.

As U.S. home prices leveled off, home-owners hit more snags trying to refinance or sell houses, particularly in areas where house prices suffered genuine declines. The number of overdue payments turned upward. The mortgage delinquency rate posted 2.87 percent in the first quarter of 2007. That was up from 2.03 percent in 2005. The foreclosure rate on subprime mortgages more than doubled in 2006 from 2005.[28] In June 2007, Countrywide Financial Corp. reported that 20 percent of its subprime mortgages had payments overdue 30 days or more. Adjustable-rate mortgages saw jumps in delinquency rates even among prime borrowers. Borrowers who had started out with introductory rates as low as 2.35 percent suddenly felt the sting of an 8.75 percent rate on an adjustable-rate mortgage. Instead of being the least part of the monthly household budget, the mortgage payment became the most variable part. By August 2006 overdue payments of at least 90 days on adjustable-rate mortgages had grown 141 percent. Many of these borrowers contented themselves with making the minimum monthly payments. They sat serenely confident that the price of their house was rising fast enough to cancel out negative amortization.

As the mortgage delinquency rate climbed, lenders tightened standards. Low documentation loans and 100 percent financing became scarcer. Lenders hiked minimum credit scores. Some lenders asked for more than one appraisal plus the opinion of the real estate broker. Doug Duncan, chief economist for the Mortgage Bankers Association, described it as, "The pendulum . . . swinging a little farther to the conservative side."[29]

Tougher lending standards threw the rod in the financial spokes of the U.S. housing market. House prices tumbled. The percent of mortgaged properties with negative equity in 2011 stood highest in Nevada at 63 percent. Las Vegas topped the state average at 66 percent. In Michigan 36 percent of mortgage property sat underwater. These numbers came from a *Wall Street Journal* article, "Second-Mortgage Misery; Nearly 40 percent Who Borrowed Against Homes Are Underwater."[30] Falling house prices were felt more keenly by home-owners who had taken out home equity loans. These home equity loans mostly remained on the balance sheets of commercial banks. That was in contrast to the first mortgages which were usually bundled into packaged securities and resold to investors.

Exotic mortgages cannot shoulder all the blame for the U.S. housing bubble. Demographics aided and abetted the process. The U.S. population was aging, swelling the ranks of people in those upper age brackets where the percentage of home-ownership stood highest. Throw in the added wealth of economic growth. A couple of decades ago two cars in a family was a mark of affluence; by the new millennium two-house families were becoming the mark of affluence. In addition, the U.S. government pushed financial institutions to help low- and medium-income families acquire homes. It also reduced capital gains taxes. Home-ownership did go up from 64 percent to 69 percent. These policies helped fuel the housing bubble that set the global economy up for a big fall.

The U.S. subprime crisis slammed the brakes on subprime lending worldwide. By the end of 2007 British lenders specializing in subprime mortgages had stopped issuing new loans. Funds for these kinds of loans could no longer be raised in international markets. In April 2008 Abbey National, part of a Spanish banking group, suspended mortgages that let buyers get into a house without a down payment. In March 2008 Britain saw the largest percentage drop in home sales since September 1992. In April 2008 a financial derivative based on property indicated investors were betting on a 10 percent drop in British property prices within a year. British observers wondered if soon the only reminder of the good old days would be the popular British TV series, *Property Ladder*, featuring flippers in the British housing market. In 2009 it would be renamed *Property Snakes and Ladders*, an allusion to the risks of flipping in a falling market.

## Housing in the Age of Speculation

The housing bubble underscored how far a speculative temper had usurped the financial planning of households and individuals. It was another episode in the trend toward more bubbles, looser regulation, faster financial innovation, and higher risks compensating for lower interest rates in meeting financial goals. The seduction of speculative motives warped the thinking of countless home buyers who had never given a minute's thought to speculating in commodities and currencies or buying stock on margin. At very low interest rates, bearing higher risks seemed the only path to wealth accumulation.

Not everyone thinks they know enough about the airline industry to purchase stock in Delta Airlines on margin. A large segment of the population, however, lives in houses. They see no mystique about the housing market. Most likely they either own a house or definitely plan to buy one someday. Learning about buying, owning, and selling a house is a normal part of household planning. For an added sweetener, low interest rates encourage households to think of home-ownership as a faster way than savings to build up wealth. Confidence in markets discourages government from considering tighter regulations as households assimilate higher risk levels.

The housing bubble furnishes another example of monetary policy feeding a bubble in one sector of the economy to undercut the effects of weakness in another area. A passion for speculation may have shared in building the bubble by distorting and narrowing the economy's response to monetary policy.

# FIVE

# Perils of Taming Inflation

## Deflation on the Radar Screen

The task of keeping inflation corralled falls to the central banks of each country. This central bank guards the value of money by holding a tight grip on its supply. Inflation signals money is losing value. Therefore the stock of money needs to be scaled back relative to the need for it. Inflation exists when prices on average are rising. A jump in the price of one product does not constitute inflation. This remains true even if the one product holds a large place in the cost of living, such as houses, or gasoline. According to Standard & Poor's U.S. house price index, house prices rose 30 percent between 2000 and 2003. The price of crude oil increased 18 percent from the end of 2000 to the end of 2003. U.S. GDP only grew 6 percent over the same time frame.[1] Despite price inflation in these crucial markets, the economy-wide inflation rate remained quite tame.

Inflation became sufficiently tame that between 2000 and 2004 fear of a new bogeyman pinned down the minds of monetary authorities—fear of deflation. By 2003 inflation rates around the world had been easing for two decades. Between 1980 and 1984 industrial economies averaged inflation rates of 8.7 percent. Over the next five years (1985–9) the average rate dropped to 3.9 percent. The next five-year segment (1990–94) saw average inflation rates clock a comparable figure at 3.8 percent. Average inflation rates for industrial economies slid again over the next five years (1995–9), registering 2 percent. These countries saw an average inflation rate of 1.8 percent over the next five-year segment (2000–04). Inflation waned dramatically among Latin American countries. These countries posted average inflation rates of 232.6 percent for the first five years of the 1990s (1990–94). For the next five years (1995–9) that number was slashed to 17.2 percent. For the first years of the new millennium (2000–04) average inflation rates for those countries quieted down to 7.9 percent. Every part of the world—Africa, Asia, Latin America, the Middle East—reported similar trends in inflation. A spurt of runaway inflation in transition countries and Latin America lifted the average world inflation rate to 30.4 percent for the first five years of the 1990s (1990–94). The last five years of the decade (1995–9) saw world inflation rates averaging 8.4 percent and then settling down to 3.9 percent for the next five years (2000–04). Such a long-term, worldwide trend of receding inflation left observers wondering if inflation might tip over to deflation. It seemed likely since it had already happened in Japan. Japan experienced average annual *deflation* of 0.8 percent for the years 2000–03.

In the early 2000s worries about deflation surfaced in central banks around the world. In 2002 economists at the Bank of England aired the possibility of deflation. They saw the U.S. and Germany as most likely candidates to join Japan in the deflation club. By 2002 economic events had taken a dire turn that left the U.S. economy with the earmarks of economies such as the U.S.'s in the 1930s and Japan's in the 1990s. The common denominator lay in an economy struggling against the backwash of major stock market crashes. In each case a preceding boom gathered momentum on the back of high rates of corporate investment and household spending. Germany faced a deflation risk because it already boasted the lowest inflation rate in the eurozone. It was argued that efforts to combat inflation in the wider eurozone threatened to push Germany into deflation. The onset of a deflationary spiral loomed less likely in the UK, but was not ruled out. Deflation already weighed on sectors of the UK economic landscape.

Wim Duisenberg paid less heed to odds favoring deflation. He was president of the European Central Bank and chaired its monetary policy meetings. He was moved enough, however, in mid-2005 to nudge upward his inflation target from below 2 percent to less than but close to 2 percent. Raising the inflation target for the whole of the eurozone lessened the chance of central bank policy pushing

Germany over the deflationary cliff. The European Central Bank cut interest rates in 2005 as the chair of the u.s. Federal Reserve System turned up the volume on deflation rhetoric. In the three preceding years the European Central Bank had cut its policy interest rate only half as much as the Federal Reserve System. As deflation worries sank roots, European Central Bank policy-makers lay under the reproach of standing with the inflation-hawk lunatic fringe. Mr Duisenberg reportedly described deflation as a "central bankers' paradise."

Among central bankers Alan Greenspan strutted and fretted the most about deflation. Early on he voiced skepticism about deflation but he came around. He served as chair of the Federal Reserve System from 1987 to 2006. In the early 2000s few if any central bankers could rival him in esteem and influence. In economic spheres his words stood shoulder to shoulder with the infallibilities of divine wisdom. Not everybody could transcend the wordy bureaucratic opaqueness that characterized most of his public utterances. His freshly minted warning of "irrational exuberance" amidst the dot-com bubble still echoed in 2003 among the scattered entrails left by that bursting bubble. In May 2005 he conceded there was "a little froth" in the housing market. More officially he said it was an "unsustainable underlying pattern."[2] The dictionary describes "froth" as a mass of bubbles or foam. In May 2003 Greenspan advised the Joint Economic Committee of the u.s. Congress that the war against inflation was won. Then he touched on threat of deflation. In his words the threat of deflation, "though minor, is sufficiently large that it does require very close scrutiny and maybe—maybe—action on part of the central bank."[3]

Greenspan conceded that rising oil and gas prices raised concerns, but argued that cutting interest rates further would be added insurance against weakening demand that might be the thin edge of the deflation wedge. He played down the adverse side effects of further interest rate cuts. In June 2003 Greenspan spoke via satellite to a panel at the International Monetary Conference. Though still insisting that deflation remained unlikely, he sounded a more determined note to resist it. He said the Federal Reserve would "lean over backwards" to prevent deflation. He further said: "We perceive [deflation] as a low probability . . . but the cost of addressing it is very small indeed."[4] Mr Greenspan went on to compare the need for insurance against deflation to a "firebreak"—the strip of land cleared to prevent the spread of a forest fire.[5] Central bankers deemed deflation more sinister than mild inflation. Falling prices and high debts brewed a bitter economic concoction, pinching profits and causing workers to face pay cuts. That was where a downdraft of deflation would leave the debt-ridden U.S. economy. Paying back debts became all the more challenging and painful for companies and households.

All right-thinking bankers hate deflation. It forces central banks to push interest rates to near zero levels. In an inflationary economy borrowing allows buyers to buy things before the price goes up. In a deflationary economy borrowing allows buyers to buy things before the price falls, and who wants to do that? With interest rates near zero, the yields on Treasury bills and commercial paper might not cover the transaction costs of buying and selling all short-term credit instruments.

Another negative angle to deflation arose from the simple fact that central banks had no experience of dealing with it. For the last 50 years central banks had thrown all their efforts into whittling down inflation rates. With inflation a central bank could always jump-start an ailing economy by pushing interest rates below inflation rates. Just about every investment opportunity takes on added charm when interest rates are below inflation rates. The central banks would have to ransack their quivers for weapons to combat a new deflation enemy.

A famous economist of the early twentieth century, Irving Fisher, painted a nightmarish deflationary spiral to explain U.S. deflation and depression of the 1930s. In 1933 he published a famous article entitled "The Debt-Deflation Theory of Great Depressions." It described a self-feeding process in which debtors sell off assets and slash spending to meet payments. Individual efforts to lighten debt burdens weaken overall demand and put downward pressure on prices. Companies and households soon see incomes falling, but most business and household costs fall as well. The debt owed, however, remains constant, and its value in real purchasing goes up as prices fall. As the real burden goes up, payments become ever harder to meet, keeping the deflationary spiral going. It is another example of what is true for the part is not true for the whole in macroeconomics. One household can sell off assets to settle debts. If all households do it at the same time, the outcome is not pretty.

Probably a few policy-makers remembered without mentioning it that deflation often brings in its wake more government regulation. Markets lose much of their charm when durable goods like houses have to be sold for less than they were bought for. Deflationary episodes such as the 1930s bring on wider and closer government regulations. Few key players in the economy eagerly waited to watch the curtain drop on deregulation.

In the 2000s deflation worries subtly and perhaps unconsciously nudged the eyes of central bankers away from inflation numbers. Central bankers went from inflation hawks to inflation doves. As long as inflation was bogeyman number one, central banks erred on the side of squashing inflation. While weighing another interest rate cut, Greenspan brushed aside rising oil, natural gas, and housing prices. For once there was no anxious rush to dampen inflation fires before they spread. History proved central bankers right about inflation. Low interest rates did not touch off a wave of inflation, at least not immediately. The determination, however, to dodge deflation as a rock of danger led to other policy excesses. Now that low interest rates no longer fed fears of future inflation, central bankers felt free to keep interest rates unusually low long after economies smoothly cruised toward full recovery. Low interest rates went from an invitation for inflation to an inoculation against deflation. The Federal Reserve went from erring on the side of forestalling inflation to erring on the side of preempting deflation. This new policy bias took low interest rates so far as to find ways to lower long-term interest rates. Central banks can dictate short-term interest rates, but long-term interest rates have a life of their own. Central banks learned that if they telegraphed to markets what they were going to do, and always did what they said they were going to do, they would acquire the power to manage long-term expectations. Long-term interest rates go in a groove strongly shaped by what future trajectory short-term interest rates are expected to follow. By carefully managing expectations central bankers piloted long-term interest rates to lower levels.

All central banks have a benchmark interest rate that acts as a policy instrument. They may dictate this interest rate directly or they may control it indirectly by stage-managing market forces. The Federal Reserve System's benchmark interest rate is the federal funds rate. It is the interest rate at which commercial banks borrow funds from each other overnight. The Bank of England's benchmark interest rate is the BOEBR (Bank of England Base Rate). It is also called the official bank rate. UK commercial banks pay this interest rate to borrow funds overnight from the Bank of England. The benchmark interest rate for the European Central Bank is called the "main refinancing rate." It closely resembles the federal funds rate. For the Bank of Japan the benchmark interest rate is called the official discount rate. It is the interest rate private financial institutions pay to borrow funds from the Bank of Japan. These benchmark interest rates carry what is called an "announcement effect." Central banks learned to sway other key interest rates just by publicly announcing their intentions.

Control over benchmark interest rates ranked among the chief tools in the central bank's monetary toolkit for reigniting a sluggish economy. In December 2000 the Federal Reserve's federal funds rate stood at 6.4 percent. That was a rather high rate aimed at taming a speeding economy riding the tide of the dot-com bubble. The bubble popped, the economy stalled, and the Federal Reserve edged the federal funds rate downward. By the end of 2001, the federal funds stood at 1.82 percent. In 2002 the Federal Reserve inched the federal funds rate down lower, finishing the year at 1.24 percent. The federal funds rate had not been that low in 40 years. In 2003, amid deflation fears, the Federal Reserve shaved off another quarter point in July. The federal funds rate remained at 1 percent until July 2004 when the Federal Reserve started edging it up. Why keep this benchmark rate so low for so long? Holding short-term interest rates near zero over a long span of time persuaded bond markets to expect low short-term interest rates.

The global economy shared in the U.S. economic slowdown of 2001. The European Central Bank's benchmark rate stood at 4.75 percent at the end of 2000. The bank shaved off one point after another, putting it a 2.75 percent by the end of 2002. In 2003 the threat of deflation reared up. The bank sliced another 0.75 percent points off. The rate remained at 2 percent points between June 2003 and December 2005. The Bank of England's benchmark rate finished 2000 at 6 percent. In 2001 the Bank of England slowly ratcheted it downward, leaving it at 4 percent by the end of the year. It remained at 4 percent until 2003 when deflation talk grew noisiest. By July 2003 this rate stood at 3.5 percent, but it did not remain that low for long. By February 2004 the rate was back at 4 percent. The benchmark rate for the Bank of Japan stood at 0.5 percent at the end of 2000. It finished 2001 at 0.1 percent points, and remained there until July 2006. Japan had deflation at the time. Switzerland's central bank, the Swiss National Bank, adopted the three-month London Interbank Offered Rate (LIBOR) in Swiss francs for its benchmark interest rate. This interest rate stood at 3.41 percent at the end of 2000. The Swiss National Bank steadily dialed it downward to 0.68 percent by the end of 2002. In 2003 the bank further tweaked this benchmark until it reached bottom at 0.24 percent in January 2004. Then this interest rate started rising, reaching 0.75 percent by the end of 2004.

Bargain-basement short-term interest rates and worries about deflation helped trim long-term interest rates. Lenders stand to enjoy a windfall gain if deflation lifts the real purchasing power of what is owed to them. As long as they are confident of repayment, they settle for lower long-term interest rates under expected deflation. In the U.S. the interest rate on 30-year fixed-rate conventional mortgage stood at 8.29 percent in June 2000. It sank to 7.16 percent by June 2001. A year later it stood at 6.65 percent. In June 2003, the month Mr Greenspan most stridently mouthed fears of deflation, it sank to 5.23 percent. It turned up mildly, experienced few transient surges up, but in June of 2005 it stood at 5.58 percent. According to a 2003 *Wall Street Journal* account,

> The Fed's preoccupation with deflation has investors piling into bonds, which will increase in value if rates keep tumbling. Ten-year Treasury notes closed yesterday at 3.29 percent, their lowest yield in 45 years.[6]

A long phase of steadily easing inflation around the world, Japanese deflation, and the highly credible voice of Mr Greenspan trumpeting deflation, neutralized what inflationary fears if any had been aroused by the Federal Reserve's easy money policies and historically low interest rates. Instead deflation was seen as the likeliest outcome. There was one market, however, where nobody expected prices to fall. The Bank of International Settlements' data for inflation-adjusted house prices shows u.s. housing prices climbing every year from the first data point in the first quarter of 1975.[7] These prices climbed in the face of 17 percent mortgage interest rates in the early 1980s. They bulldozed upward through two major stock market crashes, one in 1987, the other in 2000. Houses were one investment that could still be counted on. No amount of deflation talk from central banks could dampen the expectation that house prices were headed only one way and that was up. The u.s. housing market in 2003 was ripe for bubble formation.

### Bubbles: Piñatas or Hornets' Nest to Central Bankers

Alan Greenspan was known for not wanting to use interest rates to burst asset bubbles. He came under fire for letting the dot-com bubble get out of hand before applying the brakes of higher interest rates. He argued that bubbles are hard to identify in advance and that the brutal interest rates needed to tame them did more harm to the rest of the economy than the actual bursting of the bubble. Therefore it was better to let the bubble pop without help. Greenspan's views may have been colored by the experience of Japan's central bank. In 1989 and 1990 the Bank of Japan pushed up interest rates to prick stock market and real estate bubbles. A decade later the Japanese economy still floundered sluggish and listless.

A look at the dynamics of a bubble puts Mr Greenspan's views in perspective. A "bubble" is a species of deviate behavior that afflicts markets under certain conditions. Markets at their best can be a tidy system of rewards and penalties. The price is a reward to the producer who supplies the product. It is a penalty to the consumer who buys it. If the price goes up, the reward for producing the product rises, but the penalty for consuming the product goes up also. The higher reward for producing the product calls forth a more generous supply. The greater penalty for consuming the product cramps the demand. These forces relax tightness in supply. Therefore a higher price triggers market forces that batter the price back down. The initial increase in price might have been brought on by any number of things. In the case of houses the initial price increase might have been occasioned by a change in household preferences or a change in the average age of the population. Households start favoring houses at the expense of automobiles, or travel, or various luxury goods. As long as market behavior lies confined within the limits of this description, markets are rational institutions that mostly deserve the praise heaped upon them.

A market "bubble" implies a loss of objectivity. At the very least it is thinking driven by herd instinct. For markets to behave irrationally there must be a psychological angle to market behavior, and this enters through the role of expectations. As long as expectations are rational, market behavior remains rational. In the case of housing it is rational to study demographics and determine that family formation is about to accelerate. The higher rate of family formation can realistically be expected to lead to stronger demand for housing, and in turn higher house prices. Armed with such information, rational households aim to buy houses ahead of the future price increases. In the process households trying to beat the market bid up the price of houses, increasing the reward for building houses. More houses are built. Society gets the additional houses it needs to meet the higher rate of family formation.

A market bubble builds when buyers' expectations of future price increases are formed chiefly from extrapolations of past price increases. If rising prices lead to expectations that prices will go even higher in the future, then higher prices do not dampen demand. On the contrary they strengthen it. Every price boost vindicates expectations and becomes a pledge of even higher prices in the future. Potential buyers start thinking in terms of buying the product before the price goes up again. Given enough incentive to beat future price increases, potential buyers borrow funds if necessary. Lenders are only too happy to extend financing under these conditions. The collateral they hold appears to be an appreciating rather than a depreciating asset. Lenders see the appreciating collateral as an ace in the hole and it makes them careless. The bubble builds as price hikes fuel expectations of more price hikes. When prices stray too far from fundamentals the bubble pops. Prices overshoot the mark of what can be sustained even for a short period of time. Buyers and sellers lose confidence in house valuations. Once prices level off the bubble's days are numbered. In the U.S., bubble psychology received added impetus from the long uninterrupted upward trend in house prices. As far back as modern statistics had been collected, U.S. house prices only went in one direction and that was up. Prices had never dropped for a full year.

One tell-tale sign that house prices soared far above fundamentals was the ratio of prices to rents. It was the real estate market's version of the price-earnings ratio familiar to stock market investors. In 2005 the ratio of prices to rents in the U.S. stood 35 percent above its average level between 1975 and 2000. As this ratio rose renting became more attractive than buying for people in the housing market mainly looking just for a place to live. In Britain, Australia, and Spain the house price to rent ratio climbed above its 1975–2000 average by 50 percent or more. At these prices landlords were much better off selling property and buying interest-bearing bonds. As long as landlords remained confident of steep house price escalations in the future, they contented themselves with losing money on rent. Once that confidence had weakened the bubble sat ripe for popping.

The deflation of the bubble goes a bit easier in an inflationary economy. Then prices only need to level off for rents to catch up with prices. In a non-inflationary economy, the bubble bursts instead of quietly deflating. Optimists will insist that high prices to rent ratios are only symptoms of low interest rates. That is true to a point, but interest rates cannot remain low with speculators busily borrowing funds to buy property. Sooner or later interest rates rise above the growth rate of property prices, otherwise interest rates cannot ration limited lendable funds. Once interest rates go up, the price to rent ratio is out of line.

As the U.S. housing bubble stretched drum tight, Federal Reserve watchers anxiously waited to see if it would raise interest rates to prick the bubble. Raising a benchmark interest rate in the eyes of financial markets raised the odds favoring future deflation. That meant higher short-term interest rates did not significantly translate into higher 30-year rates. By 2004 the Federal Reserve drew fire and abuse for its policies. Wall Street grumbled that the 1 percent federal funds rate sparked asset bubbles. A 1 percent interest rate adjusted for inflation equated to zero percent real interest. In April 2004 Federal Reserve officials were staying the low interest rate course. They argued that pricking a bubble posed greater economic risks than letting the bubble deflate on its own. Once a bubble deflated the Federal Reserve could deploy monetary tools to contain the damage. The *Wall Street Journal* carried an article, "Fed Official Discounts Threat of 'Bubble' Trouble." This article quoted from a speech given by Donald Kohn, one of the twelve Federal Reserve Governors: "The balance of costs and benefits does not favor policy action to address possible imbalances."[8] Mr Kohn felt that higher wages and wealth created by new technologies should support house values.

In April 2004 the Federal Reserve's eyes were glued to commodity prices rather than house prices. The price of crude oil was 41 percent above its April 2001 level. It was bullish commodity prices that prodded the Federal Reserve to inch up the federal funds rate. In July 2004, the Federal Reserve raised it from 1 percent to 1.25 percent. The federal funds rate was pushed up in quarter notches. In February 2005 it reached 2.5 percent. That was about the time the Federal Reserve began to see a bubble in housing. Mr Greenspan told a House committee, "We do have characteristics of bubbles in certain areas, but not, best as I can judge, nationwide."[9] In April Mr Kohn gave a speech in which he said:

A couple of years ago I was fairly confident that the rise in real estate prices primarily reflected low interest rates, good growth in disposable income, and favorable demographics . . . Prices have gone up enough since then relative to interest rates, rents and incomes to raise questions; recent reports from professionals in the housing market suggest an increasing volume of transactions by investors, who . . . may be expecting the recent trend of prices increases to continue.[10]

The next month the Federal Reserve and other bank regulators sent letters to commercial banks warning them to evaluate home equity loans carefully, reminding them that these loans bear greater risk if interest rates rise and home values drop. The letter specifically mentioned interest-only home equity loans, low or no documentation loans, and higher loan to value and debt to income ratios. Mr Greenspan later insisted that the warning to banks was not an exercise in bubble pricking. Some observers saw Greenspan working the regulatory angle to rein in the housing bubble rather than painfully high interest rates.

In October 2005 President Bush nominated Ben Bernanke to replace Mr Greenspan. Mr Bernanke underscored his intention to continue the policies and strategies of the Greenspan years. On 21 November 2002, just three months after first joining the Federal Reserve, he gave a speech, "Deflation, Making Sure 'It' Does Not Happen Here" at the National Economics Club in Washington, DC. Mr Bernanke co-authored an influential study arguing that the Federal Reserve should not set interest rates to sway asset prices. In 1999, at the height of the dot-com bubble, he presented the study to a Federal Reserve conference. From all accounts Mr Bernanke planned to keep the Federal Reserve's eye fastened on inflation and economic growth, and not on speculative bubbles.

Not all scholarly research agreed with Mr Bernanke and Mr Greenspan. Some scholars concluded that house prices should matter in the conduct of monetary policy. C. A. Goodhart, an advisor to the Bank of England and accomplished scholar, was familiar with both theoretical arguments and practical operations of central banks. In an article entitled "Price Stability and Financial Fragility," he argued that central banks should weigh asset prices, and particularly house prices, in the formulation of monetary policy.[11] Not all central banks kowtowed to Mr Bernanke's and Mr Greenspan's views. While Mr Greenspan beat the drum of deflation in 2003, Ian Macfarlane, governor of the Reserve Bank of Australia, made speeches and used routine policy statements to warn that mortgage debt was rising at a fast clip, that the housing market was overheating. He minced no words that a cooling of household debt and property development lay in the long-term interest of the Australian economy.

At first Australians shrugged off signals of future interest rate hikes and kept pouring money into a housing boom. The ratio of household debt to income for Australians climbed in a decade from 56 percent to 125 percent. Purchases of second homes for investment and rental property ignited a property boom. Get-rich-quick real estate books multiplied in Australia. Television shows like *Hot Property* and *The Block* glamorized flipping. The u.s. economy barely broke out of recession before Australia's central bank started upping interest rates in May 2002. At that time talk of a global housing boom was first heard. In November 2003, the Reserve Bank of Australia raised its benchmark interest by a quarter point to 5 percent. A month later the bank raised it again by another quarter point. Australia's central bank boasted the highest rate among advanced countries. The bank kept its benchmark rate at 5.25 percent, already the highest in the industrialized world, until March 2005 when it raised its rate to 5.5 percent.

Australia's experiment with bubble popping helped brace u.s. monetary officials at least modestly to acknowledge a u.s. housing bubble. Australian house prices leveled off in 2004. A weaker housing market sapped economic growth, but did not push Australia over the economic precipice to recession. Consumer spending still grew but at half the pace. Meanwhile the IMF (International Monetary Fund) studied the outcomes of housing bubbles. It uncovered that only about 40 percent of house-price booms ended in a property bust.[12] Time would show that the Australian housing market only took a breather. According to Bank of International Settlements data, inflation-adjusted house prices in Australia leveled off in 2004 and most of 2005 before turning upward again. The Reserve Bank of Australia kept raising its benchmark rate in quarter-point increments until it reached 7.25 percent in March 2008. In September the bank switched to the rate-cutting mode.

If any central banker lay awake at night fretting about the housing bubble, it was Mervyn King, governor of the Bank of England and chairman of its Monetary Policy Committee. Deflation worries still gripped the Federal Reserve when officials of the Bank of England zeroed in on the housing bubble as its Achilles heel. By mid-2004 people in the UK were hearing warnings from Mervyn King that houses stood overpriced. In transparent speech quite different from Mr Greenspan's manner, he suggested anyone thinking of buying a house at going prices should consider the future trajectory of both interest rates and house prices. Deflation worries raged at their height in mid-2003 when the Bank of England cut its benchmark interest rate to 3.5 percent. It did not stay at that low rate for very long. In November 2003 the bank raised it to 3.75 percent, nudging it upward in quarter-point notches until it stood at 4.75 percent by August 2004. The Bank of England's Monetary Policy Committee had in mind gradually deflating the bubble rather than bursting it and sending the whole economy swirling in a wild tailspin. UK house prices leveled off in the first half of 2005, and in August the benchmark rate fell a quarter point. For a while it seemed the soft landing was on the cards. In August 2006 the Bank of England started gradually raising rates again and continued through July 2007. In September 2007 Northern Rock asked the Bank of England for liquidity support. In December 2007 the Bank of England did a U-turn and set to cutting rates.

The European Central Bank also saw risks surrounding booming house prices. After the bank's monthly meeting in February 2005, its president, Jean-Claude Trichet, vented his uneasy feeling that low interest rates were stoking the housing furnace in some countries. He remarked that current house prices in some countries "are not in our view sustainable, and certainly not welcome."[13] Despite these misgivings, the bank's top executives opted to keep the benchmark interest at 2 percent for the twentieth straight month. The bank kept its rate fixed even though the U.S. Federal Reserve had started inching its benchmark rate up from 1 percent in July 2004. Politicians begged for a rate cut to bring alive the eurozone's lumbering economies. Disparities in house price inflation across the eurozone made matters worse for Mr Trichet and his colleagues. Germany saw house price skidding 0.9 percent in the third quarter of 2004, while Spain, France, Italy, and Ireland saw them galloping upward at double-digit rates. About one-third of the eurozone's GDP comes from Germany.

The European Central Bank orchestrates a one-size-fits-all monetary and interest rate policy. It aims for the interest rate that most closely harmonizes the needs of all eurozone countries. Housing was the one eurozone industry in which price inflation bore markedly dissimilar features across countries. In no other eurozone industry did price inflation in individual countries stray so far from the all-country average. Mr Trichet further signaled that the bank saw more signs of inflation on the economic horizon than deflation, and that the bank was standing ready to hike interest rates. The European Central Bank held its rate steady at 2 percent for more than two years. It was not until December 2005 that the European Central Bank raised its benchmark rate to 2.25 percent. By then signs of inflation hushed the politicians. Inflation worries erased deflation worries and pushed aside the issue of lethargic economic growth. Between March 2006 and July 2008, the bank raised its rate eight times. It raised the rate in quarter-point upticks until it reached 4.25 percent in mid-2008. In October 2008 the bank started cutting rates.

Central banks have grown keen on managing expectations. Before raising rates, the European Central Bank spent several months sounding the inflation-fighting trumpet, and threatening interest-rate hikes. It may have hoped that undercutting the formation of inflationary expectations would remove the need for large hikes in interest rates. Expectations of inflation wrench upward wage demands and long-term interest rates. No central bank was keener on managing expectations than Mr Greenspan's Federal Reserve Bank. In 2004 Ben Bernanke co-authored a paper entitled, "Monetary Policy Alternatives at the Zero Bound: An Empirical Assessment." Two of its other authors, Vincent R. Reinhart and Brian P. Sack, also held key Federal Reserve positions related to monetary policy. The paper includes a rather candid discussion of how central banks choose their words carefully to influence long-term interest rates. A few excerpts throw light on the logic behind some of the Federal Reserve's interest rate policies during this time.

However, the success over the years in reducing inflation and, consequently, the average level of nominal interest rates has increased the likelihood that the nominal policy interest rate may become constrained by the zero lower bound on interest rates. When that happens, a central bank can no longer stimulate aggregate demand by further interest-rate reductions and must rely instead on "non-standard" policy alternatives . . . If central bank "talk" affects policy expectations, then policy-makers retain some leverage over long-term yields, even if the current policy rate [benchmark rate] is at or near zero . . . In particular, even with the overnight rate [benchmark rate] at zero, the central bank may be able to impart additional stimulus to the economy by persuading the public that the policy rate will remain low for a longer period than was previously expected. One means of doing so would be to shade interest-rate expectations downward by making a commitment to the public to follow a policy of extended monetary ease. This commitment, if credible and not previously expected, should lower longer-term rates, support other asset prices, and boost aggregate demand . . . Federal Reserve officials expressed concerns about the "remote" possibility of deflation from the latter part of 2002 through much of 2003. Subsequently, in late 2003 and early 2004, though the deflation risk had receded, the slow pace of job creation exacerbated concerns about the recovery's sustainability. Although the Federal Reserve's policy rate remained at least 100 basis points above zero throughout this period, policymakers became more specific in communicating their outlook for policy in the attempt to shape expectations . . . Policymaking by thesaurus continued through 2004 . . . By persuading the public that the policy rate will remain low for a longer period than expected, central bankers can reduce long-term rates and provide some impetus to the economy, even if the short-term rate is close to zero. However, for credibility to be maintained, the central bank's commitments must be consistent with the public's understanding of the policymakers' objectives and outlook for the economy.[14]

## An Ominous Conundrum

In April 2004 Mr Greenspan set to preparing the bond market for an upward tweaking of the Federal Reserve's key interest rate. A sudden and unexpected jump in the benchmark interest rate risked telegraphing the bond market that the Federal Reserve sees inflation coming down the pike. The outcome of a hike in the benchmark rate could be a large jump in long-term interest rates, particularly if the bond market thinks more future rate hikes will be needed than what even the Federal Reserve expects. While signaling that an immediate rate hike was not on the cards, Mr Greenspan let it be known that the current benchmark rate of 1 percent would eventually lead to higher inflation. The Federal Reserve's intent was to prevent long-term rates from rising too steeply once its key interest rate turned upward.

A subtle difference in bond market atmospherics affected the outcome of the Federal Reserve's action. The end of recession no longer signaled the return to higher inflation. The risks of long-term rates overreacting to a hike in the Federal Reserve's rate stood much lower. In the past inflation rates even at the depths of a recession remained above what most observers thought was ideal. That meant that when the recession was over, the Federal Reserve initiated monetary tightening and long-term interest rates shot up. Rates moved sharply higher because the bond market and everyone else expected inflation to be on the march. In the new bond market atmospherics every upward move in the central bank's benchmark interest rate added to the probability of deflation. Expectations of deflation pulled long-term interest rates down.

For three months the Federal Reserve dropped clues and hints of higher interest rates to come. In July 2004 it raised its interest rate a quarter-point notch, putting it at 1.25 percent. In July 2004 the interest rate on 30-year fixed-rate conventional mortgages stood at 6.06 percent. The Federal Reserve kept nudging up its benchmark rate. By the close of 2004 the rate stood at 2.16 percent. In February 2005 the Federal Reserve raised the rate to 2.5 percent. As the Federal Reserve's key interest rate went up, the interest rate on 30-year fixed-rate conventional mortgages went down, registering 5.63 percent for February 2005. On 16 February 2005, Mr Greenspan gave the Federal Reserve Board's semi-annual monetary policy report to Congress. In his testimony before the u.s. Senate's Committee on Banking, Housing, and Urban Affairs, he gave an upbeat assessment of economic conditions and went on to say:

In this environment, long-term interest rates have trended lower in recent months even as the Federal Reserve has raised the level of the target federal funds rate by 150 basis points. This development contrasts with most experience, which suggests that, other things being equal, increasing short-term interest rates are normally accompanied by a rise in longer-term yields . . . The favorable inflation performance across a broad range of countries resulting from enlarged global goods, services and financial capacity has doubtless contributed to expectations of lower inflation in the years ahead and lower inflation risk premiums. But none of this is new and hence it is difficult to attribute the long-term interest rate declines of the last nine months to glacially increasing globalization. For the moment, the broadly unanticipated behavior of world bond markets remains a *conundrum*. Bond price movements may be a short-term aberration, but it will be some time before we are able to better judge the forces underlying recent experience.[15]

The thesaurus lists for "conundrum" the following synonyms: puzzle, mystery, challenge, poser, problem, and riddle. At late as May 2005 the *Wall Street Journal* was citing Greenspan's use of the word "conundrum" in discussing why long-term interest rates had remained surprisingly low.[16] One answer to the riddle of low long-term rates might have had to do with the Federal Reserve's management of expectations. Mr Greenspan could not very easily brag that the Federal Reserve's "policymaking by thesaurus" had been all too successful in keeping long-term rates low. Airing that possibility might lay bare too much of the Federal Reserve's proactive stance on expectations management and alter the way expectations respond to certain wording.

After Mr Greenspan's use of the word "conundrum," the 30-year conventional mortgage rate gently trended upward. It was October 2005 before this interest rate entered 6 percent territory. It reached a peak of 6.76 percent in July 2006, and then again went into retreat mode. During this time lenders launched the interest-only fixed-interest rate mortgages. In April 2006 the Federal Reserve's key interest rate stood at 4.79 percent. The interest rate on one-year adjustable-rate mortgages averaged roughly one percentage point above this rate. The 30-year fixed rate stood less than one percentage point above the adjustable rate at 6.51 percent.

The real "conundrum" lay in lenders offering riskier mortgages while interest rates remained unusually low. In April 2006 the *Wall Street Journal* carried an article, "New Type of Mortgage Surges in Popularity; Fixed-Rate Interest-Only Loans Offer Lower Initial Payments but Delay Debt Reduction."[17] u.s. Bancorp unveiled these mortgages in September 2004. The president of its home mortgage unit noted that the demand for this new mortgage product was "growing every month." These loans offered the security of a fixed interest rate at a time when interest rates sat at historically low levels. Interest-only meant lower payments. Only after ten to twenty years did the borrower start paying toward the principal.

The Federal Reserve gradually edged its benchmark interest rate up in quarter ticks until it reached 5.25 percent in July 2006. That was also the month when the 30-year rate topped out at 6.76 percent. The Federal Reserve kept its key interest rate at 5.25 percent until August 2007. After reaching a peak in July 2006, the 30-year interest rate gradually sank but turned up in the following summer, touching 6.7 percent in July 2007. In August the 30-year interest rate dropped to 6.52 percent and the Federal Reserve cut its key rate back to 5 percent. By then the thin edge of the subprime crisis wedge was stubbornly encroaching.

The yield curve charts the relationship between short-term interest rates and long-term interest rates. The difference between the interest rate on ten-year treasury bonds and the Federal Reserve's benchmark interest rate is one of the ten economic barometers that go into calculating the leading economic indicator index. What is called the benchmark yield curve for the u.s. is the gap between interest rates for the two-year and ten-year Federal treasury bonds. Economic forecasters treat an inverted yield curve as a portent of recession. A yield curve turns inverted when short-term interest rates hover above long-term interest rates. Normally long-term interest rates exceed short-term rates. Banks borrow short-term and loan out long-term at higher interest rates. Investors normally demand higher interest rates before locking up funds for longer spans of time. An inverted yield curve signals that financial market participants expect weaker economic conditions ahead.

The longer a yield curve remains inverted, the greater the chance of recession. For ten straight months leading up to the recession of 2001, the Federal Reserve's key interest rate remained above the ten-year Treasury bond rate. Between July 2006 and January 2008 this interest rate remained above the ten-year rate for nineteen consecutive months. The unwillingness of long-term interest rates to rise amid climbing short-term rates produced an inverted yield curve. Some observers brushed aside yield curve recession signals and cited unique factors causing long-term rates to remain unusually low. Among other things, they cited the amount of foreign money using u.s. Treasuries as a place to park. In March 2006 Ben Bernanke, now chair of the Federal Reserve System, delivered a speech in which he addressed the meaning of the yield curve which already bordered on inversion. He indicated that in individual situations it was hard to extract exactly what signal the yield curve was sending, and for the time being he was remaining more upbeat on the economy than what the yield curve alone supported. Federal Reserve Bank of New York economists developed a forecasting model using a yield curve. In January 2007 this forecasting model suggested a near 40 percent chance of the u.s. economy entering a recession within twelve months.[18] The end of January marked the seventh straight month of an inverted yield curve. By March the ten-year interest rate minus the benchmark interest rate difference had sat negative for nine months. That month the Federal Reserve again kept its key rate unchanged and softened its anti-inflation tone a bit. Its language still left many observers thinking that another interest rate hike could be in store. This never came and in August the Federal Reserve started cutting its key rate. In February 2008 this key rate dropped to 3 percent, putting it below the ten-year Treasury rate for the first time in nineteen months.

A narrower gap between short-term rates and long-term rates squeezed bank profits. One bank analyst, Joseph Dickerson of Atlantic Equities, thought the yield curve might wreak less damage to the profits of Wachovia Corp. He said that Wachovia "is probably doing the best to mitigate the [yield] curve by being nimble and keeping home equity loans and mortgages on the balance sheet."[19]

Events were about to take a different turn. In December of 2008 Wachovia, after suffering the largest quarterly loss ever reported by a u.s. company, was taken over by Wells Fargo.

## The Uses of Forecasts

Given the imperfections of economic forecasting, prediction of deflation in 2002 and 2003 counts as a reasonably accurate prediction of the types of economic headwinds economies around the world were about to face. Given public statements of central bank officials about the threat of deflation, it is quite likely that these officials envisioned a major economic calamity as one possible outcome of trends that were developing. Deflation means higher bankruptcies and foreclosures. That part of the prediction certainly burst upon the scene with a vengeance. It seems logical that worries of higher bankruptcies and foreclosures would persuade government to tighten regulations. Government and society, however, had invested too many hopes in deregulation to turn back. The desire to sustain a given rate of return amid falling interest rates sent investors scrambling for new options and strategies. Tighter regulations only promised more hurdles standing in the way of impatient investors. Normally low interest rates in themselves should be more than adequate in nudging lenders toward tighter standards, to only fund loans where repayment went virtually guaranteed. Strange to say, as interest rates fell, lenders loosened rather than tightened standards.

We have already discussed how falling interest rates raise difficulties for savers and investors aiming to sustain a given rate of return. Now we see the thorny difficulties falling interest rates pose for monetary authorities who have an intelligent understanding of bubbles and tackle the challenges and quandaries of them with thoughtful caution. Given the spoken and probably unspoken uneasiness of central bankers, it is tempting to conclude that sidestepping disaster becomes hopeless once a bubble develops in an industry as basic as housing.

# Global Banking and Financial Crisis

## The Financial Engineering of Mortgage Banking

Brisk growth and large size are not always good news. Astronomers say that in about five billion years the sun will expand into a giant red star. As a giant red star its radius will swallow the earth's current orbit. Later it will lose its outer layers and only a small nucleus called a dwarf white star will remain. The earth will not likely survive the sun's life cycle. History offers examples of cities and small states growing into giant empires before collapsing in a trajectory that evokes an analogy with the giant red star. The red star analogy brings to mind the growth of the banking sector leading up to the subprime crisis of 2008. A banking sector spreading out at a fast clip portends ill for economic stability. It is one of the ingredients of the pre-crisis build-up. In pre-civil war U.S., wild growth in banking contributed to a major economic calamity. It shocked the freshly fledged Republic of Texas into banning banks in its constitution. Before the 2008 banking crisis, evidence of bank expansion included rising values of bank assets relative to GDP, frenzied financial innovation, rising debt to equity ratios for banks, rising debt to GDP ratios for societies, and a rising amount of bank borrowing from other banks. London ranks among the largest and oldest financial centers in the world. Its drive to maturity predates the First World War. In 1960 banking sector assets in the UK equaled roughly 40 percent of UK GDP. By 1990 that statistic stood at 220 percent of UK GDP. In 2008 that statistic reached 540 percent of UK GDP. Between mid-2004 and mid-2007 the ten largest U.S. banks saw total assets double.

The new and innovative mortgages furnished the combustible material that awaited a spark to kindle a global banking crisis toward the end of 2007. A fair amount of lax and fraudulent underwriting practices went with the origination of those mortgages. The mortgage industry came to refer to subprime mortgages as "ninja" loans (no income, no job, no assets). While accounts of what went on in the mortgage underwriting industry strains the credulity of disinterested observers, the delinquent mortgages themselves amounted to no more than a mere brush fire that set off a major financial conflagration. Between the second quarter of 2006 and the second quarter of 2007 the percentage of seriously delinquent loans in the U.S. grew from 6 percent to 9 percent. Delinquency on that order foretold no inevitable breakdown of the global banking system. The damage in global financial markets fanned out far beyond expected losses from U.S. foreclosures.

Appreciating what happened in the banking system begins with reminding ourselves how the mortgage industry evolved in the U.S. and other countries. Before the age of financial engineering, a hopeful homebuyer turned to a bank or financial institution for a home mortgage. If the loan application received a green light the borrower bought the house and the financial institution held the mortgage. The borrower owed the financial institution monthly payments. The financial institution counted the unpaid balance of the mortgage as an asset on its own balance sheet until the borrower repaid the mortgage in full. In the case of foreclosure all losses were borne fully by the financial institution. The financial institution's instinct for self-preservation assured that it only financed those borrowers who could be counted on to repay in full.

Over time the financial institution became merely the "originator" of the loan. The originator of mortgages only negotiated mortgages for a percentage fee. It sold the mortgages it negotiated to a third party who stood to shoulder the loss in the case of default and foreclosure. At first the third parties in the U.S. were chiefly Ginnie Mae, a U.S. government agency, Fannie Mae, a U.S. government-sponsored entity, and Freddie Mac, another U.S. government-sponsored entity. Later mortgage originators took to selling the mortgages to private-sector financial institutions. These third parties "securitized" the mortgages. They pooled several mortgages to create a new financial asset and sold the new asset to investors who now owned the collective payment rights of bundled mortgages. More financial engineering was at work.

"Securitization" denotes the practice of packaging a bundle of mortgages and putting the package on the market. The pool of mortgages is transferred into a trust. The trust holds the mortgages as collateral for the bonds that the trust issues. The individual mort-gages are backed by the homes and property of the borrowers. The bonds are backed by the mortgages. Thus these bonds are called "mortgage-backed securities." Like other bonds sold in the bond market, mortgage-backed securities carry ratings conferred by rating agencies such as Moody's or Standard & Poor's. The interest the bond pays comes on a pass-through basis from the monthly interest payments made on the mortgages. Payments made toward the mortgage principal go to paying off the principal on the bonds. The bond earns less interest than borrowers pay on the mortgage. The difference goes to paying the intermediaries for their financial services. The soundest mortgage-backed securities come from Ginnie Mae, Fannie Mae, or Freddie Mac. Mortgages standing for less creditworthy borrowers go to private financial institutions. These institutions sell the riskier mortgage-backed securities.

Private financial institutions, as if this process was not convoluted enough, piled on another layer of complexity. They structured an offering of mortgage-backed securities such that various bonds, backed by one bundle of mortgages, bore different priorities in the event of default. This structure involved layers of subordination. In-vestors with the least risk tolerance bought into the top layer. Bonds in the top layer were the last to bear losses in case of defaults. The bonds in the lowest layer were the first to bear losses if defaults occurred. A bundle of mortgages might be carved into as many as six layers of subordination. Other methods of parceling out risk involved over-collateralization and widening the gap between bond interest rates and underlying mortgage interest rates.

The packaging and sale of mortgage-backed securities did not fully exhaust the varied potentialities of financial engineering. The securitization process had further room to evolve in complexity.

Financial institutions bundled packages of mortgage-backed securities to invent a new financial product called collateralized debt obligations. These financial products were bonds backed by packages of mortgage-backed securities. Collateralized debt obligations could be backed by securitized bundles of mortgage-backed securities or by securitized bundles of other collateralized debt obligations. These financial products bore ratings from the same credit ratings agencies that grade corporate bonds and government bonds. The better known U.S. rating agencies were Moody's, Standard & Poor's, Fitch, and Duff & Phelps. U.S. credit rating agencies boasted the largest global presence in the market for these services. Credit rating agencies headquartered in Japan, Canada, and the UK also enjoyed a global presence. By the close of the twentieth century Moody's and Standard & Poor's kept offices in Tokyo, London, Paris, and Frankfurt. Moody's also had offices in Sydney and Madrid. Standard & Poor's kept offices in Melbourne, Toronto, Stockholm, and Mexico City. In August 2011 Standard & Poor's downgraded U.S. long-term Treasury bonds rating from AAA to AA+.

In hindsight greater caution was in order for these rating agencies. Before the subprime crisis of 2008 these agencies honored with over 90 percent of mortgage-backed securities with AAA ratings. By riskier mortgage-backed securities are meant the ones carved from subprime mortgages. To be fair, the rating agencies had little experience in mortgage-backed securities. These securities were new and came with no historical record to track. Without historical data it was hard to study performance and risks. On the other hand, the newest generation of financial analysts was trained to believe that the market price of a financial asset reflected all the available information relevant to its value. Therefore historical data brought no new information to the table that was not already incorporated into the market price. Another difficulty lay in how these agencies generated revenue. At first they sold publications of bond ratings and related material. Players in bond markets bought the publications to check the ratings various bonds carried. The companies whose debt was rated paid no fees to the credit rating agencies.

Over time various companies took to asking for credit agency ratings to comfort fickle investors. In 1970 Fitch and Moody's asked companies to pay a fee in return for receiving a rating. By 1980, fees paid by rated companies accounted for 80 percent of Standard & Poor's revenue. As companies became paying customers, paying handsome fees, credit rating agencies began to think in terms of keeping their customers happy. Leading up to the subprime crisis the credit rating agencies did this by awarding AAA ratings to securities backed by risky mortgages. As the crisis unfolded and the spotlight turned to the credit rating agencies, it became transparent that they had not covered themselves with glory.

The U.S.'s Fannie Mae only purchased mortgages that met certain underwriting standards. Mortgages that met these standards were called "prime." Mortgages that could not clear these underwriting hurdles were "subprime." The prime mortgages met the investing guidelines of the large institutional investors. That was who purchased the majority of them. Subprime mortgages required a market where investors felt freer to bear added risk. To make as many of the subprime mortgages as possible acceptable to the large institutional investors, Wall Street adopted the practice of dividing mortgage-backed securities into different layers of risks. The top layer stood the least risk of taking hits from defaults. These received the AAA rating and were sold to large institutional investors. By this stratagem large institutional investors swallowed a large share of subprime debt. The lowest layer stood to lose all its value before defaults invaded the higher layers. The higher layers must be fully paid before the lowest layer received payment. Because of higher default risks the lowest layer usually went unrated. The bottom layer paid the highest interest rate and the top layer the lowest.

Among the large buyers of the riskiest layers of mortgage-backed securities stood the hedge funds. Hedge funds had been around a while, but little was said about them during the last century. They were sufficiently private in ownership and partnership to enjoy exemption from most government regulations. As private entities their assets, liabilities, and trading activities remained hidden from the public eye. In contemporary terminology hedge funds were not transparent entities. Hedge funds invested in every species of financial asset. In the market for mortgage-backed securities hedge funds bore a marked resemblance to banks in the broad sense. They accepted short-term liabilities against themselves, and long-term liabilities against others. Hedge funds became highly leveraged, meaning they counted on a truckload of borrowed money relative to a thin stake of owner equity.

With no public disclosure of vital statistics hedge funds floated on a thin film of confidence, and with them a large source of capital for the mortgage credit market. This was how it worked: assume a hedge fund purchased $600 million of lower-layered collateralized debt obligations. It would not be unrealistic to discover that the hedge fund put up only $100 million of its own funds and borrowed the other $500 million. This $600 million represents the junk bond portion of $3 billion in mortgage-backed securities that needed to be placed. The other $2.4 billion belonged in the upper layers. It would be sold off as investment grade securities to large institutional investors. The hedge fund, by putting up $100 million of its own money, allowed $3 billion in mortgaged-backed securities to find investors. In finance jargon hedge funds ran highly leveraged.

Another arthritic joint in the system is the market. Stocks and bonds are usually traded in public exchanges. Information about prices and trading volume is transparent for anyone to see. Mortgage-backed securities and collateralized debt obligations are traded in what is called the over-the-counter market. In over-the-counter markets trading is bilateral between a dealer and customer. Information about prices and trading volumes remain withheld from the public. No transparency brings to light large or vulnerable positions. Investors have no way to see who is exposed to subprime risks. Without institutionalized market makers and dealers, trading can freeze up when major events send prices tumbling.

The liquidity of an asset has to do with how quickly it can be converted into cash. In August 2007 the market for mortgage-backed securities and collateralized debt obligations seized up. These securities became illiquid and hedge funds and other investors could not sell them. Hedge funds had borrowed large sums against these securities as collateral. As the securities became illiquid, creditors demanded more collateral from hedge funds. Without trading the market furnished no prices or benchmarks to put a value on securities at various layers of risk. Hedge funds sold off other assets to meet creditor demands and stopped trading in mortgage-backed securities. The market for these assets and related credit derivatives evaporated and issuers saw inventories go unsold and stopped packaging new issues. These issuers stopped buying subprime mortgages from the originators so bank financing that had kept many originators in business shriveled up, shoving some originators into bankruptcy. When the subprime mortgage window closed, many would-be home buyers had no other place to turn. Existing home-owners counting on refinancing as the value of their home went up could no longer qualify. The price of houses topped out and nosed over.

With the market for high-risk layers of mortgage-backed securities crumbling, lenders took a closer look at the AAA layers. These layers are also based upon subprime mortgages, but enjoy priority in payoff. Buyers of asset-based commercial paper were unnerved after discovering that the underlying assets are investment-grade rated layers of subprime mortgages. Commercial paper, essentially corporate IOUs, normally stand near the apex of pristine creditworthiness.

## Unholy Mix: Short-term Borrowing and Long-term Lending

Asset-based commercial paper furnished the financing for a new area of banking innovation. Banks set up "structured-investment vehicles" to issue asset-based commercial paper. These structured-investment vehicles in turn invested in the mortgage-backed securities and collateralized debt obligations. Citibank set up the first structured-investment vehicle in 1988. A structured-investment vehicle was a virtual bank, raising short-term money selling commercing paper, and investing long-term in mortgage-backed securities. Their official headquarters was usually a regulatory or tax haven such as the Caymen Islands. It was a virtual solution to keeping the riskier assets off a bank's balance sheet, and side-stepping heavier bank-regulated capital cushion requirements. Not as much reserve capital had to be set aside to cover liabilities. These structured-investment vehicles were often called "conduits" and became what was collectively called the "shadow banking system." In 2008 Bill Gross, founder of Pimco, a large U.S. financial firm, commented that this shadow banking system has lain hidden for years, untouched by regulation, yet free to magically and mystically create and then package subprime loans into a host of three-letter conduits that only Wall Street wizardry could explain.[1]

The subprime crisis undermined the market for asset-based commercial paper. With structured-investment vehicles unable to sell commercial paper, they faced a liquidity crisis. In December 2007 Citibank and other banks annnounced that they would bail out the structured-investment vehicles they had sponsored and consolidate their assets into their own balance sheets. This rescue boosted the capital requirement burden of the sponsoring banks, adding to the demand for credit at a time when supply was swiftly drying up.

In a summarizing nutshell, buyers of mortgage-backed securities and collateralized debt obligations sat under-capitalized and dependent upon short-term financing. The market for high-risk layers of mortgage-backed securities lived off highly leveraged buyers. Mortgage orignators needed short-term financing to fund fresh mortgages which they planned to hold only briefly. Opaqueness in over-the-counter markets masked the nature and location of subprime risks from investors. It caused investors to switch from underestimating risks to overestimating risks. Market atmospherics went from calmly shrugging off risk to weak-kneed panicking and exaggerating risk. In hindsight events would have fared far better if the over-the-counter market had kept trading alive in the mortgage-backed security market. It would have kept some liquidity in the market.

Rising delinquencies and foreclosures in subprime mortgages, in the absence of recession, raised question marks about subprime mortgage-backed securities. In too many cases repayment counted on refinancing and continued escalation of home prices. Wall Street felt the first anxiety-churning quake in July 2007 when a jolting round of credit rating downgrades hit mortgage-backed securities. Two hedge funds sponsored by Wall Street's Bear Stearns sought to liquidate large positions in these securities. When word got out Bear Stearns had to reassure rattled investors that it was not strapped for liquidity.

Evidence of wider interbank pain and turbulence occurred on 2 August. Government-owned banks in Germany announced that they would be joining in a bailout of IKB Deutsche Industriebank. The core problem lay with an off-balance sheet vehicle, Rhineland Funding. Subprime loan losses at Rhineland caused bigger banks to suspend lending to IKB or Rhineland, leading to a cash crunch at IKB. IKB sponsored two external structured-investment vehicles, Rhineland Funding Capital Corp., and Rhinebridge PLC. Rhineland was formed in 2002. Rhinebridge enjoyed a brief existence, lasting from a launch date of 27 July 2007 to October 2007 when it landed in receivership. It may go down as one of the shortest-lived AAA companies in financial history. These structured-investment vehicles issued short-term debt, commercial paper, and bought long-term mortgage-backed securities. Rhineland was set up in the U.S. state of Delaware and on the island of Jersey. Delaware offered tax advantages within the U.S. The Delaware connection straightened the path for doing business in the U.S. Jersey, a tax haven in the English Channel, favored finanical institutions. Rhinebridge PLC was based in Dublin. Dublin was not a tax haven but it was known for streamlined, light-touch regulation. Both Jersey and Dublin grew into major centers for the shadow banking system.

Rhineland raised funds issuing commercial paper, a short-term debt instrument which has to be rolled over or renewed frequently. Historically commercial paper ranked a whisker spread below U.S. Treasury bills as the safest investment. Rhineland invested these funds in long-term mortgage-backed securities, including securities backed by subprime mortgages. It sold its commercial paper in investment pools favored by U.S. municipalities. The list of investors in Rhineland's commercial paper included a school district in Minneapolis, Minnesota, the city of Oakland, California, the state of Montana, and King County in the state of Washington.

When investors learned that Rhineland commercial paper was backed by subprime mortgages, they shut the credit door on Rhineland. Suddenly, Rhineland sat without means to repay other debt becoming due. Rhineland asked IKB for a line of credit, which a conduit-sponsoring bank stood obligated to provide. IKB did not have liquid assets to meet the request. To spare IKB bankruptcy, the state-owned German bank, KFW Bankengruppe, opened up a 2.5 billion euro credit facility. IKB spent the bailout repaying its short-term borrowing—commercial paper. Instead of easing panic in the commercial paper market, this bailout announcement sounded a warning against commercial paper issued by structured-investment vehicles. The warning rocked global markets. Skittish investors now worried how far off-balance sheet vehicles masked the scale of subprime losses.

## The Zenith of Banking Crisis

On 7 August 2007 France's largest bank, BNP Paribas, announced it was suspending redemptions for three mutual funds. These funds invested in mortgage-backed securities. Just the week before BNP had indicated that the three funds were doing buisness as usual. The bank stopped both the inflow and outflow of money into these mutual funds, saying it could no longer put a value on the securities in these funds. The bank also revealed that it had recently tried to sell $60 million in mortgage-backed securities but could find no takers. Some brokers were not even answering the phone. An action of this nature by perhaps the world's largest bank shattered confidence everywhere. Fear spread that it might trigger a run on other mutual funds that had not suspended redemptions. The *Wall Street Journal* carried a story (10 August 2007) with the header, "Impact of Mortgage Crisis Spreads." It talked about BNP Paribas, but also told of Tyke Capital LLC, "a New York-based quantitative, or computer-driven, hedge-fund firm." The article claimed that the firm's largest hedge fund had lost 20 percent so far in August.[2] The firm was not returning calls to the *Wall Street Journal*. Similarities in the computer models of various hedge funds amplified fluctuations in asset prices.

The intensity of the banking crisis reached a higher pitch in September 2007 when Northern Rock, a UK bank, announced it would receive emergency liquidity support from the Bank of England. After BNP Paribas' announcement, the market of interbank borrowing and lending froze up. Banks grew afraid to loan to other banks. On 9 August, the UK's Financial Services Authority (FSA) contacted businesses it thought might have problems because of the freeze-up in interbank borrowing. Northern Rock was on their list. Northern Rock returned the call the next working day and remained in daily contact until an agreement was reached to support Nothern Rock.

The history of Northern Rock furnishes an instructive snapshot of the changing financial landscape. This bank arose from the merger of two building societies, mutual organizations that primarily held deposits of retail customers and made loans to individuals buying residences. Northern Rock demutualized in 1997. Many demutualized building societies ended up merging with banks, but Nothern Rock remained independent. It grew by leaps and bounds, expanding its assets from £15.8 billion in 1997 to £101.0 billion in 2006. It could remind one of the the the red star analogy. Nevertheless, it remained modest in size compared to other UK banks. The asset side of its balance sheet consisted mainly of mortgages. That part looked much like the balance sheet of the traditional building society model. The structure of the liability side was a different matter. Retail deposits exhibited far less growth than wholesale funds borrowed from other financial institutions. Borrowings from other banks outdistanced customer deposits threefold. Northern Rock had taken on the role of mortgage originator, chiefly originating mortgages that it planned to sell. Unlike comparable U.S. institutions it shunned the trend toward laxer lending standards, lending mainly to creditworthy borrowers. It lay more exposed than other UK institutions because its lifeblood was the ability to package and resell mortgages to investors and raise funds borrowing short-term from other banks. Structured investment vehicles accounted for £325 million of Northern Rock's investments. At first it was reported that Northern Rock did not sponsor its own structured-investment vehicle like many other banks, and did not invest in asset-backed commercial paper. It later turned out that Northern Rock did sponsor an offshore structured-investment vehicle with the winning name of Granite. It was headquartered on the island of Guernsey. Northern Rock announced toward the end of 2008 that it planned to phase out Granite.

Assurances from the Bank of England were not enough to quieten the nerves of depositors. In the words of one long-time Northern Rock depositor, "They say not to panic, but the more I'm hearing, the more I'm panicking."[3] Northern Rock branches throughout

England saw lines of depositors outside waiting to enquire about the status of bank accounts and in many cases to withdraw money. At one branch customers could not withdraw money online from the bank website. Requests for withdrawals multiplied until they jammed up the branch bank's website, leaving customers even more ill at ease. A Northern Rock branch within the heart of London's financial center saw a crowd push up against its tinted window to look inside. Northern Rock never stopped redeeming deposits. Not since the days of Queen Victoria had Britain seen a good old-fashioned bank run. Wild fears raised the specter of a panic turning viral and striking other banks.

The run lasted through Monday, 17 September even though Alistair Darling, Chancellor of the Exchequer (finance minister) gave assurances that deposits remained safe. The mistrust of official pledges did not go unnoticed. The announcement that the Bank of England had thrown Northern Rock a lifeline was what ignited the bank run. Putting a stop to the bank run became number one political priority. It happened that Hank Paulson, u.s. secretary of Treasury visited during this time. On Monday evening, Alistair Darling, flanked by Hank Paulson, gave further assurances that the government guaranteed all deposits, even beyond what was normally covered by deposit compensation or insurance. On Tuesday the lines thinned out. Adam Applegarth, chief executive of Northern Rock, pointed the finger of blame at the structured-investment vehicles. He was quoted as saying, "The way to get the freeze to thaw is for banks to come out and show what's on their balance sheet."[4] In 2008 the British government nationalized Northern Rock after private bids to take over the bank fell short of the amount needed to repay the bank's debt to the government.

In November 2007 reports bubbled up in Germany that IKB Deutsche Industriebank's problems reached beyond what was originally expected. By now the rating agencies had awakened to the issues with mortgage-backed securities. Rating downgrades slashed the value of these securities, forcing banks to write down billions of dollars in securites. The KFW group announced that it was upping from 2.5 billion to 4.8 billion euro the amount set aside for potential losses at IKB.

IKB's story sounds a recurring note. Its name, IKB Deutsche Industriebank AG, means German Industry Bank. Opened in 1924, it dedicated itself to providing long-term financing to Germany's small- and medium-sized businesses. Stable but boring would have been an apt description. On the eve of the new century IKB felt pressure to raise sagging profits amid stiff competition in a sluggish economy. An IKB unit called IKB Credit Asset Management dreamed up a strategy to broaden business through structured-investment vehicles and mortgage-backed securities. Moody's Investor Service applauded the move for intelligent and successful diversification. A less kind spin on IKB's new ventures came in a 2007 piece entitled "Dr Frankenstein of Dusseldorf." A colorful morsel from this piece reads,

So IKB began playing with the bubbling test tubes of the derivatives laboratory. The solution followed the nostrums of modern portfolio theory—namely diversification into unfamiliar foreign credit markets—while using the latest in financial engineering trickery to manage the risks and exploit a regulatory arbitrage loophole.[5]

Between 2002 and 2007 this unit multiplied eightfold the assets under its management. The list of banks courting IKB for business by some reports included Lehman Brothers Holding Inc., JPMorgan Chase & Co., and Deutsche Bank AG.

In 2004 Dirk Roethig, a top executive at IKB, told *Risk* magazine,

This adventurous portfolio building was the outcome of a carefully planned strategy. We wanted to diversify in asset classes as well as geographically because we were pretty much dependent on the German economy.[6]

The next year Mr Roethig, along with other top European bankers, sat on a panel about picking mortgage-backed securities and other asset-backed securities from the U.S. IKB was an eager buyer of what the big Wall Street investment banks were selling.

IKB's name later popped up as a victim of one of the shadier deals cooked up by Wall Street investment banks selling mortgage-backed securities. At least that is what is suggested by a complaint the u.s. Securities and Exchange Commission lodged against Goldman Sachs Group Inc. The civil law filed in April 2010 charged Goldman with defrauding IKB and other investors in the sale of a mortgage-backed security called Abacus. According to the complaint Goldman put Abacus 2007–AC1 together in February 2007, custom-tailored to satisfy the wishes of John Paulson, a leading hedge fund manager. It was an investment portfolio of mortgage-backed securities. Paulson the hedge fund manager was no kin to u.s. secretary of Treasury Paulson, who had been an executive at Goldman before becoming secretary of Treasury. John Paulson's aim was to have a mortgage-backed security that was bound to fail if any problems at all came to light in mortgage-backed securities. Goldman told investors that an independent manager was selecting the bonds. In reality Goldman let Mr Paulson pick mortgage bonds he thought likeliest to undergo losses. He zeroed in on those bonds that bore a higher credit rating than the underlying mortgages merited. These were the ratings awarded by companies such as Moody's. One report says he complained to one investor that Moody's did not want to come around on one deal and give it the higher rating he wanted.[7] Goldman designed credit default swaps as part of Abacus. These swaps allowed Mr Paulson to bet against the bonds while other Goldman clients bet the other way.

Mr Paulson's role was analagous to someone who insures his neighbor's house against fire then puts a match to it. Investors, including European banks IKB and ABN Amro, stood to gain chiefly if the bonds rose in value, but the bonds were selected to lose value. Goldman shared the bonds' credit ratings in selling the bonds, but kept secret that Mr Paulson was betting those ratings were wrong. Six months later 83 percent of the bonds underlying Abacus saw downgrades from agencies like Moody's. By early 2008, 99 percent had seen downgrades. In 2007 Mr Paulson earned $3.7 billion betting on the housing bubble bursting apart. Goldman Sachs settled its case for $550 million. In 2008 a Dallas-based private equity firm, Lone Star Funds, acquired IKB Deutsche Industriebank.

American International Group (AIG) bought into another one of Goldman's Abacus deals. This deal did not stir up an official complaint, but cost AIG billions of dollars in losses. Congress approved an $180 billion bailout to save this U.S. company. Names of other investment banks came up as culprits in these kinds of deals. In 2010 the Securities and Exchange Commision opened preliminary investigations into Morgan Stanley and Deutsche Bank for similar activities.

On 6 September 2008 two U.S. government-sponsored enterprises went into conservatorship, Fannie Mae and Freddie Mac. These institutions raised funds selling securitites, and in turn spent them purchasing mortgages originated by other financial institutions. The soundness and strength of these institutions seem essential to re-covering liquidity in the mortgage lending market. These enterprises were posting losses which threatened their ability to raise capital. The action signaled the U.S. government's commitment to keep these enterprises solvent and sustainable. It was the failure of a U.S. investment bank like Goldman Sachs that drove a wooden stake into the heart of the global financial system. On 15 September 2008 the Wall Street investment bank Lehman Brothers Holding Inc. filed for bankruptcy protection. For unclear reasons Lehman had kept a large position in riskier mortgage-backed securities. Normally these were securities it would have sold to its investing customers. It may have run into trouble moving these assets. In August 2007 the firm had shut down BNC Mortgage, an affiliated subprime lender. The credit rating agencies slashed the value of Lehman's assets, its stock price crumbled, and its investor clients staged a mass exodus. Lehman blamed some of its problems on false rumors and stock speculators selling its stock short. Short-term credit tightened more painful notches after the failure of Lehman brothers. Around the globe banks that failed or nearly failed over the next six weeks cited the failure of Lehman Brothers as the beginning of a crueler credit squeeze.

Two other Wall Street investment banks outlasted the subprime crisis after large banks took them over. Bear Stearns sponsored two hedge funds heavily invested in subprime mortgage-backed securi-ties. In July 2007 Bear Stearns reported that the two hedge funds sat broke, without significant value. Investors in arbitration claims charged that Bear Stearns had not been upfront about the funds' exposures. In March 2008 the Federal Reserve Bank of New York arranged a bailout for Bear Stearns. As part of the bailout deal JPMorgan purchased Bear Stearns for $2 per share. As late as January 2007 the stock had sold for over $170 per share.

As financing became costlier and scarcer, a new type of pain afflicted banks. Like Northern Rock the British firm Bradford & Bingley PLC originated from the demutualization of a building society. It specialized in financing apartments that investors purchased to be rented out. Tighter credit, overbuilding, and falling prices chiseled away at the returns on these investments. Rents fell below levels needed to pay mortgage payments and default rates turned upwards. About 20 percent of Bradford & Bingley's loans fit into the no-documentation category. In 2008 delinquent mortgages at double the industry average sent Bradford & Bingley's profits tumbling into red territory. Unlike Northern Rock, short-term credit issues did not trigger a liquidity crisis with this bank. It had a large retail deposit base, which is usually a more dependable and stable source of funding than wholesale markets. The problem lay in non-performing mortgages. The default rate on mortgages it acquired stood above the default rate on mortgages it generated itself. In the summer of 2008 UK bank regulators began calling around for a buyer. After credit rating agencies cut Bradford & Bingley's ratings, depositors started pulling out cash, but not at a panicky pace. Efforts to find buyers or raise additional capital lured no takers. Between 25 September and 28 September deposit withdrawals exploded from £12 million per day to £200 million per day.[8] This deposit loss forced banking authorities to act. The British government nationalized Bradford & Bingley's mortgage assets in late September and sold off the retail deposit business to Abbey National, owned by a Spanish bank, Grupo Santander.

A new depositor psychology fueled the pressure on banks. Deposit insurance went far to ease fears of tender-minded depositors. Bank runs had joined the artifacts of history. With online banking, however, depositors could now quickly and easily move deposits around. While depositors worried less about permanently losing their money, they no longer wanted even the brief inconvenience of an interruption to account access. If in doubt they opted to shift funds to a bigger bank.

Credit for the largest bank failue in U.S. history went to Seattle-based Washington Mutual Bank. It was another company that started out as a mutual company, but demutualized in 1983, becoming a public company. It ranked as the largest U.S. savings and loan association before it folded in 2008. After demutualization it grew rapidly through acquisitons. After acquiring PNC Mortgage, Fleet Mortgage, and Homeside Lending, it ranked as the third largest mortgage lender in the U.S. It acquired PNC Mortgage at the height of the subprime boom. Until mid-2007 Washington Mutual thrived packaging mortgages and selling them to outside investors. Mortgages stopped moving off Washington Mutual's balance sheet after the market for mortgage-backed securities fell apart. The bank's balance sheet showed $18.6 billion in subprime loans, $61 billion in home equity loans, and $68.4 billion in short-term adjustable rate loans.[9]

The bank laid off 3,000 workers, slashed dividends, closed 183 stand-alone home-loan offices, and raised $7 billion in added capital by selling stock at a discount. In 2007 losses led to a drop in executive pay. In December the Securities and Exchange Commission investigated Washington Mutual for making loans based upon inflated house prices. In February 2008 the bank revised its executive bonus plan to prevent foreclosure-related write-downs from hurting bonuses. In September 2008 its stock sank to $2.01 per share, compared to an all-time high of $45.

Despite deposit insurance, Washington Mutual underwent what was called a bank run in the old days. Within ten days toward the end of September, depositors hauled $16.7 billion in deposits out of Washington Mutual. The run forced the federal banking regulators to seize the bank. A few days later regulators struck a deal with JPMorgan to buy Washington Mutual.

The high-flying mortgage lender Countrywide, the largest U.S. lender by loan volume, lucked out in certain respects. Questionable underwriting methods landed Countrywide in several courts, and loans to politicians adorned headlines. The Securities and Exchange Commission sued three top Countrywide executives for falsifiying finanical statements. The CEO ended up paying a $22.5 million fine and the other two executives paid smaller fines. These fines were a small part of a larger settlement but Bank of America would end up paying the remainder. Because of its larger abuses, Countrywide ran into serious difficulty earlier than other lenders and before other banking institutions had abandoned the housing market. Country-wide sidestepped a depositor run on its savings bank in August 2007 by bringing Bank of America on board as a large shareholder. Countrywide still had to raise interest rates to hold its depositor base. In January 2008 Bank of America announced its acquisition of Countrywide. That is how Bank of America ended up paying part of the damages levied against Countrywide. In October 2008 the Bank of America settled perhaps the largest predatory lending suit in history for over $8 billion. The deal covered as many as 390,000 borrowers who had taken out mortgages with Countrywide.

Bank of America was one bank that survived 2008 stronger and more diversified. As Lehman Brothers was filing for banruptcy protection, Bank of Ameica was announcing its acquisition of Merrill Lynch. Like Lehman, Merrill went all out for the mortgage-backed security business. Unsold and hard to sell securities had backed up on its balance sheet.

IndyMac Bancorp began as a spin-off of Countrywide. It specialized in mortgages that stood between prime and subprime, called Alt-A mortgages. John Reich, Director of the Office of Thrift Supervision, pinned the blame for IndyMac's failure on Senator Charles Schumer. Late in June the Senator wrote a letter to the Office of Thrift Supervision raising doubts about IndyMac's solvency. According to Mr Reich the letter triggered a bank run on IndyMac's deposits and forced seizure of the bank.[10] IndyMac sufffered from problem loans on its balance sheet but its fate was not cast in stone until depositors made a run on the bank.

Wachovia Corp. matched the profile of the modern universal bank, encompassing a large commercial bank and securites brokerage. By gobbling up weaker rivals Wachovia Corp. leapfrogged its way to the front lines of u.s. banking giants. It boasted the second largest chain of branches in the u.s. next to Bank of America. It owned Bermuda-based BluePoint, a unit that sold credit default swaps against mortgage-backed securities which went bankrupt in August 2008. Wachovia sowed the seeds for more trouble in May 2006 when it acquired Golden West Financial Corp. This acquisition was headquartered in Oakland, California, an area where house prices cried out for a big fall. Wachovia discovered too late that it had swallowed a toxic portfolio of non-traditional mortgages heavily concentrated in California and Florida where the housing bust hit hardest. Falling prices of bank stocks kept Wachovia from raising enough capital to solve its problem. It July 2008 it stopped issuing option adjustable-rate mortgages. In late September 2008 federal bank regulators pressed Wachovia to find itself a buyer before troubling news kindled a depositor run. It soon found itself a target for stronger institutions looking to buy a "fixer-upper." In the last quarter of 2008 Wachovia posted one of the largest quarterly losses ever suffered by a u.s. company. A downward adjustment to the value of its assets accounted for a large share of the loss. u.s. bank Wells Fargo purchased Wachovia for $15.1 billion in December 2008.

## Iceland's Wild Ride

In few places did the banking crisis breed wider and deeper economic repercussions than in Iceland where the three largest banks boasted assets over ten times GDP. An Everest of bank debt dwarfed annual national income of a 300,000 population. Measured by relative size to the larger economy it ranked the largest banking crisis. Iceland's banking system was another financial house of cards unique in its own way. Iceland's economy enjoyed a robust growth, low unemployment, and income per capita above the European Union average. The government enjoyed a large budget surplus. Banks raised funds in international markets to finance a household borrowing binge. Household debt as a percentage of disposable income hovered well above u.s. and British rates. Only about 30 percent of loans were financed by domestic bank deposits. The inflow of global capital financed shopping malls and a hopping real estate market.

A booming economy enabled an inflation hawk central bank governor, David Oddsson, to keep Iceland's interest rates elevated at a time when interest rates lay unusually low around the world. Elevated interest rates kept Iceland's currency strong and imports cheap. Iceland's three largest banks, Landsbanki, Glitnir, and Kaupthing freely tapped international capital markets to finance domestic and foreign lending, but stayed clear of u.s. subprime assets. Iceland was not a tax or regulatory haven for vehicles of foreign banks, but it ideally met the needs of what was called the "carry trade." That was the label given to transactions which borrow currency in a low-interest country, say like Japan, and convert it into the currency of a high-interest rate country such as Iceland. The profit arose from differences in interest rates. The carry trade kept Iceland's currency strong and imports cheap.

To entangle matters further, the Landsbanki owned branches in London and Amsterdam. These branches held retail deposits from 400,000 UK and Dutch customers in an online saving product called "Icesave." It offered high-interest rate savings accounts. The global credit seize-up left Icelandic banks unable to roll over short-term credit. Observers judged the country of Iceland too small to support its banks. Without an inflow of capital, demand for Iceland's currency plunged, sending import prices skyrocketing. The central bank hiked interest rates which in turn pushed up mortgage payments. Iceland's economy nosed over. The crisis reached panic stage in October 2008 after the government effectively nationalized Glitnir, the third largest bank. The benchmark interest rate for Iceland's central bank then stood at 15.5 percent. A bank bailout threatened to stretch Iceland's government resources too thin. Standard & Poor's and Fitch rating agencies slashed ratings on Iceland's sovereign debt.

The Icelandic government ended up nationalizing the other two large banks. In the process it froze the deposits of Icesave. At first Iceland's government committed itself to guaranteeing Icelandic bank deposits but not UK and Dutch Icesave deposits. These deposits went uncovered by UK and Dutch deposit insurance. The British government reacted angrily and invoked an anti-terrorism law to freeze the UK assets of Icesave. This episode turned into a tense tug of war. Iceland later had to make good on the deposits as a condition for a bailout funded by the IMF and other Nordic countries.

## The Fate of Banks Swallowing Other Banks

Banks grown large on strategies of acquiring weaker rivals also ran foul of the financial crisis. Until the 1980s the Royal Bank of Scotland was a regional bank centered on retail banking in Scotland and northern England. Through acquisitions it annexed a large banking network in the U.S. and diversified its portfolio to encompass debt financing, risk management, and investment services. It could meet every need of individual, business, or corporate customers. From its acquisitions it carved out the Global Banking and Markets division, a global player in banking. Royal Bank of Scotland might have weathered its large exposure to U.S. subprime loans if in October 2007 it had not joined with Fortis, a Dutch–Belgian bank, and Santander, a Spanish bank, to take over ABN Amro, a Dutch bank. The three large banks planned to dismember ABN Amro, the Brazilian and Italian operations going to Santander, the Dutch and Belgian operations going to Fortis, and the wholesale operations and other operations, including those in the U.S. and Asia, going to the Royal Bank of Scotland. When Fortis, Santander, and Royal Bank of Scotland clinched the deal, Nothern Rock and Bradford & Bingley had already faced runs on deposits. Soon after the acquistion, Royal Bank of Scotland discovered it had inherited a toxic portfolio of defective loans. Without this misstep, the Royal Bank of Scotland would have reported a profit in 2008 instead of a £24.1 billion loss. Depositors shunning smaller banks may have helped Royal Bank of Scotland dodge a bank run. On 7 October the bank's stock price tumbled 40 percent. The British government stepped in quickly to tranquilize depositors' fear, nationalizing the Royal Bank of Scotland in all but name.

The acquisiton of ABN dealt even less kindly with Fortis, another bank fattened on acquisitions. By revenue it ranked among the largest companies in the world. Its banking operations included commercial banking, investment banking, and insurance. Fortis faced severe problems financing its share of the ABN acquisition amid a deepening global credit crunch. In September 2008 Fortis began losing deposits after business customers heard rumors of bankruptcy. Its stock prices plunged. After receiving a government bailout, its banking operations were sold to the French bank, BNP Paribas, which also bought the Fortis brand name. The Dutch government nationalized Fortis's insurance and banking subsidiaries in the Netherlands. Fortis took a new name and retained the rest of its insurance business.

The UK's largest mortgage lender in 2007 was HBOS. It burst upon the banking scene in 2001 from a merger of the Bank of Scotland and Halifax. The Bank of Scotland was the UK's oldest commercial bank. Halifax was formed in 1997 when the Halifax Benefit Building and Investment Society demutualized. It was another company with property collateral on one side of the balance sheet and the other side supported by borrowing in wholesale markets, rather than retail deposits. It shared with other banks a ballooning balance sheet. Between 2003 and 2007 its debt grew from £112 billion to £231 billion. Peter Cummings, HBOS CEO, was quoted in the press as saying, "some people look as though they are losing their nerve—beginning to panic, even—in today's testing property environment, not us."[11]

Many of HBOS's commercial property investments turned ugly. The bank appeared to be in trouble when, along with the Royal Bank of Scotland, Lloyds TSB, and others, it shared in a government bailout. Lloyds TSB took advantage of HBOS's plummeting stock to extend a takeover bid. This bank acquired HBOS only to find out later that it had acquired a mortgage portfolio more toxic than expected. The UK government approved the merger.

In March 2007 nine UK banks adorned the company list in London's FTSE 100 all share index. By April 2009 five of those nine banks had undergone partial or complete nationalization. None of the four demutualized building societies survived as stand-alone private companies. Northern Rock, Bradford & Bingley, and HBOS belong in this category. Another one, Alliance and Leicester, underwent acquisition by the Spanish bank Santander in 2008.

## The Sheltering of Swiss Banks

Switzerland, long esteemed as a hallowed island of financial probity, saw its banking system take on water amid the turmoil in global banking. No nation felt more keenly the embarrassment of a bank bailout than Switzerland. Swiss banks were bankers for the most financially sophisticated wealth in the world. The strength and security of Switzerland's banks was part of its national identity. Switzerland's status as a haven for global wealth needed no more bruises. Swiss banks had already settled a suit for secretly holding gold deposits of Holocaust victims. They were also catching grief from the u.s. government and others for conspiring with customers to hide assets and income from taxation.

According to the Swiss Banking Federation, Swiss banks never saw the dire straits of banks in other countries. It may have had a point. One of the large Swiss banks, Credit Suisse Group, brushed aside government aid in favor of raising $9 billion in private capital. Yet amidst a global banking crisis, all banks lay enveloped in a cloud of suspicion. With other European governments supporting banks and guaranteeing bank debt, Swiss banks either had to prove they stood above financial reproach, or that they enjoyed the same government support as other banks. In the third quarter of 2008 the United Bank of Switzerland saw customers yank $74 billion from its wealth management unit, business banking unit, and its prized asset management unit. That outflow amounted to a large surge in outflows over the previous quarter. The bank also faced headwinds raising funds in the interbank lending market.

All the same, the United Bank of Switzerland had helped itself a little too much to investments linked to u.s. subprime mortgages. In the year leading up to October 2008 the United Bank of Switzerland wrote off $48 billion in defective investments. Swiss banking and government officials hatched a plan in which Switzerland's central bank took over $60 billion toxic assets from the United Bank of Switzerland. Under this plan the United Bank of Switzerland bundled into a special fund these toxic assets backed by u.s. and European mortgages. The fund planned to borrow $54 billion from Switzerland's central bank, and add to that $6 billion of equity capital from the United Bank of Switzerland. Separately the Swiss government invested $5.3 billion directly into the United Bank of Switzerland. For its injection of capital the government received a bond paying 12.5 percent. The bond was convertible into roughly a 9 percent stake in the bank. The plan did not immediately set up a fund to guarantee new debt issued by either bank, as bank bailout plans in the UK and Germany had done to help unfreeze credit markets. The Swiss government kept that option open for the future. In terms of capitalization, however, it put Switzerland's two largest banks among the most bullet-proof in the world.

## The Squeezing of Bank Profits

We have already seen how savers and investors embraced higher-risk levels to preserve rates of return in the face of falling interest rates. We see another twist on this trend in the banking industry. Banks borrow short-term and lend long-term. As the gap between short-term interest rates and long-term interest rates narrowed, bank profits felt the squeeze. Recall that between July 2006 and January 2008 the Federal Reserve's benchmark interest rate hovered above the ten-year government bond rate for nineteen consecutive months. Subprime mortgages paid long-term interest rates well above short-term rates, which held out the hope of maintaining bank profits. The offshore investment vehicles allowed banks to bear more risks than domestic banks could bear without violating domestic banking regulations. It smacked of banks suspecting overly harsh and unbending regulations as the trouble rather than low long-term interest rates. Developments in the banking industry fit the trend toward more bubble-driven expansion, less government regulation, and more households and businesses playing higher-risk cards. Banking furnished another variation on the theme of growing addiction to financial engineering. It was an addiction that offered escape from lower interest rates or, in the case of banking, near flat or even inverted yield curves.

The list of countries that enacted some variety of government bank aid includes, in addition to Switzerland and Iceland, the U.S., the UK, France, Germany, Ireland, and Sweden. Soon wits were quipping of "no bank left behind," a take on the U.S. No Child Left Behind Act of 2001 concerning the education of children in public schools. Many smaller banks failed without breaking into the headlines. In the U.S. eleven banks failed and were seized by bank regulators in the five years before 2008. In 2008 25 U.S. banks failed and were seized. That number reached 140 in 2009, and 177 in 2010. These failures may partly reflect the shake-out and consolidation to be expected after the repeal of the Glass-Steagall Act.

# SEVEN
# The Rebirth of Keynesian Economics

## All Boats Drop with the Tide

The laws and machinery of whole economies such as that of France, or the UK, or the U.S. fall into a branch of economics called macroeconomics. It can be an obscure subject but the essence of the macroeconomic perspective can be grasped from a simple principle of logic first introduced in chapter One. That principle says that what is true for the part is not necessarily true of the whole. This logical principle can be seen at work at the basketball game. If one person stands up and nobody else stands up, that person can see better. That does not mean that if everybody stands up, everybody can see better. In economics the macroeconomy is the "whole." Anyone wanting strong corroboration of this simple logical principle need look no further than macroeconomics. Suppose a business cuts its price and afterwards lures more customers. Can it be inferred that if all businesses cut prices, all businesses will enjoy more customers? That inference cannot be drawn. Take another case. An almost bankrupt business persuades its workers to accept a pay cut and remain equally efficient and hard-working. That business may turn around and become profitable again. It cannot be inferred, however, that if all workers across the economy take pay cuts, that businesses on average will be more profitable. They may end up less profitable because lower-paid workers spend less. Again, if one household decides to increase its savings, that household may easily succeed. If all households decide to increase savings simultaneously, collective savings may even go down. More savings translates as less spending. Workers and businesses may find incomes shrinking as households save instead of spend. They may each end up saving less out of sheer survival.

Another clue to the macroeconmic perspective can be gleaned from the saying that all boats rise and fall with the tide. In economics the macroeconomy is the tide, and the boats are the households and businesses whose income and opportunities wax and wane with the tide. Therefore households and businesses hate to see the tide fall and love to see the tide rise. Low tide guarantees that some workers lose jobs. Job losses inescapably happen even if all workers are in every aspect equal in the eyes of employers.

The analogy of the tide leads to obvious questions such as: Where does the tide come from, can it be controlled, and what can be done to keep the tide as high as possible? Economists have insights but not always airtight answers. The tangled wheels inherent in the economic system become clearer if it is recognized that the tide analogy breaks down when it comes to the subject of regularity. The ocean tide flows in and out at predictable intervals. The macroeconomy ebbs and flows without a predictable pattern. To make sense of the macroeconomic tide, economists start with the premise that economies are buffeted by a variety of sudden and unexpected shocks. These shocks might among other things take the form of soaring oil prices, stock market crashes, rapid changes in the money supply, large changes in taxes and government spending, failure of key businesses, and wars, to mention a few. In 2008 two shocks rocked the macroeconmic system, a crumbling housing market and a breakdown in the banking system. Once this vision of the macroeconomy is accepted the next major question is what happens to a macroeconomy after a shock. Does it tend to automatically self-correct to a natural state, or does it wickedly amplify the shock into an economic nightmare? Is it stable or unstable? The question is analogous to what happens to an automobile traveling straight down a highway if the driver whips the steering wheel and then lets go of it. The car is stable if allowed to straighten out on its own. Cars are engineered to be self-correcting and stable in this manner. If the car starts swerving with ever-widening swings, it is unstable. The same issue arises in the macroeconomy.

The most popular answers given to the stability question invariably change with the state of the macroeconomy. The answer in the depths of the 1930s Great Depression took the stance that a macroeconomy amplifies shocks into something more damaging. By the year 2000 nothing like the Great Depression had occurred in 60 years. Increasingly, another answer seemed right, particularly if individual markets stood free to adjust unhindered by government regulation. An influential body of thinking developed, arguing that a free-market macroeconomy is naturally stable, that after a shock it exhibits an inborn tendency to self-correct. It will automatically, if left unharassed by government regulation of prices, adjust toward reasonable and acceptable levels of unemployment, business failures, mortgage defaults, stock prices, corporate profits, and so on.

Self-correcting adjustments take place because free-market macroeconomies break down into individual markets where the forces of supply and demand fill in gaps and restore balances. An unemployment problem signals that the supply of workers outruns the demand for workers. This imbalance prods wages toward a level where supply and demand rest in balance, and abnormal unemployment vanishes.

If a free-market macroeconomy is naturally stable, it needs minimal government action to persistently remain in a groove of prosperous growth. It is even possible that government economic policies run counter-productive. A government's short-term solutions to problems may come at the cost of other problems in the future.

The self-correcting nature of a free-market macroeconomy hardly seems surprising. All living organisms display a capacity for self-healing, and the economy is composed of living organisms. If it is self-correcting other questions remain: How steep and wild will be the downswings and upswings, and how long will it take for the economy to restore itself? Will it happen soon enough to help individuals of the current generation or will it primarily profit future generations? In a 2002 speech before the Council of Foreign Relations, Alan Greenspan, who excelled at assimilating and articulating the best wisdom of Wall Street, linked the stability of the macroeconomy with the new and complex financial instruments and derivatives. He observed:

If risk is properly dispersed, shocks to the overall economic system will be better absorbed and less likely to create cascading failures that could threaten financial stability . . . Financial derivatives, more generally, have grown at a phenomenal pace over the past fifteen years . . . These increasingly complex financial instruments have especially contributed, particularly over the past couple of stressful years, to the development of a far more flexible, efficient, and resilient financial system than existed just a quarter-century ago.

Later in this 2002 speech Mr Greenspan drops in a word of caution that helps explain his legendary reputation for wisdom:

Derivatives, by construction, are highly leveraged, a condition that is both a large benefit and an Achilles heel . . . More fundamentally, we should recognize that if we choose to enjoy the advantages of a system of leveraged financial intermediaries, the burden of managing risk in the financial system will not lie with the private sector alone. Leveraging always carries with it the remote possibility of a chain reaction, a cascading sequence of defaults that will culminate in financial implosion if it proceeds unchecked. Only a central bank, with its unlimited power to create money, can with a high probability thwart such a process before it becomes destructive. Hence, central banks have, of necessity, been drawn into becoming lenders of last resort.[1]

As the recession of 2001 receded further into the background, the new century's confidence in free markets again echoes in Mr Greenspan's utterances. Mr Greenspan expressed this confidence well in a 2005 speech entitled "Economic Flexibility."

With a masterful insight into the workings of the free-market institutions that were then emerging, [Adam] Smith postulated an "invisible hand" in which competitive behavior drove an economy's resources toward their fullest and most efficient use. Economic growth and prosperity, he argued, would emerge if governments stood aside and allowed markets to work.

Mr Greenspan gave his approving nod to the worldwide movement toward deregulation. Deregulation meant the "invisible hand" went unshackled to do its work, moving economies closer to the model envisioned by Adam Smith. In the same speech Mr Greenspan went on to say:

Deregulation and the newer information technologies have joined, in the United States and elsewhere, to advance flexibility in the financial sector. Financial stability may turn out to have been the most important contributor to the evident significant gains in economic stability over the past two decades.

Further on in his speech Mr Greenspan suggested that the new financial instruments added to the natural stability of the free-market economy.

These increasingly complex financial instruments have contributed to the development of a far more flexible, efficient, and hence resilient financial system than the one that existed just a quarter-century ago. After the bursting of the stock market bubble in 2000, unlike previous periods following large financial shocks, no major financial institution defaulted, and the economy held up far better than many had anticipated.[2]

Mr Greenspan's words voice the renewed confidence in a free-market capitalism that in the eyes of some was still getting better thanks to the latest financial engineering.

The other view was largely out of vogue during Mr Greenspan's tenure as chief of the Federal Reserve. It was the view that free-market capitalism, a free-market macroeconomic system, can become unstable and languish for years in a state of depression, and that its self-correcting forces can easily go wildly astray.

## The Tangled Wheels of Self-correcting Mechanisms

Breaking down the automatic, self-correcting adjustments into individual steps helps explain how the self-correcting process should ideally work, and how it can wander off course.[3] Suppose negative shocks rock the economy, as happened in 2007–08 when credit markets froze up and a housing bubble popped. Tight credit curbed expenditures on housing and business-investment spending, weakening the overall demand for goods and services. Slower demand meant among other things less output, more unemployment, lower profits, and more business failures.

In going over the steps in the self-correcting process it is easy to see the snags that can hold up adjustments for varying lengths of time. In the face of unemployment the first self-correcting step for recovery looks to wages. Competition between workers for fewer jobs drags down wages. Lower wages make it profitable for a wider range of businesses to hire workers. That is how it should work. The question is whether wages can be counted on to fall enough to make a difference. In practice workers put up considerable resistance to accepting wage cuts even if no employee union is actively combating wage cuts. In 2008 climbing food and energy prices strengthened this resistance. When employers hire workers at a given wage rate, there is an implied commitment that the employer will not be adjusting the wage weekly or monthly to meet changing market conditions. Employers usually find it safer to lay off workers than to cut wages. Cutting wages risks severely undermining morale and loyalty.

In time unemployed workers exhaust credit with the grocery store, the landlord, and the credit card company. They may accept lower wages out of necessity. Even if wages fall the economy may not recover back to full employment. Falling wages only help the economy recover to full employment if it allows businesses to cut prices. This is the second step in the automatic adjustment back to full employment. Otherwise falling wages mean less purchasing power for a large segment of consumers, which neutralizes the benefits of lower wages. Businesses may not be able to cut prices if the prices of other resources fail to drop proportionately. Electricity is a key resource that is often supplied by government-regulated monopolies. These companies stand unlikely to cut rates. The aftershock of the Global Financial Crisis of 2008 saw galloping oil prices as unemployment hovered at high levels. Higher oil prices subtract from the profitability of hiring more workers, canceling the benefits of lower wages. In the aftershock of the 2008 crisis food and oil prices exhibited a stubborn tendency to climb at elevated rates, cutting into the purchasing power of wages.

If the price of labor and other resources falls more or less proportionately, then in theory businesses can cut prices. Falling prices bolster the purchasing power of the money in circulation, strengthening the demand for goods and services, and leading the economy to recovery. Therefore the third step in the self-correcting process is falling prices. The economy will not get past this stage if businesses recoil from cutting prices. The chances of businesses not cutting prices run high. Beyond the production of basic commodities such as wheat or corn, producers often set their own prices. Even in the case of a basic commodity such as oil, OPEC can set its own prices. In the face of falling profits, some businesses may elect to push up prices rather than cut them. Businesses that set their own prices run the risk of sparking a price war if they cut prices. Holding prices constant or raising them is unlikely to goad rivals into retaliation. Trying to earn more profit per unit and selling fewer units may appear the more attractive option. This is the step that may disappoint those who most idealize free-market capitalism.

If the economy languishes in recession long enough businesses will cut prices. The fourth step in the rocky road to economic recovery requires that falling wages and prices strengthen demand for goods and services. Lower wages and prices allow the money in circulation to stretch further in the purchase of goods and services. Lower wages and prices, however, may not boost demand if potential buyers wait to see how far prices will fall before they make purchases. A wait and see attitude toward prices may take over in the market for household and business durable goods. In this type of market households and businesses think if they are patient they may luck into tantalizing bargains in real estate and used equipment.

With falling prices, bargain-hungry households and businesses hold onto money rather than spending it. They are waiting for the best deals to crop up. The tendency to hold money rather than spend it becomes more pronounced among creditors and financial institutions. Falling wages and prices put a squeeze on households and businesses with fixed monetary obligations, such as mortgage payments or other long-term indebtedness. The amount owed remains constant while wages and prices fall. Toxic loans and bankruptcies mount, casting doubt on whether other loans will be repaid when due or at all. Financial institutions start holding larger cash reserves to guard against the inconvenience of larger than expected rates of defaults. This is the stage where credit freezes up. Households, businesses, and banks hold redundant cash balances either for safety or in anticipation of better prices and bargains in the future.

The economy clears the hurdles at step four after the public begins spending redundant cash. At some point prices fall low enough to bring out the shoppers and banks have written down the bad debts. Therefore the demand for redundant cash balances tapers off, spending picks up, and the economy passes step four. The economy may still stumble at step five. As the demand for redundant cash balances falls, the supply of cash may also fall. Bank deposits account for a large portion of the money stock. These deposits are linked to bank lending. Deposits expand when banks grant more loans and shrink when banks grant fewer loans. As the economy emerges from step four, households and businesses will apply some of the redundant cash balances they have been holding to pay off bank loans. Unless banks promptly loan these funds to other borrowers, bank deposits contract. More likely banks will be only too glad to get their money back, and will be much more cautious about loaning it out again. Banks may even try to call in loans early. In summary, the recovery may stall at stage five if the banking system diminishes the amount of cash available for the public to use.

If the economic recovery weathers the pitfalls of steps one through five, it still has to clear another hurdle, step six. Suppose shrinkage in publicly available cash does not happen at step five, perhaps because government has taken steps to enlarge available cash. Lower prices now mean the public does not need as much cash, but the available supply has held up without shrinking. Holders of excess cash balances will invest the surplus in incoming earning assets, such as bonds. With more funds flowing into the bond market, bonds can get by paying lower interest rates without going unsold. If this portion of the self-correcting process works properly, interest rates fall. Lower interest rates boost business investment spending and other interest-sensitive spending. This process unfolds until higher spending propels the economy back to full employment. This step can hit a glitch however if wealth owners have strong opinions of what is a normal or reasonable interest rate. If this is the case wealth owners want to avoid locking in at abnormally low interest rates. If wealth owners think below-average interest rates are likely to be temporary, they hold onto their cash and wait to buy bonds after interest rates have returned to normal levels. The expectation that interest rates will be higher in the future acts as a floor that prevents interest rates from falling. If interest rates cannot fall, business investment spending cannot get the boost, and the economy cannot recover.

If interest rates remain below average long enough, the wealth owners revise expectations and allow interest rates to drop further. At step seven falling interest rates lead to economic recovery unless interest rates drop to zero or bump against a floor right above zero. If negative interest rates are required to restore full employment, then full employment is out of reach, unattainable. That is how things can go wrong at step seven.

If interest rates cannot drop low enough to give business invest-ment spending the needed boost, the economic recovery completely stalls out. Instead of rebounding to full employment, the economy spirals further into depression. Keeping costs down plays a large role in business survival. If business equipment and other capital goods suffer falling prices, the businesses that purchase these goods at the lowest prices enjoy the lowest costs. If the businesses that postpone the purchase of plant and equipment the longest end up with the lowest costs, then even zero interest rates prove inadequate to reignite business-investment spending. As long as household spending remains below normal, businesses are likely already to own redundant plant and equipment.

Thus the macroeconomy, instead of rebounding to full employ-ment, slips into an irreversible downward spiral that signals the onset of longer-term depression. Potential purchasers withhold spending until prices fall further. The longer spending sits postponed, the more household spending and business-investment spending weaken, fueling unemployment and accelerating the fall in prices. The faster prices fall, the higher the rate of loan defaults and bankruptcies. As the rate of bad debt climbs, banks hold onto more cash as a precaution against the risk of more debt going unpaid. To hold more cash, banks tighten credit, which further depresses business investment expenditures. Prices, incomes, and output fall further with less investment expenditures, piling higher a mountain of bad debt. With more defaulting loans, banks hoard more cash by tightening credit again. Matters go from bad to worse.

In 1999 it appeared that the economies of the u.s., Europe, and maybe even Japan approximated the stable free-market macroeconomies envisioned by classical economists such as Adam Smith. By 2008 these same economies bore the stamp of the unstable economy in the hypothetical example just outlined.

In the early to mid-twentieth century, John Maynard Keynes, an influential British economist, popularized the idea that free-market macroeconomic systems are unstable but that the public sector's budget can be used as a stabilizing balance wheel to keep the system on a growth path. Part of the instability problem, according to Keynes, lies in management of the public sector's budget. As a macroeconomic system enters into recession, government tax revenue shrinks. This prompts the government to balance its budgets by slashing government spending and hiking taxes. One small government acting alone can balance the budget by this policy. If all small governments act in chorus to implement this policy, or if one large government alone implements it, things will not go well. Then the policy runs up against the logical principle that what is true for the part is not true for the whole. That principle frustrates the effort to balance the budget. Forcing everyone all at once to pay higher taxes has the same economic impact as everyone all at once deciding to increase savings. Keynes argues that a large government should do the exact opposite to stabilize the system. As tax revenue drops in the face of recession the government should pile on more government spending, at least not raise taxes, and perhaps cut taxes. The government turns its budget into a balance wheel to offset fluctuations in private-sector spending. Using the government's budget as a tool of economic stabilization is called fiscal policy. The other key tool is monetary policy, which has to do with adjusting the money supply and interest rates. Keynesian economics is the name attached to a school of economics which argues the macroeconomic system is unstable and that in severe recessions fiscal policy wields much more firepower than monetary policy.

As confidence in the stability of free-market macroeconomic systems strengthened, Keynesian economics lost out as a credible policy option. The newer view was admirably expressed by an influential economist of the later twentieth century and after. Alan Blinder served a stint on the President's Council of Economic Advisors and on the Board of Governors of the economic system. He was a bit too questioning to go along with what passed for conventional wisdom within the Federal Reserve System. He never gave up on Keynesian economics and talked up the cash for the clunkers program in the U.S. to help the ailing automobile industry. The U.S. government bought high-polluting older cars and scrapped them. In 2006 Blinder summed up the state of fiscal policy:

> Today's conventional wisdom holds that discretionary changes in fiscal policy are unlikely to do much good, and might even do harm. Why is that? First, the lags in fiscal policy, especially the inside lags, are long—perhaps longer than the duration of the typical recession. Second, the effects of the most plausible fiscal policy weapon, changes in personal income taxes (or transfer payments) are likely to be weakened by deploying it on a temporary basis. And third, an obviously superior stabilization weapon—namely monetary policy—is readily available.[4]

In 2008 the fiscal policy had its day in court. By the end of 2008 the U.S. Federal Reserve had already pushed its policy interest rate to roughly zero. By May 2009 the European Central Bank had its policy interest rate at the historically low value of 1 percent. The Bank of Japan's key interest rate had stood below 1 percent since 1995. By March 2009 the Bank of England's benchmark rate stood at 0.5

percent. The Swiss National Bank had the three-month Libor rate in Swiss francs below 1 percent by January 2009. Central banks had pushed interest rates about as low as they could go. These benchmark interest rates are short-term. Monetary authorities still had some room to maneuver long-term interest rates down, but not much. Monetary policy bumped against its operational limits.

## Gathering Forces for Fiscal Stimulus

In 2008 both the IMF and the OECD called for fiscal stimulus packages. It had to be a collective action, otherwise one country's stimulus might primarily have the effect of stimulating some other corner of the world. The IMF suggested a stimulus on the order of 2 percent of world GDP.[5] The OECD favored government spending over tax reductions, which it regarded as less effective. The IMF recommended both. It recommended added government expenditures, including investment type and transfer-payment type expenditures. For taxes it recommended both tax-rate deductions and tax rebates, including reductions and exemptions for unemployment insurance contributions.

For most countries the amounts spent rescuing the financial institutions dwarfed the fiscal stimulus packages, which were separate. For the U.S. the fiscal stimulus package and the amount spent rescuing financial institutions stood roughly equal in 2009, right at 5 percent of GDP. Other developed countries opted for fiscal stimulus packages closer to the 1 percent range, averaging 1.4 percent for eighteen of the most developed countries. The same developed countries that enacted smaller fiscal stimulus packages spent more as percentage of GDP rescuing financial institutions. The UK spent 22 times more on rescuing financial institutions than on fiscal stimulus, Spain eighteen times more, France seventeen times more, Germany seven times more, and Portugal six times more.[6]

Developing countries shared in this trend to meet the global financial crisis with fiscal stimulus packages. China adopted a fiscal stimulus package equal to 13 percent of GDP, but Malaysia adopted a fiscal stimulus package equal to about 1 percent. In the Middle East, Saudi Arabia adopted a stimulus package equal to about 9 percent of its GDP.

The move toward fiscal stimulus received a hearty endorsement at a Washington DC summit of the G20 in November 2008. This group is composed of the largest developed and emerging economies: Argentina, Australia, Brazil, Canada, China, France, Germany, India, Indonesia, Italy, Japan, Korea, Mexico, Russia, Saudi Arabia, South Africa, Spain, Turkey, the UK, and the U.S. These countries pledged rapid fiscal stimulus to shore up economies. Some observers doubted whether the U.S. could be counted on to keep its pledge. The process of transitioning from one presidential administration to another was underway, making it harder for U.S. officials to speak with authority. It was also a lame-duck U.S. Congress. What the U.S. would ultimately enact seemed more in doubt than usual.

While waiting to see what the U.S. would do, European countries set to work enacting fiscal stimulus plans. On 26 November 2008, the European Commission unveiled a plan for coordinated fiscal stimulus across the European Union. The plan provided for temporary cuts in employment and sales taxes and larger support for the low-paid and jobless. The commission urged member countries to aim toward fiscal stimulus programs equaling about 1.5 percent of GDP. It also said that European Union rules capping budget deficits at 3 percent of GDP would be relaxed. Europe had more built-in Keynesian policies than the U.S. Its higher tax rate meant that tax revenue automatically fell faster in downturns. Europe's more generous unemployment benefits meant government spending automatically rose faster in upswings. Aggregate government budget deficits of all European Union countries amounted to only 0.6 percent of aggregated GDP, largely because Germany had roughly a balanced budget. Both France and Italy ran budget deficits close to 3 percent of GDP. In the U.S. the Bush administration opened with a balanced budget for 2000 and finished in 2008 with a budget deficit at 2 percent of GDP.

The idea of fiscal stimulus met a chillier reception in Germany than in other parts of the European Union. The European Central Bank still had room to cut interest rates significantly. Germany's stiff-necked attitude toward inflation tended to downplay the threat of unemployment and depression. Still, Germany's cooperation remained crucial, otherwise countries less able to afford deficit spending would be priming the economic pump partly for Germany's profit. In December 2008 the German government enacted a stimulus plan equal to about 1.3 percent of Germany's GDP. In U.S. dollars it measured roughly $39.6 billion. This stimulus package stressed incentives for public and private investment. The German government cringed at measures for cutting taxes and making cash payments to consumers. The small size of the stimulus drew derision.

The size of Germany's stimulus disheartened other European governments who were hoping Germany would lead a Europe-wide effort for fiscal stimulus. German chancellor Angela Merkel came to be known as "Madame Non" for her opposition to Germany's larger involvement in European fiscal stimulus. By late December rapidly deteriorating economic conditions, widespread fears of job losses, and international pressure coaxed Germany into more aggressive action. In January the German government beefed up its stimulus package to the $67 billion range. It added tax cuts and breaks, bonuses of 100 euros per child, and a cash-for-clunker cars program. The government decided to accelerate spending on infrastructure and other public works, but shied away from further enlarging its stimulus plan until President Obama's new administration enacted a stimulus plan.

Other European countries enacted stimulus plans toward the end of 2008: Sweden equivalent to about $1.01 billion; Portugal 2.18 billion euros for 2009; and France 1.3 percent of its GDP equating, in U.S. currency, to a $33 billion package. The French plan provided for spending on infrastructure projects and investments in state-controlled enterprises. It also included a one-time payment of €200 to low-income households, and an incentive to trade in old cars. The French government also planned to buy 30,000 unfinished houses in 2009 and help finance the construction of another 70,000 houses.

The UK was among the first to wave the banner of fiscal stimulus. On 24 November 2008 the British government announced a stimulus package to the order of £20 billion, or $29.73 billion. The package cut the value-added tax for one year from 17.5 percent to 15 percent, and provided debt guarantees for small businesses. It also extended tax breaks for low-income workers and moved up spending on infrastructure projects. The package provided for a future hike in tax rates for highest-income earners. The top rate was upped from 40 percent to 45 percent, effective after the next election. The UK's package amounted to about 1.5 percent of GDP spread across 2008, 2009, and 2010. The UK stimulus packages would probably have been larger if the government had not already spent a hefty sum bailing out banks. The UK was another country where a large public sector and high tax rates generated a large amount of automatic stimulus— the stimulus from falling tax revenue in recession and rising government expenditures of cyclical spending such as unemployment insurance.

In December 2008 Japan rolled out its newest stimulus plan. This embraced a loan plan for laid-off temporary workers and measures to assist businesses in raising short-term capital. A government-backed bank would buy the debt of businesses.

The re-enthronement of Keynesian economics did not precisely begin in 2008. One trait shared by Barack Obama and George Bush Jr was that they both took office amidst ailing economies and both started out recommending large fiscal stimulus packages. In George Bush's case much of his stimulus took the form of temporary tax cuts, which Keynesian economists usually regard as the puniest way to boost demand for goods and services.

In February 2008 the U.S. government enacted a fiscal stimulus plan at an estimated cost of $152 billion for 2008. This act provided for tax rebates on low- and middle-income individuals and families. The rebates ranged between $600 and $1,200. It also embraced tax incentives to encourage business investment. By the end of 2008 the global economy had sunk into a much deeper crisis, and European governments had already enacted fiscal stimulus packages. In February 2009 the U.S. enacted its newest fiscal stimulus package. Its estimated costs stood in the range of $787 billion. Tax incentives accounted for $288 billion. This package provided for direct spending on infrastructure, education, health, energy, added unemployment and social welfare benefits.

Only China developed a package of fiscal stimulus rivaling in scope and weight the U.S. stimulus, and it was unveiled much sooner. China announced its package on 9 November 2008, a Sunday after a G20 meeting in Sao Paulo, Brazil. A week later the G20 held a summit in Washington DC. Measured in U.S. currency the plan called for stimulus spending to the order of $586 billion. It was a bit less than the projected $787 billion U.S. stimulus, but the Chinese economy is only a third the size of that of the U.S. As revised in March 2009, road, railway, irrigation, and airport projects accounted for 38 percent of the total amount. Another hefty slice went to reconstruction of areas hit hard by earthquakes in 2008. Rural development and technological advancement received a share of the total allocation. Rural development included resettling nomads and providing safe drinking water. Earmarks for 5.3 percent of the total allocation went to energy savings, cutting gas emissions, and various environmental engineering projects.

Few programs signal more clearly the global element in economic policy-making than the program that in the U.S. went by the popular name of "cash for clunkers." This part of fiscal stimulus packages was aimed at directly stimulating the industrial sectors of the global economy. It had the added benefit of taking older and thus gas-thirsty, high-emission automobiles out of service, providing an incentive for replacing them with new ones. In the U.S. rebates up to $4,500 were paid on the purchase of a new car. A higher improvement in gas efficiency correlated with a higher rebate. The rebate in effect went to purchase the trade-in, which the government took and scrapped. The U.S. program only lasted for a few months in 2009. The UK offered a rebate of £2,000 on the trade-ins that were at least ten years old. The program began in 2009 and lasted through March 2010. Germany boasted the largest plan for scrapping older automobiles. Its program lasted throughout 2009, and cost twice as much as the U.S. equivalent. The government paid 2,500 euros for trade-ins of at least nine years old. To qualify the cars had to be traded in on a new automobile. France started its program in January 2009. It offered graduated rebates depending on the gas mileage and emission standards of the new automobile in the deal. Unlike the U.S., UK, and German plans, the French plan required the new automobile to meet certain emission requirements. The rebate for an electric automobile equaled 5,000 euros. The minimum rebate was 1,000 euros. The level of emissions was the main consideration in the size of the rebate. Traded-in automobiles had to be at least ten years old. The French government made a deal with the Irish government to make the offer good in Ireland on cars traded in for new French-built cars. Canada called its program "retire your ride." It gave up to 300 Canadian dollars or a public transit pass. The trade-in had to have been built in 1995 or earlier. Italy started its clunker program in January 2007, and renewed it in January 2009. This program also put a premium on environmentally friendly cars. It ended in December 2009. Spain also had a program that stressed emissions. Japan launched a clunker program lasting from April 2009 through March 2010. The new cars had to meet government standards for environmental friendliness and fuel efficiency. The trade-in automobiles had to be at least thirteen years old. The rebate equaled 250,000 yen, equivalent to roughly $2,500. The Netherlands designed a clunker program that added a premium for residents of Amsterdam. Norway had operated its own version of a clunker program going back to 1978. Under this plan the buyer of a new automobile paid a "Vehicle Scrap Deposit Tax." When the vehicle was scrapped, the tax was refunded. Other countries in 2009 with some sort of a clunker program included Austria, China, Ireland, Luxembourg, Portugal, Romania, and Slovakia.

The u.s. government took seriously the destruction of old clunkers. It required that the oil be drained and that motors be injected with sodium silicate. A scandal surfaced in Germany where the government only required the clunkers be hauled to a junkyard and it was discovered that about 50,000 German clunkers went as illegal exports to Africa and Eastern Europe.[7]

Almost all the G20 countries enacted fiscal stimulus packages aimed at propping up the global economy. The announced size of the measure was at times misleading. Governments tended to include in these announcements measures that had been planned before the scale of the crisis became clear. According to a Brookings Institution study, total stimulus funds allotted for expenditure in 2009 was $689 billion.[8] This amount only included the new measures that were brought forward after governments recognized the intensity of the crisis. This amount equates to about 1.4 percent of the combined GDP of these countries and barely above 1.1 percent of global GDP. The IMF had called for combined fiscal stimulus equaling 2 percent of global GDP. Three countries, U.S., China, and Japan, accounted for 39 percent of the G20. The same three countries topped the list of countries expected to contribute the most fiscal stimulus in 2010. These countries, along with Saudi Arabia, planned to spend as much or more in 2010 as in 2009. According to the Brookings study, France had one of the lightest stimulus packages for 2009 spending, measuring only 0.7 percent of French GDP. As a percentage of domestic GDP, the Brookings study puts for 2009 the U.S. stimulus package at 5.9 percent, Saudi Arabia's package at 9.4 percent, China's at 4.8 percent, Spain's at 4.5 percent, and Germany's at 3.4 percent. The only G20 country reporting no stimulus spending was Turkey. Countries reporting less stimulus spending percentage-wise than France were Brazil at 0.5 percent, India at 0.5 percent, and Italy at 0.3 percent.

## Summing Up

Governments faced with the formulation of fiscal policy and stimulus packages muddled through, torn between advocates of tax cuts and advocates of enlarged government expenditures. Countries whose stimulus packages took shape in multiple waves of announcements graduated toward greater reliance on government expenditures, and less on tax cuts. The U.S. stimulus enacted in January 2008 involved virtually all tax cuts. The 2009 U.S. stimulus relied more heavily on added government expenditures.

In theory either tax cuts or added government expenditure boost total demand for goods and services. Many economists who advocate tax cuts, however, are not Keynesian. They simply want to downsize the government. Putting the government on a diet seems a perfect way to do it. They also think taxes harm incentives to work, save, and bear risks. The idea that faster government spending effectively stimulates the economy is pure Keynes. The shift toward greater confidence in government spending above all signals the rehabilitation of Keynesian economics.

In two G20 countries, Brazil and Russia, tax cuts, according to the Brookings study, accounted for 100 percent of total stimulus in 2009.

In Argentina, China, India, Italy, Mexico, Saudi Arabia, and South Africa tax cuts accounted for 0.0 percent of total stimulus. In France tax cuts only accounted for 6.5 percent of total stimulus. In the UK tax cuts accounted for 73 percent of total stimulus, in Germany 68 percent and Indonesia 79 percent. At the lower end of the tax-cut scale stands Japan at 30 percent, the U.S. at 34.8 percent, Spain at 36.7 percent, Australia at 41.2 percent, and Canada at 45.3 percent.

The global drive toward laissez-faire capitalism gained momentum in the 1990s. The prevailing ideology argued that production could only prosper where initiative was free. The warm embracement of Keynesian economics indicated things were not all well and good in the era of globalization. In 2008 Warren Buffett, world famous investor, wrote in an annual newsletter, "You only learn who has been swimming naked when the tide goes out."[9] Deregulation, financial innovation, and low interest rates coaxed more households and businesses into swimming without a swimsuit. Some were not only swimming naked, but in piranha-infested waters. More technically, they bore greater risks to sustain accustomed rates of return amid falling interest rates. In the eyes of many, government intervention was distasteful, but not as distasteful as the tide receding while swimming without a bathing suit. Even the staunchest critics of government intervention were content to see a resurrection of Keynesian economics if it held out the hope of keeping the tide from retreating. The large tax cuts the U.S. enacted in 2001 had not fulfilled expectations. The U.S. tax cuts of early 2008 seemed to pack little bang per buck. The same countries that rallied to the banner of deregulation, privatization, free trade, and financial liberalization now marched in Keynesian lockstep.

EIGHT

# China and India Knock
# at the Door

## The Wisdom of Ancient China

The renaissance of laissez-faire capitalism, the wave of privatization and government deregulation that swept the global economy toward the end of the last century, was directly felt in China. Before this fresh invigoration of capitalism, China was communist. If communism was a religion, as some claim, then the Chinese were fundamentalist. Some observers might say the West stirred in China a zeal for capitalism. The Chinese would point out how far they have applied their own pragmatic thinking and energy to the assimilation of laissez-faire capitalism.

One of the humors of history is that it was the Chinese who first infected Western Europe with a passion for laissez-faire. In the seventeenth century Jesuits in China began sending translated works of Chinese philosophers and descriptions of Chinese government to Europe. France received the greatest impetus from cross-fertilization with Chinese civilization. None less than Voltaire heaped high praise on works of Chinese philosophers. It is widely known that Adam Smith adopted the principle of laissez-faire from the French Physiocrats. Not so well known is that the Physiocrats derived the concept of laissez-faire from translations of Chinese philosophers and books about Chinese government. Francis Quesnay (1694–1774) gets credit for founding Physiocrat economics. The Physiocrats' debt to the study of Chinese civilization is evident in a book Quesnay wrote on China, *The Despotism of China* (1767).

Through China the concept of laissez-faire goes back to Lao-tze, the founder of Taoism. He is a legendary Chinese philosopher who lived sometime between 600 and 400 BCE. One scholar combines paraphrases and quotes to describe concisely the libertarian philosophy of Lao-tze and a later Chinese philosopher, Chung-tze:

> To the individualist Lao-tze, government, with its "laws and regulations more numerous than the hairs of an ox," was a vicious oppressor of the individual, and "more to be feared than fierce tigers . . . The more artificial taboos and restrictions there are in the world, the more the people are impoverished . . . The more laws and regulations are given prominence, the more thieves and robbers there will be." . . . Chuang-tze reiterated and embellished Lao-tzu's devotion to laissez faire and opposition to state rule: "Good order results spontaneously when things are let alone."[1]

With this philosophical heritage, no one should be surprised that China thrived more than any other economy transitioning from communism to capitalism. China started the new century leaving many wondering if it might once again consume (China would say civilize) her conquerors. Revolutions clear out much rubbish, and chaos is a transition. Many times has China died and been reborn. Both had happened within the memory of people still living. China was now becoming the greatest rival and customer of the West.

Perhaps China prospers better than other transition economies because it is an old hand at both communism and capitalism. The Chinese Emperor Wu (140–87 BCE) nationalized the land and natural resources, subjected trade and transportation to government direction, levied an income tax, and built canals that connected rivers and irrigated fields. The government accumulated stockpiles of goods when prices were falling and sold them when they were rising. An American historian quotes Szuma Chien, a Chinese historian of the era, as saying Wu Tu took these actions to prevent private individuals from

> reserving for their sole use the riches of the mountains and the sea in order to gain fortune, and from putting the lower classes into subjection to themselves . . . the rich merchants

and large shopkeepers would be prevented from making big profits . . . and prices would be regulated in the empire.[2]

The experiment ended when alternating droughts and floods caused shortages, and prices climbed beyond control.

A later Chinese emperor, Wang Mang (r. CE 9–23) was an accomplished scholar and millionaire who seized the throne. He nationalized the land and divided it equally among the peasants. He also sought to regulate prices by hoarding and venting stockpiles of commodities. He made low-interest loans available to private enterprise. He was assassinated and his reforms repealed. A thousand years later the socialist sun rose again in China. Premier Wang An-shih (r. 1068–1085) is quoted as saying:

> The State should take the entire management of commerce, industry, and agriculture into its own hands, with a view to succoring the working classes and preventing them from being ground into dust by the rich.[3]

He nationalized commerce, advanced low-interest loans to rescue peasants from money lenders, and furnished seed and other aid to new settlers. He undertook great engineering projects to control flooding and provide public employment. He appointed district boards to regulate local prices and wages. He granted pensions to the aged, unemployed, and poor. The rich poured out their resources to undermine the system. The premier's brother argued that between human corruptibility and human incompetence, government control of industry was doomed to fail. Another episode of drought and flood, crowned with the arrival of a terrifying comet, persuaded Wang An-shih to repeal his reforms and yield power to the opposition.

A culture oozing with Confucian philosophy merits some of the credit for China's prosperous transition from socialism. China and East Asia stand almost unique in having a philosophy exert a heavy influence on values and morals. In most countries morals and values stay moored to religions and not philosophies. Confucianism is a secular philosophy but its morals and values are a common denominator in the various religions and sects of China. After Asian capitalism came alive in the post-Second World War era, scholars and observers began to wonder if Confucian philosophy gave capitalism an edge not shared by non-Confucian countries.

The West did not always look kindly on Confucianism as a forward economic force. In 1905 Max Weber published an influential book entitled *The Protestant Ethic and the Spirit of Capitalism* in which he argued that capitalism and Protestantism cohabitated uniquely well. They shared in a spirit of rationalism that grew out of the application of reason to theological issues. After finding Catholicism less congenial than Protestantism to the development of capitalism, Weber went on to compare European with non-European cultures. He concluded that the religions and values of India and China hindered the development of capitalism. In the case of Hinduism and Buddhism, he argued that these religions lacked in the spirit of rationality. The otherworldliness of these religions also undermined the drive toward creative work in the world. Confucianism survived the otherworldliness test. Its hub was this world, a necessary ingredient for prosperous capitalism. Confucianism fell short in the asceticism that capitalism requires to encourage delayed gratification. What capitalism needs, according to Weber, was asceticism without otherworldliness. It was also observed that Confucian-trained government officials furthered isolationist government policies and shunned modernization along Western lines. The weight of tradition and worship of ancestors left China and other Asian countries less open to modern ideas.

Economic renewal and prosperity inspired a new trust in Confucian culture and values. A re-evaluation of Confucianism discounted the backward government policies of Confucian-trained government officials. Instead it underscored the cultural values of a population that absorbed and learned to live by Confucian principles without receiving a formal education in Confucian philosophy. What workforce would not be improved by the Confucian focus on this world, on self-cultivation, discipline, hard work, frugality, and education? The Confucian commitment to family, political order, duty, and avoidance of litigation supplied a useful antidote against the wild individualism that capitalism fosters. What's more, Confucian societies esteemed education and self-improvement. Rapid technological advance gave the fast learners an advantage over the slow learners. Thanks to Confucian values, China and other East Asian societies enjoyed a larger share of populations belonging in the faster learner category.

## Unleashing China

When a country with such a rich historical and philosophical background meets and assimilates technology-driven market capitalism, things are bound to happen. A hint of what is happening can be gleaned from the high GDP growth rates that China invariably clocks. A normal GDP growth rate for an advanced, developed country such as the U.S. sits around 3 percent. When economies report GDP growth on the order of 10 percent, double digit growth, they rank as star performers, classed as economic miracles. Japan stands out as an economic miracle remembered from times past.

Between 1983 and 1988, the Chinese economy, according to data set on the IMF's website, posted double digit GDP growth every year except 1986 when growth was only 8.8 percent. One year, 1984, China's GDP leaped forward an eye-popping 15 percent. China had some slow years but growth remained above what would be considered normal growth in the U.S. or Europe, and often entered double digit territory. After 1991, even in the slow years China's economic growth never fell below 7 percent. In 2001, while the U.S. economy floundered in recession, China galloped at 8.2 percent growth. From that year onward annual growth inched upward until in 2007 China posted a jaw-dropping 14.2 percent GDP growth. In the aftershock of the global financial crisis of 2008, China remained in the high growth column, posting growth of 9 percent or higher as the U.S. and European economies limped and stumbled. The same signs of a busy hothouse of economic development show up in China's share of world trade. That also has also been on the march. Between 1979 and 2003 China watched imports and exports bounding upwards at an average annual rate of 15 percent. That statistic stands out when put against the 7 percent average annual expansion of world trade over the same interval.

As China's economy grew, China's communist government steadily implemented reforms favoring private-sector development.

Between 1978 and 1984 China decentralized farming to the house-hold level, raised agricultural prices, and allowed high-performing state enterprises to pocket profits as a reward. The success of these reforms led Chinese officials to undertake further reforms between 1984 and 1988. These reforms targeted the urban industrial sectors. They allowed enterprises more control over prices and wages. They also opened up to foreign trade and investment fourteen major cities in coastal areas. In 1992 the Communist Party officially decreed the compatibility of the market system with the ideals of socialism. The establishment of a socialist market economy became official government policy. From 1998 onward China entered the era of globalization. In 2001 the World Trade Organization approved China's membership. As a condition of membership China liberalized foreign trade and investment. Foreign banks won the right to conduct business in China. Tariffs, subsidies, and other forms of trade protection saw large drops.

The exchange rate between the currencies of two countries largely determines the price of one country's goods and services in the other country. Exchange rates can be determined in free markets. Under a free market an exchange rate fluctuates amid shifting market forces. In practice governments vary in the latitude they give their own domestic currency to fluctuate against other currencies. China's official currency is the renminbi. The yuan is the primary unit of the renminbi. The more yuan a U.S. dollar buys, the further a dollar stretches buying Chinese goods. In 1988 one U.S. dollar only bought 3.7 yuan. Over time China gradually devalued its currency. The dollar bought more yuan in 1995 than in 1988 because China's renminbi had depreciated against the U.S. dollar. By 1995 one U.S. dollar equaled 8.3 Chinese yuan. From 1995 until 2005 China held its exchange rate pegged to the dollar. Over these years the exchange rate remained fixed at $1 = 8.3 yuan, regardless of market forces. The depreciation of the renminbi slashed the cost of Chinese goods in U.S. markets and pushed up prices of U.S. goods in China. China's pegged exchange rate policy meant that China's currency shared the U.S. dollar's fate in foreign exchange markets. If the dollar fell against the Japanese yen or the European euro, China's currency fell also against those currencies. If the dollar climbed against other currencies in foreign exchange markets, China's currency in percentage terms climbed an equal amount.

To appreciate the upshot of China's exchange rate policy, it helps to recall the U.S. dollar's exchange rate experience since 2001. In December 2001 one U.S. dollar equaled 127.6 yen. The dollar steadily lost value against the yen. By December 2004 one U.S. dollar equaled only 103.8 yen. This change in exchange rates meant that Japanese goods cost more in the U.S. and U.S. goods cost less in Japan. Since China pegged its currency to the U.S. dollar, the same applied to China's goods. They sold cheaper in Japan while Japan's goods cost more in China. A look at the exchange rate between the U.S. dollar and the European euro reveals a similar trajectory. In December 2001 one U.S. dollar equaled 1.12 euros. By December 2004 one U.S. dollar equaled 0.74 euro. The result was that U.S. goods sold for less in the eurozone. Since China's currency remained pegged to the dollar, China's goods also sold for less in the eurozone. While eurozone goods and Japanese goods sold for higher prices in the U.S., the price of China's goods relative to U.S. goods went unchanged.

A weighted index of the dollar against major currencies shows that the U.S. dollar lost 26 percent of its value between December 2001 and December 2004.[4] Low U.S. interest rates clear the path to a weak U.S. dollar. The dollar tends to gain strength as it becomes a ticket to higher interest rates. A weaker U.S. dollar tips the balance of world demand in favor of U.S. goods. Regardless of whether a customer lives inside or outside the U.S., a weakening of the dollar makes the U.S. goods a better buy relative to non-U.S. goods. Between 2001 and 2004 the U.S. economy, however, did not get as much of a boost as it could have because China's goods enjoyed the same price advantage as U.S. goods. A weaker U.S. dollar also rendered China's goods less costly in other countries because China's currency was pegged to the dollar.

China's currency peg irked the U.S. and many European countries who felt that China's goods wielded an unfair advantage in world markets. For every year between 2002 and 2006 China's exports to the rest of the world grew at feverish rates above 20 percent. In 2004 China's exports grew a white-hot 28 percent. Exports grew in all countries over the same time frame, but no major economy matched

China's export performance. Among the IMF's list of advanced countries only Estonia reported export growth near that of China. The larger economies of Europe ran nowhere close, nor did Japan. As early as 2003 U.S. officials opened discussions with China over its currency policy. China showed signs of studying the issue. It invited top U.S. economists to Beijing to share their expertise. One Nobel Prize-winning U.S. economist, Robert Mundell, advised China to make no change in its exchange rate policy.[5] China sent representatives to the U.S. Federal Reserve System for training on exchange management. China sounded a typical defensive note after U.S. secretary of Treasury John Snow visited Beijing in September 2003. Chinese officials indicated that China might change its exchange rate policy, but never under U.S. pressure.

Between December 2001 and December 2004 U.S. imports of Chinese goods grew by 130 percent. The sharp growth occurred while the U.S. economy labored against the headwinds of the 2001 recession. Anger in Congress reached boiling point in April 2005. One bipartisan proposal in Congress called for a 27.5 percent tariff on imports from China. By now U.S. officials had grown weary of pleading for patience with China. In May 2005 U.S. officials quietly began traveling to China and opening discussions with a broader range of Chinese officials, including central bank officials and Communist Party officials. The U.S. Senate withdrew its tariff threat after hearing that the Chinese stood ready to act. In July 2005 China raised the exchange of the yuan relative to the dollar a modest 2.1 percent. It was a small adjustment but a beginning. By June 2008 the yuan had moved up to a point where it took 6.8 yuan to purchase one U.S. dollar. That compared favorably with the 8.3 yuan it had taken to buy one U.S. dollar between 1995 and June 2005. The yuan now stood 20 percent higher than before devaluation began, raising the cost of China's goods to the rest of the world.

The rising value of its currency helped tame China's stampeding export growth. In 2007 export growth fell to 18.1 percent. In 2008, the year of the financial crisis, export growth fell to 8.5 percent. After pushing its exchange rate up to 6.8 yuan per dollar in June 2008, China suspended further upward adjustments until mid-2010. In 2009 China's exports fell 10 percent, as the global recession threatened to suck China into its downward spiral. To immunize against the infection of global recession China enacted an aggressive fiscal stimulus. Between 2008 and 2010 China's government debt as a percentage of GDP went from 16.9 percent of GDP to 33.8 percent. Between September 2008 and December 2008 China's central bank slashed its one-year rate from 7.2 percent to 5.3 percent. In 2009 China saw annual money supply growth numbers on the order of 35 percent. For 2008 and 2009 China posted GDP growth barely below 10 percent. For 2010 GDP growth inched slightly above 10 percent.

To inoculate itself against global recession China in 2008 did what the U.S. did in 2001. It kindled a housing boom. Not that China had completely missed the global housing boom that ended in the 2008 crisis. At least parts of China, particularly Beijing and Shanghai, had shared in the pre-2008 boom. Those cities saw house prices rising 15 percent to 30 percent.[6] Like the U.S. government the Chinese government had to take steps to cool its housing market. Foreigners were buying luxury apartments and later selling them for handsome profits. In 2006 the Chinese government rolled out new regulations which prevented foreigners from buying a home until they had lived in China for one year. These new rules also prevented foreigners from owning more than one home at a time.

The government succeeded in taking some steam out of the run-up in house prices that ended in 2008. By December 2008 China's house prices were falling as much as 30 percent in some areas.[7] While prices fell, China dodged the wave of foreclosures that savaged many advanced countries. Down payments as high as 30 percent kept home-owners solvent. Many home-buyers had paid cash. The Bank of International Settlements database of property prices showed China's land price index peaking in March 2008 at 116.5. The index steadily fell, reaching a trough in March 2009 at 101.5.

Just as the government's policies to cool the housing market seemed to be working as planned, the global financial crisis displaced fear of a housing bubble with fear of an imported recession. China's housing policy did a quick U-turn. In October 2008 the government stepped in with smaller down payment requirements and lower interest rates for first-time buyers. The government goaded banks into granting more loans. In January and February 2009 house prices stabilized and started inching up. In April 2009 Mei Jianping, a finance professor at a Beijing university, was quoted as saying, "The Chinese Housing Market may have a good chance to be among the first ones to see real signs of picking up."[8] By August 2009 the stock of unsold housing was down to a level that inspired the *Wall Street Journal* to carry a story billed as, "Is China the Next Real Estate Bubble?"[9] By this time China's banks owned a large portfolio of mortgage loans, creating a vested interest in keeping house prices headed up. The government saw the healthy housing sector as the one glittering rainbow until the global economy rebounded. Another *Wall Street Journal* article, "China Takes Hard Road on Housing," opened with the statement, "Deciding whether a bubble is inflating in Chinese property is like nailing jelly to a wall."[10]

Between January 2009 and January 2010 the average prices of Chinese houses grew 11.3 percent in a 70-city sample. China's government now began to raise taxes and tighten credit for purchases of second homes. It tried not to engineer another housing slump as it had in 2008. Tax revenue from rising property taxes was helping support local governments. The Chinese government wanted no part of a massive U.S.-style housing bubble that might pop, dragging the housing sector and perhaps the Chinese economy underwater for no telling how long.

After learning that banks had granted loans measuring more than a trillion yuan in the first two weeks of 2010, Chinese bank regulators pressed banks to dial back the lending. By March 2010 the government had unwrapped its next budget. By now the government looked to wean the Chinese economy from stimulus spending. The budget tapered off expenditures on public housing. Part of China's stimulus strategy had boosted government spending on social security, education, and health. Expanding government programs in these areas freed households to undertake more consumption spending. Spending in these areas saw smaller cuts. Meanwhile China's central bank kept its benchmark interest rate at 5.3 percent.

Government housing and mortgage policies irked urban Chinese who saw house prices climbing out of reach. In April 2010 the State Council issued a statement about booming property prices:

A number of factors driving up prices are appearing, strengthening expectations of inflation. The problem of excessive increases in housing prices in some cities is particularly acute.[11]

The southern island province of Hainan saw the largest leap in house
prices. This free-wheeling island was becoming the fashionable playground for China's fresh money elite looking for nice beaches in a
tropical setting. The finely tuned antennae of speculators zeroed in
on luxury properties. The provincial capital of Haidou saw house
prices breeze upwards by 64.1 percent between March 2009 and
March 2010. Annual house price growth in the resort city of Sanya
posted a comparable 57.5 percent rate. The capital of the southern
province of Guangdong witnessed house prices climbing a heady
20.3 percent within a year. By the end of the first quarter of 2010
property loans had surged 44.2 percent from a year earlier. Loans to
individual home-buyers had climbed 54.3 percent.[12]

To quiet a mounting housing bubble, the Chinese government
raised the minimum down payment on second homes from 40
percent to 50 percent. Mortgages for third homes also faced stiffer
obstacles. It urged banks to approve mortgages for non-residents
only if they had paid local taxes and welfare-benefits fees within the
last year. The government accelerated construction of subsidized
public housing, and took steps to enlarge the supply of available land.
Another new policy required developers to get government approval
before accepting down payments on unfinished properties. The
government authorized banks to turn down mortgage applications
of home buyers who already owned two or more properties. The
government claimed to have unearthed evidence that developers
were hoarding property to illegally hoist up prices. The government
vowed certain punishment for offenders.

By June 2010 house prices felt the weight of the government's
efforts to rein in the housing market. House prices in June fell by 0.1
percent against May prices, the first month to month drop since
February 2009. The government judged it was tightening at about
the right tempo, but did relax restrictions on mortgages for third
homes. By the fall of 2010 the global economic recovery was displaying signs of faltering with the debt crisis in Greece undermining

the forces of recovery. The global economy owed much of what it had in the way of rebound to China's swift bounce back from recession. China had become a vital engine of global growth. China's imports grew 20 percent in 2010, a rate well in excess of import growth in the u.s., Japan, the UK, France, or Germany. In addition China's import growth remained modestly positive in 2009 at 3.7 percent. France in 2009 saw imports sink 10 percent, Germany 9 percent, Japan 15 percent, the UK 12 percent, and the u.s. 13 percent. Given weak growth in the u.s. and Europe, Latin America and Africa now looked to China to buy their raw materials. One product China imported from Canada and the u.s. was lumber which fed China's growing building activity. Canada's board feet of lumber shipped to China grew from 210 million in 2006 to 1.6 billion in 2009. u.s. logs shipped to China grew from 256,000 cubic meters in 2007 to an estimated 2.4 million in 2010.

Even with some adjustment in China's exchange rate, the global economic recovery threatened to be brutally brief if China's growth faded. It turned out government measures only took some steam out of China's housing market. In August and September of 2010 house prices again turned upward. Public resentment heated up over unaffordable housing. In September the government announced measures against land hoarders. Some developers owned land that lay undeveloped a year after it was purchased at auction. The government barred these developers from entering bids at upcoming auctions. Toward the end of September the government took further steps to combat speculation. It ordered banks to halt mortgage lending after the second home. Banks could grant no mortgages for the third home and beyond. Banks were also asked to take special care that other consumer loans did not go to buying property. The government put in place tax breaks that favored home purchasing. It also announced plans for future reform of real estate taxation. In October China's central bank raised its interest rate from 5.3 percent to 5.5 percent.

In February 2011 the Chinese government announced that it was ditching the country's widely followed index of national property prices. The government suspected the index played a part in igniting public anger over unaffordable housing. The government announced

a proposal for a new property index. Professor Xianian of the China–
Europe International Business School quipped,

> It's just like changing the scale of a thermometer, and then
> telling the patient they no longer need to take medicine for their
> fever, and the whole family cheers that the illness is cured.[13]

Even concerning basic numbers such as GDP, skepticism and uncer-
tainty about China's official economic and financial data remained
widespread.

In 2010 China's housing market still sizzled, pumping up prices 37
percent in Beijing, 37.9 percent in Chongqing, and 47.1 percent in
Hangzhou. China's central bank raised its key interest rate three
times in 2011. The last increment in July 2011 raised it to 6.5 percent.
In May 2011 bankers upped minimum down payments for first
houses to 40 percent in the hottest housing markets and to 60 percent for second houses. By mid-2011 China's housing-led recovery
drove a China-led global recovery. Beijing now boasted the costliest
real estate market in the world when measured against the income of
its citizens. A real estate bubble now loomed as China's biggest economic risk, making it a large risk for the global economy. Signs that
the government's tighter policies were finding traction came to light
in April 2011 when home prices fell in certain areas. By September
2011 only 23 of 70 large and mid-sized cities reported higher house
prices in August than in July.

Many of China's trading partners felt disheartened that China's
growth had not done more to spur global economic recovery. In July
2010 China began to let the yuan gradually inch up again, making
foreign imports a bit less costly in China, and China's exports a bit
less threatening in global markets. The change came in baby steps. In
June 2010 the yuan stood at 6.8 per dollar; by June 2011 it stood at
6.4 per dollar. China's trading partners wanted China to evolve toward a consumption-driven economy rather than an export-driven
economy. A consumption-driven economy required higher incomes
for households. These households in turn developed a taste for
imported goods, particularly if the government took steps to open up
foreign trade.

China's policies become clearer when viewed as an effort to avoid Japan's experiences in the 1980s. Like China in the 2000s, Japan in the 1980s had come under international pressure to raise the value of its currency. Also like China, Japan enjoyed large trade surpluses and foreign exchange reserves, excess liquidity and soaring asset prices. In 1985, France, West Germany, Japan, the U.S., and the UK signed the Plaza accord. This accord pledged these countries to depreciating the U.S. dollar against the Japanese yen and West German mark. Japan turned to expansionary monetary and fiscal policies at home to cancel the domestic impact of a rising yen and falling exports. Japan's expansionary policies at home had the desired effects. Just as Japan stood ready to tighten policies and dampen the boom, the Dow Jones crashed in October 1987, marking the beginning of a global slowdown. Japan slashed interest rates to vaccinate itself against global recession. The low interest rates touched off booms in property and stocks. When these bubbles burst apart the Japanese economy entered a prolonged era of weak-winged growth that had not ended in 2012.

Unlike Japan in 1987, China had already instigated monetary tightening when the global financial crisis of 2008 struck. Its central bank had raised its key rate by nearly two percentage points between 2006 and 2008. Once the global economy plunged into recession, China hurriedly backtracked and turned to unusually expansive monetary and fiscal policies. Like Japan in the 1980s its asset prices rebounded quickly. To avoid a repeat of Japan's experience China took pains to curb speculation in the housing market. It adjusted its exchange rate, but at the speed of hot lava.

By 2012 the global economy has much riding on developments in China. If China's real estate market crashes, China's hot growth screeches to a crawl. The global economic recovery flickers out and the U.S. and Europe enter an even broader and deeper downturn.

## Unlocking India

India was another emerging country that joined the ranks of economic miracles. Like China it angled for the economic holy grail that promised the fruits of capitalism while dodging its pitfalls. India shared in the renaissance of free-market capitalism that swept the world in the 1990s, but with its own twist. In 1914 India's international trade as a percentage of GDP stood at 20 percent. After gaining independence in 1947, India maintained highly protectionist trade policies. By 1970 India's international trade as a percentage of GDP had dropped to 8 percent. Between 1991 and 2003 India largely dismantled custom duties on foreign trade. By the mid-1990s India's international trade once again reached 20 percent of GDP. Foreign trade received a further boost from lower transportation costs. Innovations in telecommunications and computer networking opened up new opportunities for trade in computer-based services.

Capital flows can take the form of loans, portfolio investment, or foreign direct investment. The acquisition of tangible, physical capital belongs in foreign direct investment. It can range from the construction of new plant and equipment to the purchase of an existing operation. The Indian government undertook liberalization of capital flows between India and the rest of the world. Foreign private sector financing arrived in 1975. In 1995 India started gradually opening up portfolio investment and foreign direct investment. For portfolio investment India started by allowing certain classes of foreign investors to buy into its stock market. Hedge funds prominently figured among the unwelcome. Much foreign direct investment came from foreign private equity funds. These funds made financial investments in Indian firms whose stocks were not traded on a public stock exchange. At first the share of foreign ownership faced government-imposed limits, but the limits varied from sector to sector. Gradually the government lifted limits sector by sector. By 2000 most sectors allowed 100 percent foreign ownership, but not all. The city of Mumbai matured into India's financial center. By financial flows it grew to rank among the top ten financial centers in the world.

India's capital account has yet to shake itself free of overgrown and ossifying bureaucratic nuisances and rigidities. A single account of all Indian capital controls runs into thousands of pages describing detailed rules. Yet actual capital flows give India the features of a more open capital account.[14] Between 2000 and 2005 capital inflows averaged 2.73 percent of GDP. For the years 2006 through 2010 that number climbed to 4.55 percent. Capital account regulations particularly displayed bias against short-term foreign borrowing. It was short-term foreign borrowing that led to Iceland's debacle.

Several factors helped open up India's capital flows beyond the cautious policy gradualism that India exhibited in this area. Financial engineering multiplied the capabilities of the financial system to outwit capital controls. The creation of synthetic corporate bonds circumvented controls against short-term foreign borrowing. Almost any kind of transaction became possible with the proper mix of financial engineering and legal wizardry. Another opening factor took the form of illegal capital flows. Some of this happened through miss-invoicing on the trade account. A third factor had to do with the increasing sophistication of Indian firms. Some Indian firms eluded capital controls by reinventing themselves as multinational corporations. With these reforms and innovations India's economy rode the crest in the tide of global growth. In 2005 India's GDP growth punctured the 9 percent territory. It dropped back to the 6 percent range amidst global crisis and recession but in 2010 India savored 10 percent GDP growth.

India as a potential economic miracle drew attention in early 2002 when Dr Sanjay Saini, an Indian radiologist working at Massachusetts General Hospital, saw a solution to a u.s. shortage of radiologists. Why not email medical images, such as x-rays, CT scans, MRI scans, and ultrasounds to India where radiologists are in abundance? Indian radiologists' earnings are about one-tenth those of their u.s. counterparts. When word got out, Dr Saini received some ugly emails. u.s. radiologists fumed about "radiologists' sweatshops" abroad. This anecdote sums up much of the difference between India and China. India just happened. The high-tech revolution seemed custom-tailored for India.

It might be argued that China owes its success to a determined government, sound macroeconomic fundamentals, low inflation, high savings, and trade surpluses. The same cannot be said of India. Inflation in India steadily heated up from 2006 onward, touching double digit levels in 2010, and clocking a blistering rate near 11 percent in 2011.[15] While China reports large current account surpluses every year, India reports current account deficits from 2005 to the present. The current account in the balance of payments largely reflects the trade balance, but it also includes cross-country flows of investment income and monetary transfers, such as government or private aid. The U.S. and UK invariably register current account deficits. Rising oil prices and the Western taste of younger, urban consumers feed India's trade deficit. Both China and India save a large share of income, but China more so than India. China reports national savings rates above 50 percent of GDP, while India reports savings rates of 34 percent of GDP.

In India an observer will miss the balance between public and private goods often seen in emerging countries with a recent communist past such as China. One observer described India's urban development policy as follows:

> But as reflected in the state of most Indian cities, little attention is given to their well-being and advancement. The dire and unbearable conditions of our cities are the result of slow and small-scale interventions to ever worsening conditions. They are the result of a complete lack of long-term strategic thinking . . . there has been a virtual collapse in the basic urban services of housing, water, energy, healthcare, etc. India's cities today are characterized by widespread poverty, poor health and sanitation, crumbling infrastructure, environmental degradation and poor quality of life . . . The sectors of water, solid waste management, transport, electricity and sanitation are some of the areas that need immediate focus. What is the point of a designer shower system in your new house if you don't have water in it.[16]

Another area where a divergence in economic philosophy between China and India shows up is currency. This divergence may owe less to differences in government policy and more to the success of India's private sector in eluding government controls. Historically China pegs its exchange rate to the dollar. The U.S. constantly hammers China to let its currency float to free-market levels. If China's exchange rate is pegged at an artificially low level, China's goods sell in the U.S. at artificially low prices. China arouses wide suspicion that it holds its exchange rate down to favor its exports. The U.S. claims no such issues with India. India's currency fluctuates with market forces.

Further liberalization of capital controls would allow the rupee to undergo wider fluctuations. In January 2002 it took 48 Indian rupees to purchase one U.S. dollar. By July 2005, when China finally agreed to let its currency rise, India's currency had already undergone appreciation. By then it took only 43.4 rupees to buy a U.S. dollar. By the end of 2007 it took only 39.3 rupees to buy a U.S. dollar. An influx of foreign investment gradually strengthened the rupee. In 2008 foreign investors dashed to the exit door, and the rupee sank. By April 2009 it took 51 rupees to buy a U.S. dollar. Foreign investors flocked back in 2009, again bidding up the rupee. By April 2011 the rupee stood at 44 per dollar.

China defends its currency policy by saying that the undervalued yuan allows China to attract more factory jobs, and so doing more to alleviate the poverty of its poorest citizens. India counters that its policies allows a stronger flow of financial investment into India. These financial flows give Indian companies access to lower-cost capital, and underwrite Indian entrepreneurs.

Unlike China the secret of India's rapid economic development lies in growing consumer demand driven by rising wages. While the rest of the world may complain that foreign-produced goods face a frosty reception in China, it cannot lodge that complaint against India. In 2007 China's imports grew 8 percent while India's grew 16 percent. The year of the financial crisis, 2008, China's imports grew 3.8 percent while India's grew 10.8 percent. In the first year of recovery, 2009, India's imports grew 8.3 percent while China's grew another 3.8 percent. In 2010 India's imports sprinted 16.5 percent which barely lagged China's belated but sharp rebound of 19.8 percent. Nevertheless the common denominator between China and India lies in the large role played by exports. In the crisis year of 2008 India's exports grew at 10.6 percent against China's 8.5 percent. During 2009, the year of global recession, India's exports grew a very modest 0.67 percent, which looks strong against China's negative growth of -10.3 percent. The next year, 2010, China's exports rebounded a hefty 24 percent while India's exports posted a lively 22 percent jump. A world-class high-tech sector strengthens India's export performance.

Like most central banks, the Reserve Bank of India aggressively slashed interest rates to inoculate India against the contagion of global recession in 2008–09. The rate cuts started from a high of 9 percent. Six separate cuts in the latter part of 2008 and the early part of 2009 brought the key rate down to 4.75 percent. The Bank of England, the European Central Bank, the Bank of Japan, and the U.S. Federal Reserve System kept interest rates at historically low levels throughout 2009, 2010, and 2011, but not India's central bank. Early in 2010 India's central bank started raising rates, a necessary measure to combat inflation. By the last quarter of 2011 the central bank's key interest rate stood at 8.5 percent.

India's stock market mirrored India's buoyant economy. The index for the Bombay Stock Exchange grew more than threefold from the end of 2003 through the end of 2007, bolstered by an influx of foreign buyers. It lost half its value in 2008, partly because foreign investors jerked large sums out of the market. This kind of capital flight suggested that capital controls had lost their grip. Capital outflows also sent India's currency crashing downward 25 percent. The stock market snapped back quickly, partly because foreign investors made a beeline back to India. In November 2010 the index matched its previous high, but traded slightly lower in 2011.

The Bank of International Settlements does not report data on property prices in India. Data on house prices are sketchy, but India did partake in the pre-subprime property boom, including a boom in luxury apartments. Shopping malls, houses, and business parks sprouted up. Global capital helped underwrite the boom, including names like Goldman Sachs, Wachovia, Citigroup Venture Capital, and Tishman Speyer, a U.S. real-estate company. Indian real-estate companies tapped global capital markets to raise funds. They sold equity through Initial Public Offerings, and raised funds in sub-markets of the London Stock Exchange.

In 2007 New Delhi's government approved 100 percent foreign direct investment for private developers launching new townships and housing complexes. Developers also received permission to buy land directly from farmers and other landholders. Since 1957 Indian regulations had required developers to go through the Delhi development authority to acquire land. These actions were part of a government plan to turn New Delhi from a chaotic city into an organized, clean, world-class metropolis. India's Supreme Court ruled that the government must study power and water supplies before approving the addition of third floors to existing buildings and launching plans for more roads.

India's housing market tumbled amid global financial crisis. Early in 2008 developers found credit tougher to secure. Prakash Chakravarti, editor of a weekly report from Thomson Financial, is quoted as observing,

> A few months ago real-estate companies were raising capital like there was no tomorrow . . . If sentiment has affected the market so badly it raises questions about their ability to raise capital for expansion going forward.[17]

As the credit crunch battered demand, developers did not want to build more units. In October 2008, high tide of the crisis, stories bubbled up of developers offering jewelry vouchers, free parking, and even new BMWs as sweeteners on the sale of $600,000 luxury flats. In 2009 reports surfaced of prices falling 35 percent to 45 percent for new residential properties.[18]

Like China, India in 2009 looked for economic salvation in a vigorous housing recovery. It was a vital part of the plan to keep the Indian economy afloat amidst the global economic downdraft. India had no shortage of people needing homes. Developers started building smaller and more spartan apartment units away from big-city land prices. These less costly apartments chiefly targeted potential buyers that had no credit history or proof of permanent residence. Many banks might have feared to tread into this mortgage market given the U.S.'s recent experience with subprime mortgages, but in India two government-owned banks, the National Housing Bank and the National Bank for Agricultural and Rural Development, waded into these waters, agreeing to underwrite mortgage companies serving these home-buyers. With a 25 percent down payment and employer confirmation of employment, these home-buyers qualified for loans at interest rates only modestly above those paid by borrowers with established credit histories. Who would have thought another subprime-driven housing boom would be in the making so soon? According to a press account in March 2010,

> The Indian version of Forbes magazine lists the 100 richest Indians. Apart from the usual suspects, what intrigued us was that most of the new entrants in it were from the real estate industry. India is a services-based economy as a lot of people were from technology or other export services and products. But real estate?[19]

By 2010 India's property boom had reasserted itself with a wild vengeance. Prices turned around and spiked upward like a diver returning to the surface. The boom centered in Mumbai and the National Capital Region, including New Delhi and neighboring cities like Gurgaon and Noida. Once again apartments popped up for the super rich. Legal changes allowed construction of taller buildings. A bubble-fed explosion of new apartment construction seemed destined to end in a bubble-bursting housing glut. At any time a hike in interest rates could prick the bubble. Worries abounded that the urban infrastructure might not support the housing expansion.

By June 2011, climbing interest rates were bleeding the demand for housing. India's central bank had raised its key lending rate ten times over the previous sixteen months, putting the rate at 7.5 percent. India's financial capital of Mumbai had piled up a three-year overhanging stock of unsold housing. Prices had not budged much, but some developers offered discounts as buyer eagerness waned.

The Asian growth engine downshifted in 2011. Rising interest rates to combat inflation sapped economic growth. The IMF projected 7.8 percent GDP growth for India in 2011, compared to 10 percent for 2010. The IMF projected 9.4 percent GDP growth for China in 2011. That was down from 10.3 percent in 2010.

## Dodging the Pitfalls of Success

China and India did not make the complete story of Asia. Even outside of Asia countries like Australia and Brazil had helped pull the global economy out of a steep slump. Australia was another economy growing on the back of a housing boom. Rising commodity prices and housing booms gave the developing economies a second wind that spared the global economy a deeper and more prolonged decline. After the global financial crisis of 2008 the world turned to developing countries to lead the global economy out of the slump. If the undertow of the European debt crisis pulls the global economy under, housing booms in these countries will falter. That is the prospect that threatens to send the global economy tumbling into an even prettier mess.

China and India appear as economies that have blossomed under deregulation. While economic growth eased in the U.S. and Europe with lighter regulation, it gathered momentum in China and India. Like the U.S. and Europe these countries grew upon the back of low interest rates and housing booms that did not last. Unlike the U.S. and Europe, they quickly snapped back to roaring growth from global financial crisis. The fast rebound can partly be chalked up to a boom in commodity prices, which helps countries with large agricultural and mining sectors. Manufacturing is the primary victim of soaring commodity and raw material prices. Therefore the more industrialized countries flounder.

On the surface it may seem that China and India profit from deregulation more than others. It is likelier, however, that when commodity prices soar, developed countries, being highly industrialized, will face stronger headwinds than developing countries. If commodity prices happen to crash, some developing countries that are now booming may enter their own time of troubles. Another point recalls that the economies of China and India, despite some deregulation, are still highly regulated when measured against the economies of Europe and the U.S. Who is to say that some developing countries may not find ways to dodge the pitfalls of capitalism as it has been practised in the U.S. and Europe?

# NINE

# Commodity Prices Take Flight

## The Financialization of Commodity Markets

The economic recovery that began in 2001 bore a congenital weakness that fated it to a rickety and feeble life even if the financial system had not fallen to pieces. The troubling nemesis was soaring commodity prices. According to the World Bank, it was the strongest commodity boom since 1900.[1] Shortages of vital raw materials signaled a failure of economic coordination and foresight. Bottlenecks and imbalances of this kind seemed quite incongruent with the adaptability and performance expected of the market system in an age of market idealization. After all, the much vaulted market system rewarded participants for gathering as much information as possible, never wasted information, and used it efficiently. If any institution could be counted on to supply the economy with the resources it needed, it had to be the market system, or so its champions believed. Either the market system mishandled the work of coordination and foresight, or it lay blindsided by sharp and unforeseeable shocks.

By commodities is meant the most primary of products: oil, coal, natural gas, wheat, corn, cotton, rice, sugar, soybeans, coconut oil, pork bellies, milk, coffee, natural rubber, copper, tin, iron ore, and so on. Commodities are mostly agricultural products and industrially used raw materials. Raw steel is a commodity while a finished automobile is a manufactured product. If the price of steel rises faster than the price of automobiles, profits of automobile companies feel the squeeze. Commodities trade on exchanges similar to stock exchanges. The largest commodity exchanges are in London, New York, and Chicago. Other large cities boast commodity exchanges specializing in commodities produced in their region. Wheat is traded on the Kansas City Board of Trade, and rice on the New Orleans Commodity Exchange. Businesses buy commodities directly from suppliers or through commodity exchanges. Physical traders are traders who plan to actually take custody of a commodity. Other traders buy commodities for speculative or other financial reasons and never plan to take custody of them. Like stock prices, commodity prices can be run up by speculators. A long and steady run up might end in a sudden and stomach-churning crash. Speculators find in commodity markets all the usual tantalizing tools awaiting their skillful hands, such as options and futures. Commodity prices fluctuate freely unless a group of organized suppliers regulate production to stabilize prices at a level favorable to producers. The Organization of Petroleum Exporting Countries is a good example of organized suppliers regulating production. These groups hardly ever stop prices from rising, and prices may occasionally fall despite their best efforts to the contrary.

Commodity markets, like financial markets, share in the latest innovations of financial engineering. It has led to what is called the "financialization of commodity markets." Financialization draws a wider range of investors into commodity markets who never intend to take delivery on an order of commodities. Exchange-traded commodity index funds, hedge funds, and mutual funds provide an open conduit for excessive financial market speculation to induce waves in commodity prices. Cousins of commodity-based exchange-traded funds are the commodity-based exchange-traded notes. These are debt instruments in which the issuer agrees to pay as interest the return of a commodity index fund, minus management expenses.

Commodity-based exchange-traded funds popped up on financial markets in 2004, quickly gaining traction with investors. These funds are bought and sold on regulated exchanges just like shares of corporate stock. They allow ordinary investors to add commodities to a financial portfolio without taking custody of any commodities. Trades are handled through ordinary brokerage accounts like other financial assets. Commodity-based exchange-traded funds are available for individual commodities. The list includes aluminum, Brent oil, coffee, copper, corn, cotton, crude oil, gasoline, gold, heating oil, lean hogs, live cattle, natural gas, nickel, silver, soybean oil, soy-beans, sugar, wheat, and West Texas intermediate crude oil. Rather than invest in one commodity, investors diversify into baskets of commodities. A basket can be an all-commodity fund, or can focus on agriculture, energy, grains, industrial metals, precious metals, petroleum, livestock, or softs (agriculturally grown commodities such as cotton).

The passion for managing risks skyrocketed to such lofty heights that commodity-based exchange-traded funds passed as ways for households to hedge against rising food and gasoline prices. In citing reasons for investing in commodities, particularly food commodities, a *Wall Street Journal* article states, "Also, these specialized investment products can be used to help lessen the pinch of rising food costs at home." A gasoline exchange-traded fund was held out as a tool for families to hedge against the rising cost of gasoline during summer vacation months. The fund was designed to rise in value at the rate that gasoline prices rose at the pump. Not all financial advisors recommended commodity exchange-traded funds. The same *Wall Street Journal* article quotes Jeff Ptak, director of exchange-traded securities analysis at Morningstar Inc. as saying, "I can't think of a prudent reason a typical [individual] investor would utilize products like these. They're far too specialized to suit main-stream investing purposes."[2] All the same many investors saw commodity funds as an intelligent and useful diversification.

In March 2008 Lehman Brothers, the investment bank fated to close in September 2008, unwrapped two new exchange-traded notes based upon commodities. A broad commodity note is designed to follow energy, metals, agriculture, and livestock. An agricultural note is designed to follow grains like corn, soybeans, and wheat, and soft commodities such as coffee, cotton, and sugar. Goldman Sachs, Bear Stearns, and other financial giants had already rolled out similar financial products, claiming notes have some advantage over funds.

Oil is only one commodity among many that shared in a com-modity price boom between 2001 and 2011. The case of oil illumi-nates the issues faced in the study of commodity prices. It lays bare the difficulty of pinpointing the forces driving oil prices upward. At times it seems the global economy owes high oil prices to the concentration of oil reserves in politically volatile areas, which leads to periodic disruptions of supply. This explanation holds one drawback: it fails to explain the correlation of prices between commodities that seem to have little in common. It throws no light on a key task, which is seeing clear to the bottom why the price of a particular commodity marches in phase with the prices of most other commodities. In fact the price of oil is not unique in having ready at hand one-time events to explain its fluctuations. Often the blame for price surges in one commodity is cast at the door of one-time natural events, such as mad cow disease, avian flu, hurricanes, freezes, droughts, or wars.

Oil prices climbed fourfold between 2001 and 2008.[3] Prices backed off after the financial crisis of 2008 but finished 2010 at levels three times above those of 2001. Some of the oil-price escalation was put down to the war in Iraq, but war could not account for all commodity price inflation. During the same time frame prices of food commodities almost doubled. Beverage commodities, including coffee and tea, saw prices more than double. Agricultural raw materials, including materials such as cotton, grew roughly 20 percent. The price of metals vaulted upward threefold. The IMF's index of all primary commodities climbed roughly threefold between 2001 and 2008. The boom gained intensity until it faltered amidst the 2008 financial crisis. Of the 47 commodity prices tracked by the IMF, 25 in 2008 peaked at above 50 percent higher than their average prices for 2006. Another nine peaked 25 to 50 percent above average prices for 2006.[4]

Unlike houses, commodities are highly tradable goods and usually sell internationally in U.S. dollars. Comparing these numbers with generalized U.S. inflation rates gives an indication of primary commodity inflation relative to inflation in general. U.S. consumer prices grew 21 percent between 2001 and 2008. Perhaps more revealing prices of capital equipment grew 10 percent. Prices of consumer durables fell 12 percent.[5]

An economy with stable prices normally sees some prices rising and others falling. These price adjustments only manifest the normal operation of a market economy redirecting resources to where they are most wanted. Such price activity does not reflect on the purchasing power of a unit of money. A generalized rise in the prices of all goods, however, suggests erosion in the value of a unit of money. Prices rise on a wide scale not because of shortages in goods, but because of excess money in circulation. Rarely are all or practically all prices rising, but it has been known to happen. Climbing prices across a broad range of goods suggest rapid money supply growth. The hint becomes more glaring if gold is one of the commodities whose price is climbing. Gold is one commodity often held as a surrogate for money. Paying a higher price for gold is often but not always tacit admission that the value of a unit of money has diminished, particularly since gold pays no interest.

## The Igniting of Commodity Booms

It is not obvious that other commodities act as surrogates for money, but that is the case for businesses needing these commodities. An oil refinery that regularly purchases crude oil can at any moment invest surplus cash either in Treasury bills or oil futures contracts. If the refinery worries about money losing its value, it opts for the oil futures contracts.

A key measure of U.S. money stock, which goes by the colorless bureaucratic name of M2, grew by a factor of 1.5 between 2001 and 2008, about half the growth rate of the primary commodity index. A narrower measure of the U.S. money stock, M1, grew by a factor of 1.25. The money stock grew by a larger factor than consumer prices, reflecting that the economy needed a larger money stock to accommodate economic growth. A fundamental theory in economics argues that if the money stock doubles and level of GDP output remains constant, prices on average must double. In practice growth in output eases some upward pressure on prices. Therefore, if the money supply doubles, prices almost, but not quite, double. Prices change proportional to changes in the money stock. An assumption that GDP remains constant simplifies matters. Then a doubling of the money stock doubles prices. A doubling of prices implies that on average prices double, but does not imply that all prices double. A few prices may even drop. That can happen if other prices rise fast enough to more than cancel out the effect of falling prices. Average prices still double in that case. For the years 2001 through 2008 overall consumer prices grew by a factor of 1.2. This factor is in line with expectations since the money stock measures grew by factors between 1.25 and 1.5. Overall consumer prices approximate an economy-wide average. The data for these years shows capital equipment and consumer durable goods prices growing at below average rates and commodity prices growing at much higher rates. This data suggests that prices in some economic sectors react quicker and more vigorously to money stock growth than prices in other sectors.

The above-average growth for commodity prices and below-average growth for capital equipment calls for a bit of reflection. The main goal of accelerated money growth lies in a reduction in interest rates, which in turn boosts demand for capital equipment and consumer durables. Lower interest rates sweeten the profits expected from capital equipment purchases. A relative elevation of commodity prices, however, subtracts from the profits earned from operating capital equipment. Capital equipment is less useful and profitable if energy and raw materials are not to be had at reasonable prices.

A nineteenth-century Irish economist, John Cairnes (1823–1875), observed that crude material prices, compared to finished manufactured-good prices, exhibited higher sensitivity to faster money stock growth.[6] He attributed the discrepancy in price inflation to differences in responsiveness of supply to price changes. He argued that supplies of crude materials sat unresponsive to price changes. Higher prices only called forth larger supplies after a lengthy span of time. Therefore stronger demand caused prices to rise instead of output. The opposite occurred in the market for manufactured goods. He collected data from several countries that lent support to his hypothesis. Frank Graham (1890–1949) discovered a similar phenomenon during Germany's post-First World War episode of hyperinflation. Raw material markets saw prices react quicker than markets for finished goods.[7] Michael Bordo came upon a similar pattern of bullish commodity prices unleashed by money stock growth.[8] He accounted for the behavior of commodity prices by differences in price flexibility between various markets, which he tied to differences in contract length.

Other reasons beside the one cited by Bordo help explain why prices of manufactured goods fluctuate less. Commodity prices are free to change and do change daily. Take the automobile as an example of a manufactured good. If Toyota changes the prices of automobiles daily, consumers will ask Toyota to make up its mind. Toyota fixes the price of its automobiles. Rival automobile manu-facturers watch Toyota's price-setting behavior and judge Toyota's aims accordingly. If Toyota cuts the prices of its automobiles, rival companies may view Toyota's price cut as an aggressive act against them. In retaliation they might slash their own prices and do no telling what else. Compared to a price war, holding prices constant looks reasonable. Similar considerations prevent Toyota from raising prices. If Toyota voluntarily raises prices, rival companies may think they can hold prices constant and undersell Toyota without pro-voking a price war. In summary, market conditions corner these companies into a strategy of infrequent price changes.

Purists in monetary theory argue that money stock changes lead to proportional changes in the level of prices, but leave untouched relative prices between goods and services. According to this view, discrepancies between commodity price inflation and capital-good price inflation remain a puzzle that begs for explanation. One explanation suggests that during some interim period of price ad-justment commodity prices overshoot the mark to counterbalance sluggish price adjustments in other sectors, such as capital-good production. If some prices do not change, then other prices must undergo larger adjustments to keep the overall price level propor-tional to the money stock. If the rate of money stock growth leaps by an extra 10 percentage points, then eventually all prices rise by an extra 10 percent. During an interim period, however, inflation for some commodities rises faster than 10 percent. This offsets the tendency for prices to rise at rates below 10 percent for other com-modities. Commodity prices become more flexible to compensate for less flexibility in other prices. This theory has been put to the test and found viable.[9]

Interest rates are another factor accounting for heightened com-modity price sensitivity to money stock changes. Monetary author-ities accelerate money stock growth to peg interest rates at lower levels. Inflation-adjusted interest rates enter into the carrying cost of holding commodities. This carrying cost can be expanded to embrace the cost of holding subterranean commodity reserves waiting for future extraction. Slashing inflation-adjusted interest rates subtracts from incentives to extract commodities. It is easier to see this effect when considering a hike in inflation-adjusted interest rates. The faster resources are extracted, the faster they can be exchanged for money that can be put in interest-earning assets. When money pays low interest, there is no hurry. When money pays high interest, there is hurry. Looked at another way, the higher the interest rates, the higher the opportunity costs of holding inventories. As interest rates go up, speculators turn to Treasury bills to the exclusion of commodity contracts. The higher interest rates go, the more commodity prices fall. Commodity prices bottom out when speculators expect commodity prices to start rising at a rate in excess of the rate of interest. This analysis needs minor fine-tuning since the interest rate is not the only opportunity cost of holding commodities. To foregone interest income must be added storage costs and the risk premium attached to investment in commodities. Commodity prices stabilize at a point where the benefits of holding commodities balance the opportunity costs of holding commodities, including foregone interest income. To test this theory Jeffrey Frankel performed regression analysis on the log of real commodity prices against inflation-adjusted interest rates for 23 commodities.[10] In nineteen of 23 cases the expected negative relationship turned up. In eleven of nineteen cases the statistical chance of the interest rate coefficient not being negative stood very small.

Periodic surges in commodity prices have also caught the eye of economic historians. Walt Rostow (1916–2003) dated worldwide surges in commodity prices going back to 1790. These surges lasted around fifteen years and were followed by periods of weak commodity prices. According to Rostow commodity prices boomed between 1790 and 1815, 1848 and 1873, 1896 and 1920, and 1935 and 1951. Another surge began in 1972.[11] During these phases prices in general climbed, but not as fast as raw material prices.

The commodity boom that began in 2001 spawned the conventional and expected explanations of its origin. According to one economist,

The commodity price boom was the culmination of demand and supply pressures that *atypically coincided* across most primary commodities . . . "Classical" supply shocks, such as bad weather, pests, and disease, helped push up prices: drought in Australia and the Ukraine raised wheat prices; floods in the mid-west of the U.S. raised corn prices; while Cyclone Nargis raised the price of rice by reducing production in Myanmar.[12]

The *Wall Street Journal* reported the findings of a survey of economists on the cause of booming food and energy prices. Fifty-one percent of respondents largely pinned the blame for rising energy prices on strong demand out of China and India. The next most significant culprit was supply interruptions, which was cited by 15 percent of respondents as the prime cause. Forty-one percent of respondents saw strong demand behind rising food cost. Twenty percent focused on supply interruptions to explain rising food cost. Only 11 percent of economists saw the potential of a bubble born of speculation.[13]

Governments banned exports to put a lid on domestic food prices. In 2008 India banned exports of non-basmati rice and wheat. Kazakhstan and Pakistan joined India in banning wheat exports. China imposed quotas and taxes on the export of grains. Russia, Ukraine, and Argentina levied export restrictions. Vietnam temporarily suspended exports of rice in 2008. Vietnam and the Philippines saw evidence of hoarding. Weather and poor crops may have played a modest role in food prices. Australia suffered back-to-back droughts in 2006 and 2007. Droughts in Eastern Europe and North Africa in 2007 cut into global grain production. In 2008 flooding damaged crops in the U.S.'s Midwest.

Commodities are highly tradable goods. Most commodities trade internationally in dollars. Since commodity prices are international, depreciation of the U.S. dollar against other currencies leaves commodities costlier in the U.S., but not necessarily in other parts of the world. Currency depreciation holds one link between commodity prices and easy money policies. Some observers argue that depreciation of the dollar contributed to a global boom in commodity prices. This argument begins with the premise that many developing countries do not like to see the dollar depreciate relative to their domestic currency. Therefore, they either peg domestic currencies to the U.S. dollar or prevent domestic currencies from undergoing large appreciation relative to the dollar. The U.S. dollar depreciating relative to the Chinese yuan is equivalent to the yuan appreciating relative to the dollar. If the dollar depreciates relative to emerging country currencies, then goods from emerging countries become costlier in U.S. markets, hurting exports from emerging countries. To hold relative exchange rates constant, emerging economies must accelerate money supply growth at home to cancel the exchange rate effects of faster U.S. money supply growth. To keep exchange rate fluctuation within bounds monetary policies in emerging countries mirror U.S. monetary policies. Donald Mitchell of the World Bank found that between January 2002 and June 2008 the depreciation of the U.S. dollar boosted food prices about 20 percent.[14]

The commodity price spiral that left even seasoned traders and industry executives flat-footed and scratching their heads was the price of oil. On 10 December 1998 crude-oil futures finished at a low point of $10.72 per barrel on the New York Mercantile Exchange. Fallout from the East Asian financial crisis coupled with an unusually warm winter sent oil prices tumbling in 1998. OPEC cut production and prices reached $25 per barrel in 1999. In 2003 the second Iraq war cramped production in one of the world's largest oil producers and in 2004 global demand shot up to 2.8 million barrels a day. China ranked the biggest culprit, now sucking up oil to power steel mills and other factories. Oil prices made history on 2 January 2008 when the New York Mercantile Exchange registered a benchmark crude futures contract of a record $100 a barrel. The next day a *Wall Street Journal* article analyzed oil's march to a tenfold increase in price. After citing factors such as China, war in Iraq, and lagging exploration, the article went on to discuss the role of financial innovations:

The ease of trading has helped attract a flood of new money. Oil markets were once dominated by physical traders—firms that needed to take delivery of the crude oil to run through refineries or trade with partners. Most of the new market entrants have no interest in ever taking delivery of a barrel of oil . . . The new money comes from hedge funds seeking profits in sharp oil-price moves, pension funds seeking diversification and a hedge against inflation, and Wall Street Commodity desks risking their own capital . . . The number of oil futures bets outstanding on Nymex [New York Mercantile Exchange] has quintupled since 2001. Because oil has been rising at the same time dollars at stake in the main oil-futures benchmark, not including options, rose from roughly $7 billion in 2001 to more than $145 billion, calculates Ben Dell, energy analyst at Sanford C. Bernstein & Co.[15]

In February 2008 benchmark oil futures for the first time finished above $100 for two consecutive days. Another *Wall Street Journal* piece addressed oil prices:

After a two-week-long run-up fueled largely by supply concerns, prices roses as speculative money flooded the market . . . "The funds are buying into this," said Mark Waggoner, president of Excel Futures, a commodities broker in Huntington Beach, Calif. "With the expiration of the March contract, the market becomes extremely volatile," he added.[16]

By 20 April crude-oil futures had rammed through to the neighborhood of $117 per barrel. On 21 April 2008 the *Wall Street Journal* carried a c10 page article headlined: "'The Mother of All Bubbles'? Oil's Record Run Baffles Bears." By this point analysts were expecting oil prices to fall back at least to $80 and possibly to $40 per barrel.

The wildly upward march of oil prices lit a fire under the U.S. Congress. One senator wanted to ban large pension funds and financial institutions from investing in futures markets. Defenders of speculation argued that speculators cannot drive up oil prices without taking custody of oil and holding it off the market. On 15 July 2008, a U.S. Senate committee heard Ben Bernanke give the Federal Reserve's required semi-annual monetary policy report to Congress. Mr Bernanke's testimony covered factors behind the run-up in oil prices. He told the committee:

Our best judgment is that this surge in prices has been driven predominantly by strong growth in underlying demand and tight supply conditions in global oil markets . . . On the supply side, despite sharp increases in prices, the production of oil has risen only slightly in the past few years. Much of the subdued supply response reflects inadequate investment and production shortfalls in politically volatile regions where large portions of the world's oil reserves are located. Additionally, many governments have been tightening their control over oil resources, impeding foreign investment and hindering efforts to boost capacity and production. Finally, sustainable rates of production in some of the more secure and accessible oil fields, such as those in the North Sea, have been declining . . . The decline in the foreign exchange value of the dollar has also contributed somewhat to the increase in oil prices . . . However, the price of oil has risen significantly in terms of all major currencies, suggesting that factors other than the dollar, notably shifts in the underlying global demand for and supply of oil, have been the principal drivers of the increase in prices . . . Certainly, investor interest in oil and other commodities has increased substantially of late. However, if financial speculation were pushing oil prices above the levels consistent with the fundamentals of supply and demand, we would expect inventories of crude oil and petroleum products to increase as supply rose and demand fell. But in fact, available data on oil inventories show notable declines over the past year.[17]

The IMF in the October 2008 issue of its *World Economic Outlook* agreed with Mr Bernanke that speculation was not elevating commodity prices, or causing higher volatility. This report found greater volatility in commodity prices since 2003 but could not trace it to the financialization of commodity markets.[18]

This study did conclude that financialization of commodity markets had strengthened the links between commodity prices, causing a greater tendency for commodity prices to fluctuate in step with each other. The linkages between commodity prices had grown closer for all commodities, but particularly for financialized commodities.

Investors purchasing commodity exchange-traded funds were often buying baskets of commodities. Instead of buying into one commodity, they were buying into several at once. Tendencies for commodities to boom across the board were first observed at least as far back as the nineteenth century. Recall earlier studies that concluded the secret to wide commodity booms lay with money supply growth.

This same *World Economic Outlook* issue did not quite agree with Mr Bernanke's assessment of the part played by the Federal Reserve policy in global commodity prices. It found that the loose u.s. monetary policy had helped fuel the commodity boom but cast the blame on other countries who kept domestic currencies tied to the dollar. These countries heavily managed exchange rates to keep exchange rates between the dollar and their domestic currencies within certain bounds. In some cases they outright pegged exchange rates with the u.s. dollar. The Federal Reserve put out of court the link between low interest rates and commodity prices, and exonerated speculation as the culprit. For those who want to shun monetary explanations of commodity booms, it is necessary to find other explanations for the correlation between price inflation across different commodities. Commodity exchange-traded funds can explain some of the correlation. Oil prices offer another possible link between prices of various commodities. Few commodities can be produced or extracted without an expenditure of energy.

An even tighter link is possible between oil prices and food prices. The u.s. enacted legislation effective January 2005 which gave tax incentives for the use of biodiesel fuel made from agricultural products. A European Union directive also stipulated that member countries take measures to expand the use of bio-fuels. These policies strengthened demand for corn and oil seeds. To expand production of corn and oil seeds, farmers took land out of the production of wheat, soybeans, and other crops, hurting supplies of these crops. The International Food Policy Research Institute credited bio-fuel demand for 39 percent of the rise in corn prices between 2000 and 2007, 22 percent of the increase in wheat prices, and 21 percent for rice.[19] Mitchell concluded that bio-fuel demand may have driven between 60 and 70 percent of the escalation of corn prices through early 2008.[20]

## Speculation Grabs Headlines

Few prices capture headlines more than food prices. Grain prices directly impact the price of food. Indirectly grain prices enter into food prices by affecting the cost of feeding livestock. Food inflation heated up in 2005. Between January 2005 and June 2008 maize prices exploded almost threefold, rice prices stampeded 170 percent, and wheat prices leaped up 127 percent. Over the same time frame, palm oil prices tripled and soybean oil prices almost tripled.[21]

Investors in PowerShares DB commodity Index Tracking fund, a commodity-based exchange-traded fund, saw its value climb 52 percent between May 2007 and April 2008. This fund covered commodities ranging from wheat and corn to heating oil. On average commodity-based exchange-traded funds rose 34 percent over the same time frame.[22]

Official institutions gave speculators little credit for booming commodity prices. The press is not gospel and interpreting market activity through its prism falls way short of scientific observation. A large number of press reports corroborating each other, however, merit consideration. It is another case of where there is smoke there might be a problem. In November 2005 the *Wall Street Journal* carried a piece about the sugar market. Its header read, "Sugar Futures Climb on Buying by Producers and Speculators."[23] It was small-sized speculators in this case. Later that month the same newspaper led with the header, "Sugar Prices Hit Contract Highs as Speculators Buy."[24] In this analysis speculative buying drove the price hikes. Three years later similar articles still appear. A *Wall Street Journal* piece led with the header, "Sugar Futures Fall as Speculators Exit." The same article made a brief mention of developments in the silver market. Bill O'Neil of Logic Advisors is quoted as saying, "Silver continues to be a wild speculative playground."[25]

Speculators busied themselves particularly in the coffee futures market, according to the press. This market clearly shows that speculators can drive prices down as well as up. A September 2003 *Wall Street Journal* piece opened with the header, "Commodities Report: Coffee Soars as Speculators Buy Back Their Short Positions."[26] Another header from January 2004 read, "Commodity Report: Coffee

Futures Trickled Down as Speculators Pocket Profits."[27] In March 2008 a *Wall Street Journal* story pointed the finger of suspicion at speculators and commodity funds for driving up coffee prices. According to this story:

> Coffee prices are on the march, and the costs of the milk, sugar, and even paper cups also are climbing. But whereas other commodities like copper or oil have been pushed up by demand from developing countries, coffee is a different case. Demand has only edged up, and much of the recent surge is due to speculators hopping into the commodity . . . Just as in oil and metals markets, investment funds have played a big role in the coffee run-up. On Intercontinental Exchange Inc.'s ICE Futures U.S., the world's main coffee-trading arena—formerly known as the New York Board of Trade—coffee's open interest, the number of unclosed positions, has shot up 50% over the past year. It is now at an all time high of 191,977 contracts, according to the Commitments of Traders Report, published by the Commodity Futures Trading Commission. The increase in trading is widely attributed to investment funds.[28]

By investment funds this article is referring to commodity-based mutual funds and exchange-traded commodity funds.

### Commodity Prices Bounce Back

The Global Financial Crisis of 2008 put an end to the housing boom and threw the global economy into recession. Unlike housing and many other sectors that continued to sag after the recession, commodity markets came alive with vigor. The synchronized rebound of commodity prices underscores their tendency to share the same upswings and downswings, to march to the same drummer. The IMF's All Primary Commodities Index peaked in 2008, posting 172.3 for the year.[29] It tumbled 30 percent in 2009, posting 120.7 for the year. By 2010 some economic sectors still sat in the tank but not commodities. This index of primary commodities in 2010 clawed its way back and then some to 152.2, a 26 percent rebound. By the second quarter of 2011, this index had leapfrogged its previous high, registering a value of 201.6. The food component of this index peaked at 157 in 2008. It skidded in 2009, posting 134 for the year, but turned around in 2010, posting 149.4. The second quarter of 2011 saw this index standing at 186.5, a rally of 19 percent above its previous peak in 2008. The beverage component of food, which includes commodities such as coffee and tea, did not even pause for a breather in 2009. It posted 152 for 2008, a modest increase of 154.4 for 2009, 176.2 for 2010, and 213.4 for the second quarter of 2011. It had soared 40 percent since 2008. The metals component of this index peaked in 2007 at 183.3, before slipping back to 169 in 2008. It bottomed out in 2009 at 136.5, and outdistanced its previous high in 2010, registering a value of 202.3. For the second quarter of 2011 this number stood at 241.8, a nice jump from the previous year. The petroleum component of this index peaked at 182.1 in 2008. It went into freefall in 2009, registering a yearly value of 116.2, a 36 percent drop. This index component bounced back to a level of 148.5 in 2010. Then it pressed ahead to post a value of 207.3 for the second quarter of 2011. The index for agricultural raw materials charted a similar pattern. Every single commodity group rebounded significantly by the end of 2010, and posted new highs in 2011.

In November 2010 China clamped price controls on food to hold prices down. It also awarded subsidies to truckers and retailers to tame food prices. China had its own concerns about internal speculation. China's National Development and Reform Commission issued a tough statement promising to severely punish agricultural traders and producers who spread fictitious price information, hoarded products in short supply, or manipulated futures markets.

In 2011 speculators drew holy censure for running up commodity prices. Pope Benedict XVI denounced food speculation. In 1 July 2011 he asked delegates of the UN Food and Agriculture Organization meeting:

How can we remain silent when even food has become the object of speculation or is linked to a market that, without any

regulation and deprived of moral principles, appears linked
solely to an objective of profit?[30]

The growth of exchange-traded funds was thought to be part of
the problem. On 12 April 2011 Europe's Financial Stability Board
issued a report entitled, "Potential financial stability issues arising
from the recent trends in Exchange-traded funds." This report cited
the remarkably rapid and broad financial innovation in exchange-
traded funds. In April 2011 the IMF issued a report on global financial stability which suggested that the growth of exchange-traded
funds did pose risks to the stability of the global financial system.
With regard to commodity-based funds it said:

> The recent increase in commodity price volatility has been
> partly attributed to the strong flows into commodities-based
> funds, particularly gold ETFs, amid mounting concerns that the
> flows are distorting prices away from fundamental factors.
> Gold ETF funds received net inflows of around $12 billion in
> 2009 and another $9 billion in 2010 as prices surged 62 percent
> in the two years to over $1,400 an ounce. However, flows
> sharply reversed course in January 2011, with $3 billion in out-
> flows in one month alone, driving prices sharply lower. Such
> dynamics raise concerns that a reversal of investor flows from
> other commodity-based funds could potentially increase
> volatility in the broader market and influence price action in
> related sector indices. Data show that assets under manage-
> ment in commodity-based funds (including mutual funds,
> ETFs, and index-linked funds) stood at over $320 billion in
> 2010:Q3.[31]

The promoters of exchange-traded funds could thank low interest rates for the growing popularity of their product. Low rates drove
investors into the arms of ever riskier and more complex financial
products, including those based upon commodities. This logic would
suggest a linkage between low interest rates and booming commodity prices. The Federal Reserve, however, cringed at the suggestion
that lax monetary policy and low interest rates bore responsibility

for setting off a commodity price boom. On 11 June 2011, Ben Bernanke gave a speech to the International Monetary Conference in Atlanta, Georgia:

> Another argument that has been made is that low interest rates have pushed up commodity prices by reducing the cost of holding inventories, thus boosting commodity demand, or by encouraging speculators to push commodity futures prices above their fundamental levels. In either case, if such forces were driving commodity prices materially and persistently higher, we should see corresponding increases in commodity inventories, as higher prices curtailed consumption and boosted production relative to their fundamental levels. In fact, inventories of most commodities have not shown sizable increases over the past year as prices rose; indeed, increases in prices have often been associated with lower rather than higher levels of inventories, likely reflecting strong demand or weak supply that tends to put pressure on available stocks.[32]

The debate over the role of speculation simmered despite assurances of respected voices such as Ben Bernanke. In July 2010 the U.S. Congress enacted the Dodd-Frank Wall Street Reform and Consumer Protection Act. This Act empowered the U.S. Commodities Futures Trading Commission to apply tighter regulation to commodity speculation. The commission brought forth its first proposal in January 2011. Wall Street welcomed this proposal with bared fangs. The commission received about 15,000 letters from various interested parties.[33] Those eager to see more controls on speculation may owe the *Wall Street Journal* for nudging the commission into action. In the weeks leading up to the commission's vote, it published data that the commission had collected from firms engaged in commodity trading. The data had been entrusted to the commission in confidence and participating firms had never expected it to see the light of day. The commission collected the data in an effort to understand the forces driving gyrations in the oil market. It exposed the big players in the commodity rally of 2008. The names of Goldman Sachs, Yale University, and a Danish pension fund adorned this list. The stock market has rules about public disclosure, but the commodities markets do not. Wall Street firms cried foul and asked for a probe into how this information fell into the hands of the *Wall Street Journal*. They claimed releasing this information wickedly exposed their secret trading strategies.

It was October before the commissioners voted 3–2 to adopt new rules that curbed speculative bets on 28 different commodities, including oil, gold, and natural gas. The vote split along party lines with three Democrats in favor and two Republicans against. Wall Street lobbied to the last minute trying to dilute the new rules. One rule barred a firm from acquiring more than 25 percent of a commodity's estimated supply deliverable in the short term. Firms were restricted to a smaller proportion of longer-term contracts. Critics fumed that the 25 percent rule was far too watered down.

In October the European Commission also advanced proposals for tighter regulation of financial markets. It covered a wide range of financial products, including derivatives and commodities. It proposed that commodity traders publish a weekly breakdown of stakes in various commodity markets. The key question was how much sway speculators held on commodity prices if after buying commodities they sold them before taking possession. Buying makes prices go up but selling makes them go down. Buyers in markets watch other buyers and often suspect them of having hidden information. Speculators entering a market can produce the same effect as someone spreading false rumors of an impending shortage. It undermines resistance to rising prices and prices end up going higher. If end-users remain convinced prices are moving up, they buy in advance to beat the increases. Inventories should climb as end-users stock up. Here the expectations of the end-users loom important. End-users may not stock up if they think the price run-up is driven by speculation and likely to prove temporary. With the economy weak and expectations of generalized inflation low, end-users of commodities cannot count on commodities prices continuing to rise; they are more likely to expect a crash in commodity prices. With expectations of deflation, interest rates cannot go low enough to justify holding commodities as an inventory investment. Therefore inventories do not rise in the face of rising prices.

Letting speculation off the hook does not clear the Federal Reserve of all suspicion. Research for over a hundred years leading up to the boom suggested a link between monetary growth and quickened commodity price inflation. More than one theory has been advanced to account for this connection. Answers that central banks give while taking heat for soaring commodity prices may not prove to be the most scientifically valid. It is an issue, however, that must wait until the boom is over before it can be settled to everyone's satisfaction.

## The Unquenched Thirst for Speculation

The continuing boom in commodity prices laid bare a passion for speculation that went unabated amid the scattered debris of collapsed bubbles in housing and dot-com. Historically commodity markets had been the elite province of the most experienced speculators. Financial engineering and financialization of commodity markets cleared the path for a wider range of investors to enter commodity markets. These swelled the ranks of investors who might want to swim without their swimsuit if they found a high-tide market. These were another instance of investors striving to maintain accustomed rates of return amid falling interest rates. By entering commodity markets these hopeful investors bore higher risks since commodity markets have been known to crash. In the case of housing, speculators could persuade themselves that house prices only go up. Not so in the case of commodities. Those looking for specimens of crashed commodity markets need only go back to the 1980s.

# TEN

# The Weakening of the Labor Market

## The Labor Market through Macroeconomic Lenses

The labor market presents another case where the macroeconomic perspective throws a vital shaft of sunlight on thorny issues. Recall that the essence of the macroeconomic perspective distills down to the straightforward logical principle that what is true for the part is not necessarily true for the whole. If only one worker out of all workers takes a pay cut, that worker is less likely to end up unemployed. If all workers take a pay cut, however, the unemployment rate may not drop, and might even go up. Earning a college degree decreases the chance that an individual goes without a job. Statistics show that college graduates enjoy a lower unemployment rate than high school graduates. From that statistic it might be inferred that if everybody earned a college degree, the unemployment rate would go down. Education levels, however, have moved up over the years, and society still suffers cruel episodes of elevated unemployment.

It is said that all sides of a problem cannot be seen from one angle. In the case of unemployment the personal angle cries for center stage. Unemployment invites scrutiny of the person without a job: perhaps that person has poor work habits; maybe they miss work too much, or never get to work on time; or are not a team player when they do get there. Maybe they cannot pass a drug test or have criminal record, or never graduated from high school. Needless to say countless personal traits may hold back a person in the job market.

There is another angle from which unemployment can be seen. It is the macroeconomic angle. This puts the spotlight on the economy as a whole. It asks if the cause of unemployment lies with the economy.

The first step in exploring the macroeconomic angle is to assume that the workforce is homogeneous. What if all workers are equally attractive in the eyes of employers? There is no differentiation into doctors, lawyers, hairdressers, agricultural laborers, and scientists. All workers are equally educated, talented, creative, innovative, experienced, motivated, loyal, cooperative, dependable, and honest. The next step is to explore under what conditions such a labor market and economic system will undergo episodes of high unemployment. Under what confluence of circumstances would some workers be thrown overboard, put out of work, even if all workers looked and performed equally well for employers? If individuals end up unemployed under these conditions, it is not because of personal failings. The cause lies with the workings of the macroeconomic system.

This standardization of workers clears the field for pinpointing where the labor market may go astray. If all workers are the same, they are all paid the same wage. The absolute level of the wage does not matter as much as the wage relative to prices. If the wage jumps tenfold it means nothing if prices also jump tenfold. It is the real wage that counts, the wage divided by the price level. With these simplifications unemployment becomes a matter of supply and demand. Unemployment signals that the supply of workers outruns the demand for workers. Under the pressure of unemployment wages drop relative to prices, making the employment of workers more profitable. As firms bring on board more workers, unemployment shrinks. The unemployment rate never drops to zero because some individuals are always in between jobs. It drops to some level found to be normal or natural from long-term experience.

It is not hard to see now the labor market just described adds another rheumatic joint in the macroeconomic system. Wages are not that flexible in the first place. When a firm hires an employee at $20 per hour, it implies that the wage will be no lower than $20 for quite a while, at least a year. If the firm announces a lower wage at the beginning of the next week, or even the next month, the worker feels cheated. The company has to show itself to be in dire straits before workers even grudgingly go along with a pay cut. In some cases the implication of a steady wage carries a legal sanction in collective bargaining agreements. In other cases minimum wage laws put a floor under wages. For these reasons wages show little sensitivity to imbalances in the labor market. In the face of unemployment wages drop over time, but not promptly. Unemployed workers resign themselves to lower wages after they lose hope of finding a job that pays as well as the job they lost.

Another difficulty with the labor market lies with the behavior of prices. At the onset of recession prices may fall before wages fall. The real wage equals the ratio of wages to prices. It is real purchasing-power wages. Falling prices without falling wages sends real wages skyward. Rising real wages in the midst of recession spells more unemployment. This scenario furnishes a case of unemployment in an economy of standardized workers. Even though all workers stand equal in the eyes of employers, some workers get the pink slips because of rising real wages. In practice of course the more vulnerable employees see the exit door first, but that leaves unchanged the fact that somebody faces unemployment even if all workers are of the same caliber.

In advanced economies stabilized by monetary and fiscal policies, prices may never fall in recession. Monetary authorities expand the money supply however much it takes to preempt deflation. These economies often exhibit an inflation bias that pulls wages up during booms. If wages carry upward thrust from the prior boom, it may still be difficult for real wages to fall even if prices do not drop. The unemployment rate belongs with what economists call lagging indicators. It is one of the last signals that hints at recession. After the stock market has crashed, and GDP growth winds down, the unemployment rate creeps up at a leisurely pace. Once an economic cycle bottoms out, and economic activity turns up, the unemployment rate straggles behind, one of the last indicators to show light at the end of the recession tunnel. It may sink lower even after the economy turns around and perks up. It lags because firms are accustomed to a certain amount of fluctuation in sales data. They are not lusting to give workers the boot if sales drop for one month. Hiring workers consumes time and pushes up costs. They do not want to lay workers off until they are sure they do not need them. They cannot afford to be laying workers off one week, and rehiring the next. It takes time to plan and execute a lay-off. Only after firms are convinced the economy has crossed the recession threshold do they lay off workers. A reverse logic comes into play once an economic upswing is underway. Firms want to make absolutely sure the economy has turned the corner to recovery before recruiting more workers.

The tendency of firms to hoard labor affects the behavior of the labor market. Firms try to keep workers they like and consider a good fit. They find ways to rid themselves of workers who do not fit so well. Most of the workers they have they want to keep. Moreover, in a recession firms may retain more workers than they need. It keeps them poised to take advantage of an upswing when it comes, but it delays rehiring at the end of the recession. Labor costs are obviously a large consideration in this matter.

Expectations enter into labor hoarding and the labor market. If a recession lasts longer and goes deeper than expected, then firms wake up to the fact that they have been hoarding too much labor. When the upswing comes, these firms do not step up hiring because they start the upswing with too many redundant workers. Growth in employment remains muted. Fears of a double-dip recession or prolonged depression heighten the chance that firms postpone decisions to hire more workers.

## Toward Jobless Recoveries

While the unemployment rate trails behind other economic variables, it eventually recovers if other economic variables remain long enough on the path of recovery. The recovery from the 1990–91 recession earned the distinction of a jobless recovery. In the typical economic expansion between 1960 and 1989, the U.S. economy needed eight months of expansion to recover its recessionary losses in employment. Real GDP recovered lost output within less than six months of expansion. A new pattern of recovery marked the 1990–91 recession. Firstly, real GDP took nine months of recovery to regain lost output. But the bigger story was what happened in the labor market. It took 23 months for the labor market to regain its employment lost during recession. It was labeled a "jobless recovery." Roughly speaking a jobless recovery is one in which employment growth remains zero or negative during the first year of the recovery. The jobless recovery of 1991–2 gave only an ominous hint of things to come. After the 2001 recession it took 38 months of expansion before employment losses of the recession were replaced. In many respects the 2001 recession was tame. GDP recovered its lost ground in only one quarter, three months. In jobless recoveries employment growth registers much weaker than expected given the strength of GDP growth.

According to the National Bureau of Economic Research the last U.S. recession began in December 2007 and ended in June 2009. Total civilian employment in the U.S. peaked in January 2008 at 146,407 million. It fell to its lowest point in December 2009 at 137,960 million. Employment continued to fall six months after the National Bureau of Economic Research dated the end of the recession. By October 2011, 27 months after the recession ended, U.S. employment had only recovered to 140,302 million. The recovery from the last recession far over-qualifies as a jobless recovery.

Other countries shared in the jobless recovery. In France employment peaked at 25.9 million according to the IMF.[1] By 2010 the number sank to 25.6 million. The IMF forecasted 25.7 million in 2011. The French unemployment rate stood at 7.8 percent in 2008 and 9.7 percent in 2010. The IMF expected France to finish 2011 at 9.5 percent unemployment. Employment numbers portray an uglier state of affairs in Spain. Spanish employment peaked in 2007 at 20.6 million with the unemployment rate standing at 8.3 percent. By 2010 Spanish employment stood at 18.7 million and the unemployment rate stood at 20.1 percent. The IMF expected the numbers to slightly deteriorate for 2011. The jobless recovery virus spared Germany in the 2010 recovery. Between 2002 and 2006 German employment remained below the 39.3 million reported in 2001. Employment steadily increased every year afterwards, including 2008 and 2009. In 2010 employment stood at 45.5million. After reaching double-digit levels in 2004, 2005, and 2006, the German unemployment rate began creeping down. It inched up to 7.7 percent in 2009 compared to 7.6 percent in 2008. In 2010 it registered 7.1 percent. The IMF forecasted 6 percent for 2011.

Japan's employment in 2007 stood at 64.1 million, roughly level with 2001. Employment sank every year afterwards, posting 62.6

million in 2010. Japan's unemployment numbers posted a slight drop in 2010 but the employment numbers did not bear the features of a recovering labor market. Employment still trended downward. The UK saw employment sink from 29.4 million in 2008 to 29 million in 2010. Over the same time frame the unemployment rate leaped up from 5.5 percent to 7.8 percent. Ireland's employment reached a peak in 2007 of 2.12 million after climbing every year since 2001. From 2008 forward Irish employment inched down, registering 1.8 million in 2010.

Australia and Brazil paint a happier picture. By 2011 Australia's employment had posted annual growth every year of the new millennium. It even eked out modest growth in 2008 and 2009. A slowdown in job creation sent Australia's unemployment rate spiking upward in 2009 but it trended downward in 2010. The IMF's database does not report employment numbers for Brazil but it does show unemployment reaching a trough of 7.9 percent in 2008. It spiked to 8.1 percent in 2009. In 2010 the unemployment rate was 6.7 percent, the lowest Brazilian rate of the new millennium.

A jobless recovery implies one of two things. It can mean employed workers are putting in longer days, raising the average number of hours each employee works per week. It can also signal an increase in the output per hour worked, which is an increase in productivity. Boosts to hours worked per week are not a large factor. Improvements in productivity drive the jobless recoveries. Jobless recoveries are not the only troubling stain on the new labor markets. The phenomenon of job polarization has reared its head. Job polarization means that a disproportionate share of job growth occurs in both high-skilled, high-wage occupations and low-skilled, low-wage occupations. From 1979 to 1989 employment grew in the U.S., but it grew faster in middle-skill, middle-wage occupations.[2] From 1989 to 1999 trends flip-flopped and the high-skilled, high-wage occupations saw the fastest employment growth. The share of total employment in these occupations grew. To a lesser extent the same trend showed itself in the lower-skill, lower-wage occupations. This group modestly raised its share of total employment. The middle range of occupations lost ground as a share of total employment. For the 1999–2007 time frame, the high-skilled, high-wage occupations remained roughly constant as a share of total employment. The middle-skill and middle-wage level occupations again lost ground as a share of total employment. The fastest growth occurred among low-skilled, low-wage occupations. This group captured a larger share of total employment.

The u.s. suffered no monopoly on the trend toward job polarization. A study of sixteen European Union countries uncovered the same annoying trend.[3] This study covered the years 1993 to 2006. All sixteen countries saw middle-skill, middle-wage occupations lose ground as a share of total employment. France and Austria saw the largest decline in middle occupations as a share of total employment. The smallest decline happened in Portugal, only a 1 percent change. On average middle occupations lost about an 8 percent share of total employment across Europe. This average percentage was derived by averaging the percentage loss per country without weighting countries differently according to size. In thirteen of the sixteen countries the high-skill, high-wage occupations acquired a larger share of total employment. The unweighted average gain in the high-wage share of total employment registered around 6 percent. The low-skill, low-wage occupations for eleven of the sixteen countries gained in share of total employment. All sixteen countries saw low-skilled, low-wage occupations grow in size relative to middle occupations. The unweighted average gain in share of low relative to middle occupations measured 10 percent.

In the u.s. managerial, professional, and technical occupations belonging to the highly educated, highly paid classifications saw solid employment growth from 1979 onward. These groups saw no absolute decline in employment during the 2007–09 years when total u.s. employment fell by eight million workers. The middle occupations in the u.s. suffered absolute declines in employment between 2007 and 2009. The decline held true for both middle white-collar occupations often filled by females and middle blue-collar occupations often filled by males. The declines ranged from 7 percent to 17 percent. Service occupations in the u.s. devote themselves to helping, caring for, or assisting others. These occupations include food preparation, cleaning services, personal care, and protective services. These occupations often require no post-secondary education, and in most cases command wages below those paid in other occupations. These occupations grew at double-digit annual rates through the 1990s. These double-digit growth rates continued in the millennium up to 2007. Even during the slump years of 2007 through 2009 these occupations eked out modestly positive growth.

One analysis claims that advanced countries paid for surging trade with low-wage countries by hollowing out middle-income occupations. Freer trade encourages countries to specialize in goods and services where they wield a comparative advantage. Wealthy countries can afford the education systems that graduate large numbers of highly educated and skilled workers. Developing and emerging countries hold vast armies of unskilled and uneducated workers. The abundance of these unskilled workers holds wages down in these countries. Hourly manufacturing wages paid in China equal a tiny fraction of wages paid in the u.s. In turning out goods and services skilled workers and unskilled workers complement each other. They are used together. Enlarging the accessible supply of unskilled workers renders the skilled workers more valuable. In response, the wages of skilled workers go up. Opening up trade with China, Mexico, and similar countries has vastly enlarged the usable supply of unskilled workers.

The above explanation accounts for the rising wages of highly skilled and educated workers. The wages of this group in advanced countries have gone up despite a rising supply of college-educated workers. This theory does not account for strong growth in low-skill, low-wage occupations. It cannot account for this growth unless the low-wage occupations have grown in importance to meet rising demand for services from the high-wage occupations. That explains why immigrants often say they take jobs that nobody else wants. These high-paid workers need lawn care, child care, restaurant meals, and other services. This explanation may hold a piece of the puzzle.

Researchers have studied this hollowing out of the middle occupations. Their verdict points to innovations in information and communication technologies as the guilty party. Information and communication technologies have seen rapid innovation and plummeting prices. Like other technologies, information and communication technologies are labor-saving devices. Some researchers have concluded that this technology has mainly replaced labor in the middle occupations. This new technology enhances the productivity of highly educated and skilled workers who are adept at abstract and creative thinking and analysis and whose work cannot be replicated by machines. It cannot displace the high-wage, high-skill workers. The middle occupations are a different matter. Instead of increasing the productivity of workers in the middle occupations, this technology has displaced them. Many of these middle occupations involve jobs that can be reduced to a set of instructions. Assembly-line workers belong in this category. Robots can be designed to perform the same tasks. Certain clerical tasks—those of bank tellers, payroll clerks, and paralegals—can be performed by this new technology. Occupations that involve a large component of routine and mechanical activity stand to be replaced by this new technology. Meanwhile, recessions and stiffer competition from imports press companies to innovate faster out of necessity. The lower end of the skill and wage spectrum includes a number of service occupations that go without risking displacement from technology. Cab drivers, janitors, and gardeners are examples that come to mind. Employment in these industries grows as wealthier societies demand more of these services.

Researchers tested the argument that faster investment in information and communication technologies correlates with rising demand for the most educated workers, and falling demand for workers with intermediate levels of education.[4] Their findings came from analyzing data of eleven countries—the U.S., Japan, the UK, Austria, Finland, Germany, France, Spain, Denmark, the Netherlands, and Italy. The database stretched from 1980 to 2004. Much of the less technical analysis was based upon comparing 1980 statistics with 2004 statistics. It separated workers into three different occupation groups based upon education. The high-skill workers had a college degree; middle-skill workers had a high school diploma with perhaps some college. Industries that upgraded information and communication technology substituted collegeeducated workers for middle-skilled workers. The relative wage difference also grew wider in industries reporting faster growth in technology upgrades. The share of wage outlays going to the high-skilled group grew the most in the UK, which happened to be the country that saw the largest increase in information and communication technology intensity. The U.S. came in second in the growth of information and communication technology usage. It placed third in the largest increase in wage outlays going to high-skilled workers. All countries exhibited a negative correlation between information and communication technologies intensity and the share of wage outlays going to middle-skilled workers. Japan was the only country not to show a positive correlation between information and communication technology intensity and the share of wage outlays going to high-skilled workers. This same study also found that expenditures on research and development exerted a similar effect on labor market polarization but not quite as strong. This study tested for the effects of foreign trade and off-shoring of jobs. It found these variables were not needed to explain labor-market polarization. The study did not rule out that these variables were important if innovation became a strategy for staying one step ahead of foreign competition. Companies faced a choice between becoming more technologically sophisticated, moving overseas, or going under.

The U.S. recession of 2001 followed a period of high business investment in business equipment. This equipment embodied the newest and cleverest advances in information technology, telecommunications, and computer networking. During the recovery GDP growth was partly driven by firms still assimilating this new technology. Assimilation of technology enabled firms to expand output without hiring more workers, making for a jobless recovery. The subsequent recovery and expansion gathered steam without the stimulus of high business investment spending. It was driven by a housing boom. Since investment in business equipment remained subdued from 2000 until the recession of 2008–09, businesses had plenty of time to catch up on the assimilation of new technology. Therefore to sustain output growth in recovery after the late 2000s recession, businesses were expected to depend more on hiring new workers and less on innovative applications of technology.

This logic sounded airtight, but productivity data belied the logic. In the second quarter of 2009 U.S. non-farm business productivity jumped 6.8 percent at an annual rate. The third quarter registered 5.2 percent growth in productivity, the fourth quarter 5 percent growth at an annual rate. The first quarter of 2010 saw annualized productivity growth of 2.7 percent. U.S. annualized GDP growth went from -6.7 percent in the first quarter of 2009 to 3.8 percent for the fourth quarter of 2009.[5] U.S. productivity numbers dropped off in 2010 and 2011, but GDP growth also dropped. Falling productivity amidst falling GDP invariably occurs because of the effects of redundant labor. U.S. GDP grew at an annualized 3.9 percent in the first quarter of 2010. From that high rate growth tapered off. For the first quarter of 2011 GDP annualized growth registered a mere 0.36 percent. Growth modestly rebounded the next two quarters, but never broke into 3 percent territory again. This data suggested that surges in GDP were likely to be attended with productivity surges at the cost of employment growth. The unemployment rate faced a long road back. Large productivity gains raised the GDP growth necessary to lower unemployment rates. After 2008 firms in advanced countries stood eager like never before to find technological solutions for cutting costs. Not since the 1930s had firms had more reasons to innovate as quickly as possible if cost could be slashed.

## A Digression on Technology Assimilation

A historical perspective on the assimilation and diffusion of new technologies throws light on what was happening in labor markets after 2008. It is worth remembering that in the early phases of the technological revolution, economists were struck at the small effect the wave of major innovations was having on productivity statistics. It is called the "productivity paradox."

This "productivity paradox" puzzled Robert Solow, a professor of economics at the Massachusetts Institute of Technology and perhaps the most famous theorist on economic growth in the post-Second World War era. In 1987 he won the Nobel Prize for his analysis of economic growth. He formulated a model now called the Solow growth model. In the year that he received the Nobel Prize he wrote a review of the book, *Manufacturing Matters: The Myth of the Post-Industrial Economy* by Stephen Cohen and John Zysman. In this review he touched on the failure of productivity statistics to reflect computer-age innovations:

> What this means is that they [the authors], like everyone else, are somewhat embarrassed by the fact that what everyone feels to have been a technological revolution, a drastic change in our productive lives, has been accompanied everywhere, including Japan, by a slowing down of productivity growth, not by a step up. You can see the computer age everywhere but in the productivity statistics.[6]

Solow's observation suggests a lag in the assimilation and diffusion of technology. From 1979 to 1989 U.S. output per hour grew at an average annual rate of 1.2 percent. During those years U.S. firms invested vast sums in computer equipment. From 1998 to 2003 U.S. output per hour grew at an average annual rate of 3.45 percent. Between 1947 and 2010, the year posting the fastest growth in output per hour was 2002. That growth rate was 4.6 percent. That year was also a year of a jobless recovery.

Productivity surges in recoveries partly because firms hold redundant labor during recessions that is used more efficiently as production is stepped up in recovery. After a phase of rapid technological advance another factor enters the equation. An economic recovery presents a perfect juncture for a firm to extract more work out of fewer workers by fully exploiting new technologies embodied in the high investment of the prior boom years. Before hiring new workers a firm decides between widening and deepening technology applications or hiring more workers. The firm chooses the least costly alternative to sustain output growth. Firms may make these decisions without consciously choosing between technology and people. More marketing goes into persuading firms to use technology than to use people. Studies on the assimilation and diffusion of ground-breaking technological innovations suggest it takes a while for the full economic impact to be felt.

In 1990 Paul David published a scholarly paper, "The Dynamo and the Computer: An Historical Perspective on the Modern Productivity Paradox." It studied the history of electricity for insights into the productivity paradox. Edison introduced the carbon filament incandescent lamp in 1879 and the Edison central generation station in New York and London in 1881. In 1900 the age of electricity stood as far distant from these key inventions as the computer age stood in 1990 after the introduction of the 1,043-byte memory chip in 1969 and Intel's silicon microprocessor in 1970. In 1899 electric motors supplied less than 5 percent of factory-driving power in the U.S. Not before the early 1920s did factory electrification give a measurable boost to U.S. manufacturing productivity. In comparing the computer with the electrical generator, David wrote:

> In both instances, we can recognize the emergence of an extended trajectory of incremental technical improvements, the gradual and protracted process of diffusion into widespread use, and the confluence with other streams of technological innovation, all of which are interdependent features of the dynamic process through which a general-purpose engine acquires a broad domain of specific applications . . . Moreover each of the principal empirical phenomena that make up modern perceptions of a productivity paradox had its striking historical precedent in the conditions that obtained a little less than a century ago in the industrialized West, including the pronounced slowdown in industrial and aggregate productivity growth experience during the 1890–1913 era by the two leading industrial countries, Britain and the United States . . . the transformation of industrial processes by the new electric power technology . . . did not acquire real momentum in the United States until after 1914–17, when regulated regional utility rates for electricity were lowered substantially in relationship to the general price level.[7]

This paper did not address the obvious question: Did the rapid spread of this transforming technology have anything to do with the decade-long episode of elevated unemployment in the 1930s? A definitive answer to this question perhaps lay beyond reach. It was an intriguing question to ask given what was happening in labor markets in 2010. The weak labor market in 2010 of course followed the rapid and ubiquitous spread of information and communication technologies from 1995 onward.

From what is said above it seems that productivity statistics may not always bring to light everything that is going on with new technology. It also appears that investment in information and communication technologies may bear part or all responsibility for softening the labor market. A review of the boom in these new technologies allows the issue to be viewed from yet another angle. Part of the story lies in the tumbling prices of the new technologies. The cost of computers in 1987 stands over twelve times above the cost of computers in 2002, a breathtaking 92 percent plummet in price.[8] Prices dropped every year from 1987 through 2009. Between 1995 and 2009 prices fell another 50 percent. Prices of communication equipment did not start dropping significantly until 1995. Between 1995 and 2002 prices dropped 21 percent. By 2009 these prices were less than half what they were in 1995. Software sees the smallest drop in prices. Between 1995 and 2009 software prices fell 9.4 percent.

Falling prices failed to keep businesses from spending larger amounts on information and communication technologies acquisitions and upgrades. Between 1995 and 2000 U.S. business investment spending on these technologies grew an average of over 25 percent a year.[9] Between 2000 and 2009 annual growth in business investment on these technologies cooled to a 4.4 percent annual average. That 4.4 percent must be compared with negative growth in overall business-investment spending for those years. U.S. GDP growth over that time frame also remained well below its long-term average of 3 to 3.3 percent per year. The share of total U.S. business investment spending going to these technologies went from 16 percent in 1995 to 30 percent in 2000. By 2009 expenditures on these technologies accounted for 44 percent of total business investment. As a share of U.S. GDP, business investment in these new technologies went from 1.93 percent in 1995 to 4.67 percent in 2000 and to 6.03 percent in 2009.

The heady investment spending on information and communication technologies between 1995 and 2000 mirrored the dot-com bubble that burst in 2000. After that bubble popped annual investment spending on these technologies settled down to a more leisurely pace. Still, each year's investment spending enlarged the total outstanding stock of equipment and software even if spending in some years trended downward, as it did in 2001, 2002, and 2003. Another revealing statistic measures the value of the accumulated stock of information and communication technology investment per worker. Between 1995 and 2000 the value of the accumulated stock of these investments used by each worker roughly doubled. Between 2000 and 2009 the accumulated stock per worker grew 82 percent, no small amount.[10]

The displacement of some workers in the labor market by technology does not alone account for a jobless recovery. As recounted above reductions in employment in middle-skill, middle-income occupations have been offset by growth in the high-skill, high-income occupations and the low-skill, low-income occupations. Some workers must settle for lower-paying occupations, but that is at least partially offset by other workers capturing higher-paying occupations. For the most part that is what eventually happens. The unemployment rate, however reluctantly, subsides in every recent economic recovery. It doggedly lingers at elevated rates before subsiding because of the expectations of workers. Unemployed workers have a history of earning certain wages. On becoming unemployed they look for work in pay ranges that they have been led to believe are reasonable for them to expect. If the first job opportunity an unemployed worker lands upon pays better than the job the worker just lost, the unemployed worker snatches up the new job at once. If the first job opportunity pays less than the job the worker just lost, the worker is likely to regard the job as beneath them and turn away. Before accepting a lower-paying job, an unemployed worker first gives up on finding a job that pays as well or better than their last job. The availability of unemployment insurance may encourage the most conscientious and ambitious of workers to extend a job search in the hope of landing a job that pays as well or better than a previous job.

## Expectations Matter

The effect of worker expectations reinforces the tendency for unemployment rates to remain stubbornly elevated long after economic recovery is underway. It reflects the resistance of workers feeling pushed into lower-paying occupations. The unemployment rate remains elevated partly because workers lengthen the duration of unemployment hoping to land an acceptable job.

The assimilation and diffusion of information and communication technologies aggravates the difficulty of unemployed workers landing an acceptable job. It is an issue that has drawn the interest of scholars. One study links rates of technical change to odds of displaced workers finding new employment after losing a job.[11] Higher computer usage and intensity of research and development in an industry lowers the chances of displaced workers finding a new job. Older and less skilled workers face the most difficulties getting a new job after displacement. Another study concludes that workers closer to retirement see less incentive to acquire new skills necessary for computer usage. It also finds that computer-using workers retire later than non-computer using workers. This study concludes that computer use decreases the probability of retiring.[12] Another study links the rate of technological change to the average length of time a person remains unemployed before finding a job.[13] This study measures computerization by investment per worker in office, computing, and accounting equipment. It concludes that computerization lengthens the average period of unemployment. It also finds that in duration of unemployment older workers suffer more than younger ones. These findings are based upon u.s. data.

The u.s. Bureau of Labor Statistics reports data on the average number of weeks an unemployed person goes without a job. It shows that in 2000, the height of the dot-com boom, the average duration of u.s. unemployment stood at 12.6 weeks. That number continued to grow during the recovery, peaking at 19.6 weeks in 2004. By 2007 this statistic stood at 16.8 weeks before climbing sharply, registering an average of 33 weeks in 2010. For the 55–64 age bracket of workers, the average duration of u.s. unemployment stood at 18.4 weeks in 2000. It peaked in 2004 at 26 weeks before skidding steadily, reaching 21.9 weeks in 2008. Then it turned up sharply, posting 41.2 weeks in 2010.

The website for the OECD (http://stats.oecd.org) reports average duration of unemployment in months. For the G-7 countries— Canada, France, Germany, the UK, Italy, Japan, and the u.s.—this

data shows that in 2001, a recession year, the average length of unemployment stood at 3.2 months. It reached a peak in 2004 at 4.5
months then dropped until it turned up again in 2008. In 2010 this
number stood at 7.4 months. For 55-plus workers the numbers are
higher, reaching 8.9 months in 2010.

## Fitting the Pieces of the Puzzle

It is now abundantly clear how the labor market fits into the big
picture. During the 1990s commodity prices were cheap and the
Federal Government moved toward a balanced budget. These trends
eased pressure on monetary authorities, enabling the u.s. to enjoy a
relatively fast monetary growth and falling interest rates. These
trends, coupled with a long stretch of continuous GDP growth,
touched off a stock-market boom. Early in 1997 the Federal Reserve
edged interest rates up, hoping to preempt inflation that might break
out after a long expansion. In August 1997 the East Asian Financial
Crisis struck. The price of oil plummeted 50 percent to $11 per
barrel. Crashing currencies cheapened imports into the u.s. economy. In 1998 and 1999 the Federal Reserve backpedaled and cut
interest rates to immunize the u.s. from the contagion of the financial crisis, a policy not dissimilar to China's in 2009 to shield itself
from the global financial crisis of 2008. Low interest rates coupled
with low inflation kicked off a speculative frenzy in the u.s. stock
market. In December 1997 the u.s. NASDAQ index stood around
1,500. In March 2000 it strutted into 5,000 territory.

The booming stock market furnished new and old firms with an
abundance of cheap money. Just as prices are falling for information
and communication technology, firms are swimming in money for
capital expansion. Stock market finance enables firms to purchase
massive amounts of new information and communication equipment. The stock market also acts through another channel to feed
the boom in this new technology. Rising stock prices leave households wealthier, bolstering a strong demand for goods and propelling
economic growth. Corporate profits soar, putting firms in an even
better position to acquire new equipment. Much of this equipment
and software wields more processing power and capabilities than

companies know how to use. The engineers designing the new equipment and software are far ahead of the market and the current needs of businesses. High technology companies count on supply creating its own demand. In time businesses will catch up and learn how to use all the capabilities of the new technology. As they do, they will need fewer employees. Before the bubble pops, enough new investment in this labor-saving technology occurs to impart a large upheaval in the labor market.

After the jobless recovery of the early 1990s raw materials and commodities were cheap. Economic growth created enough jobs to eventually absorb displaced workers. The jobless recovery was followed by an unusually long phase of steady economic growth. Even then some of the jobs did not pay that well. After the jobless recoveries of the early 2000s, commodity prices start spiking. Thanks to booming commodity prices economies meet with headwinds that prevent the creation of jobs on a scale needed to absorb workers displaced by technology. Economies cannot grow as fast as they did in the 1990s. Unemployment rates stubbornly hover at high levels.

The labor market affords a revealing case of how bubbles and speculation affect the real, non-financial sectors of the economy. Individuals who have never invested in financial markets share in the turmoil caused by speculation. The NASDAQ or dot-com bubbles arise from economic policies aimed at shielding the U.S. economy from recession and financial crises abroad. The bubbles create waves in the labor market that do not go away that quickly.

# ELEVEN

# String of Sovereign Debt Jitters

## The Sages Speak on Public Debts

Sovereign debt crises present a case where it is hard to miss the macroeconomic perspective—what is true for the part is not necessarily true for the whole. In the case of public sector budgets this principle can play cruel pranks on governments laboring to balance budgets. One small government within a large economy can reduce its deficit and balance its budget by raising taxes and cutting government spending. If all the small governments concurrently raise taxes and cut government spending, they face an uphill effort. Combined deficits may well go up instead of down, at least in the short-run. If a government happens to be large compared to the whole economy, the outcome will be the same as if several smaller governments act concurrently. A large government may find raising taxes and cutting government spending widens a deficit. At least the deficit grows worse before it gets better. Similar logic applies to downgrades of credit-rating agencies. A rating agency downgrading the debt of one government may redirect the flow of capital to better uses. Downgrading several governments almost at once may lead to a different outcome.

The series of sovereign debt crises offers the most visible example of the logic behind the macroeconomic perspective working itself out in the open. These successive crises wear the aspect of a toppling row of dominoes. Each falling domino knocks over the one next to it. Toppling the first domino sets off a chain reaction that does not end until the last domino falls. Lengthening the domino chain by adding dominoes does not change the end result. It only lengthens the time it takes for the process to complete itself.

Classic writers of the first rank have put in a kind word for public debts. Montesquieu in *The Spirit of Laws*, published in 1748, wrote, "Some have imagined that it was for the advantage of the state to be indebted to itself: they thought that it multiplied riches by increasing the circulation."[1] This line of reasoning appears at a time when gold and silver circulate as money and act as a store of wealth. Government bonds give households and businesses another store of wealth. These bonds free up gold and silver hoarded as a store of wealth and let them flow into circulation as a medium of exchange. Alexander Hamilton, first secretary of Treasury of the U.S., subscribes to roughly the same view. He holds out interest-bearing government bonds as a place for businesses to park capital when it is not in use.

In the twentieth century economists saw government debts as sometimes necessary to offset excess savings. It is argued that wealthy societies naturally evolve to a stage where savings are high and investment opportunities low. This stage supposedly occurs after a large stock of infrastructure and developed property is in place. Public debt is necessary to absorb excess savings generated at full-employment output. Otherwise demand for output falls short of supply, and the economy irreversibly spirals downwards.

Scholars and thinkers have highlighted the sunnier side of public debts, but there is a seedier side. Amidst the sovereign debt crises of 2011 an article by Carmen Reinhart and Kenneth Rogoff, published in the *American Economic Review*, put sovereign debt crises in historical perspective.[2] This article draws conclusions from a data set on sovereign debt defaults stretching back to 1800. The authors identify five episodes of serious foreign debt crises. During these episodes at least 20 percent of the sampled countries default. The sample covers 70 countries in Africa, Asia, Europe, Latin America, North America, and Oceania. The first episode comes toward the close of the Napoleonic Wars. That episode is short-lived and only slightly over 20 percent of countries default. The second episode breaks out in the second half of the 1820s, stretching nearly to 1860. During a portion of this episode nearly half of all countries sit in default, including all countries in Latin America. Another episode erupts in the 1870s and lasts through much of the 1880s. At its worst, over 35 percent of countries end up in default. The Great Depression of the 1930s opens the fourth episode, which lasts through the early 1950s. This episode has two peaks, in each of which well over 40 percent of countries default. The last episode dates from the early 1980s to mid-1990s. At its peak, over 35 percent of sampled countries sit in default.

A budget deficit and a public debt represent two different things, but they are related. A budget deficit equals the amount government spending outruns government revenue for a set time period, such as a year. Likewise a budget surplus equals the amount government revenue outdistances government spending. The public debt equals the accumulated budget deficits of past years minus the accumulated surpluses. A public debt mounts up if annual budget deficits over a span of years outweigh budget surpluses.

In public debt as in private debt a large consideration lies in the amount of income available to repay it. An individual sinks no deeper in debt if the amount owed doubles, but the individual's income also doubles. The debt must be measured against the ability to pay. If debt rises faster than income the odds of default go up. Economists measure the degree of a government's indebtedness by the ratio of government debt to GDP. In 1946 the U.S. public debt stood at 121.7 percent of GDP. Economic growth and inflation helped bring the percentage down. By 1982 U.S. public debt was down to 32.5 percent of GDP. It then marched steadily upward. In 2008 the U.S. public debt stood right at 70 percent of GDP, but it commenced rising faster.[3] Between wars, slow growth, and economic stimulus, U.S. public debt as a percentage of GDP finished above 100 percent in 2011.

The U.S. has never officially defaulted on its debt but in 1971 it did suspend the convertibility of dollars into gold which could be counted as a default. In August 2011 Standard & Poor's stripped the U.S. Treasury of its AAA credit rating, lowering it to AA+. This put the U.S. Treasury's credit rating below that of a dozen other countries. Standard & Poor's numbered among the same credit rating agencies that honored mortgage-backed securities with AAA ratings before the subprime crisis. Japan's saw its credit rating downgraded in January 2011 from AA to AA-. Japan's public debt as a percentage of GDP stood in the 200 percent range, far above that of the U.S. Japan's economy lay depressed for decades and still offered few signs of turning around.

The financial crisis of 2008, coupled with a global economic downturn, weighed heavily on public finances in several advanced countries. Fiscal deficits gaped much wider as lethargic economies churned out less revenue for tax coffers. While tax revenue shrank, governments beefed up and padded spending by stimulus programs and official bailouts of financial sectors. From the close of 2007 to the close of 2010 average budget deficits widened from 1 percent to 8 percent of GDP for member countries of the OECD. Gross government debt ballooned from an average 73 percent of GDP to 97 percent.[4]

In a discussion involving interest rates it helps to know what a "basis point" is. It takes 100 basis points to equal one 1 percent point. In the eurozone the interest rate paid by German government bonds is considered the benchmark rate. Bonds issued by other euro sovereign governments pay basis points above or below the German interest rate, depending upon risks and other factors. Sovereign debt stress was most keenly felt in the euro area. From the introduction of the euro in 1999 until July 2007 interest rates between various government bonds within the euro area varied little. The narrowness of the spread between interest rates was perhaps unjustified and unrealistic, but it went unexamined until the subprime crisis started to unfold. With the opening of the subprime crisis in late 2007 sovereign debt underwent closer scrutiny. Particularly after the rescue of Bear Stearns in March 2008 investors linked the sovereign debt risks with banking sector weakness. Investors now expected governments to bail out banks, dragging governments deeper into debt.

## Greece

Eurozone rules required member countries to hold deficit spending to no more than 3 percent of GDP. The latest and cleverest in Wall Street financial engineering and magic lent an obliging hand to eurozone countries, particularly Greece and Italy, wanting to mask indebtedness from eurozone overseers. Financial derivatives developed by Goldman Sachs, JPMorgan Chase, and other banks permitted politicians in Greece and Italy to envelope government borrowing in a shroud of financial abracadabra. In November 2009, three months before Athens became the vortex of global financial jitters, the president of Goldman Sachs headed a fieldtrip of bankers to Athens equipped with a financial instrument that would push Greece's health care system debt far into the future. Athens said no thanks to Goldman's ingenious proposal this time, but it had heartily welcomed Goldman's help in the past.

When Greece joined the eurozone in 2001 its public debt already stood above 100 percent of GDP. Greece's budget deficit fell outside the 3 percent of GDP deficit limit required by the eurozone. Skeptics hinted that Greece wedded to the eurozone would not be a marriage made in heaven. Goldman Sachs gladly stepped up as Greece's deliverer. It helped Greece secretly borrow billions, giving Greece the appearance of meeting the eurozone's deficit rules without raising taxes or cutting spending. It was an original sin that drew down its own punishment. The deal entailed a loan hidden as a currency trade. It involved a kind of financial derivative known as a swap. Goldman received $300 million in fees for the 2001 Greek trans-action.[5] The Greek deals were even honored with names from Greek mythology. The 2001 deal went by the name of Aeolos, god of the winds. It gave Greece an upfront cash advance in return for rights to future landing fees at Greek airports. In trade for cash Greece mort-gaged highways and bartered away lottery proceeds for years to come. The lottery revenues went to a 2000 deal named Ariadne. These underhanded deals gave Greece a fig leaf because they were not recorded as loans. They were liabilities hidden from public view. With a twinkle in the eye the Greek government slyly classified these deals as sales and not loans. That sleight of hand did not silence critics. Banks such as Goldman and JPMorgan earned handsome fees for these deals. It was not as if European Union officials sat innocent to what was going on. In 2000 European finance ministers hotly debated the disclosure of derivative deals that equated to creative accounting. The Ministers decided against taking action at first, but in 2002 they decided to require disclosure of many entities, such as Aeolos and Ariadne. The Greek government had to restate these transactions as loans and not sales. In 2005 Goldman sold an inter-est rate swap, another offspring of financial engineering, to the National Bank of Greece. In 2008 the bank with Goldman's help turned the swap into a legal entity called Titlos. Titlos issued bonds that the bank utilized for collateral in borrowing from the European Central Bank. According to Eurostat, the European Union's statistics agency,

> [In] a number of instances, the observed securitization operations seem to have been purportedly designed to achieve a given accounting result, irrespective of the economic merit of the operation.[6]

In 2007 Greece's government deficit according to Eurostat stood at 6.4 percent of GDP, well above the eurozone limit of 3 percent. Government deficits as a percentage of GDP for all eurozone countries averaged less than 1 percent. Deficits in the eurozone expanded to 2 percent of GDP in 2008, while Greece's deficit grew to 9.8 percent. In 2009 Greece first issued a ball-park figure for deficit spending on the order of 13.6 percent, but that number was later revised upwards to 15.4 percent. By 2009 government deficits for all eurozone countries averaged on the order of 6.3 percent of GDP.

In April 2010 Standard & Poor's slashed Greece's sovereign debt rating from BBB to BB+, putting Greek bonds at junk status. The interest rate spread between the Greek ten-year bond and the benchmark German ten-year bond widened to a gaping 682 basis points after the downgrade. Before the downgrade the spread stood at 625 basis points. By May 2010 the Greek government faced default. A giant question mark hung over its ability to roll over debt. As conditions for a bailout loan package the IMF, the European Central Bank, and the European Commission pressed Greek officials to tighten budgets, raise taxes, and privatize some government activities. The Greek government proposed savage cuts in wages, pension plans, jobs, and welfare. The cuts were to be implemented over two years, and amounted to 10 percent of output for each year. The Greek government agreed to aim for a 20 billion euro reduction in its annual budget deficit over three years. In May 2010 the IMF, European Central Bank, European Commission, and the Greek government reached an agreement for a Greek bailout. It made available 145 billion euros in loans in return for assurances that the Greek government would keep its promises of spending cuts, tax hikes, a harder line against tax evasion, and privatization plans. Out of this agreement came the formation of a eurozone bailout vehicle known as the European Financial Stability Facility. This vehicle was set up to guarantee bonds issued by European governments with troubled finances. It could issue AAA-rated bonds.

The Greek public had already displayed its unhappiness by strikes and protests. The new government austerity measures brought anger to boiling point. A May protest led to three fatalities after protestors took to the streets hurling gasoline bombs. The protest was part of a general strike that shut down airlines, schools, and hospitals. Austerity measures helped send the Greek economy tumbling. In the second quarter of 2010 Greek GDP was down 3.7 percent on a year-to-year basis. Gross investment in fixed assets, as opposed to inventory investment, was down 18.6 percent.

Greece achieved some progress toward its budget goals. In 2010 its budget deficit as a percentage of GDP came in at 10.5 percent. Despite deep economic recession government revenue eked out a slight gain. By November 2010 civil servants and pensioners had suffered cuts of more than 20 percent. Deficit reduction measures pushed the Greek economy deeper into recession territory. In 2010 GDP shrank by 4.3 percent. In both 2009 and 2010 Greece endured the highest inflation rate of eurozone countries leaving Greek goods relatively more expensive in other countries and goods from other countries relatively less costly in Greece. For 2011 the IMF predicted Greek GDP would shrink another 5 percent.

For 2010 Greece's public debt as a percentage of GDP stood at 143 percent. Japan's public debt stood above 200 percent of GDP, but Japan was not dependent upon foreign investors. Greece had chalked up an unenviable history of financial mismanagement, and investors distrusted government statistics in Greece. By October 2011 Greece once again faced default. French president Nicolas Sarkozy and German chancellor Angela Merkel brokered an agreement with Charles Dallara representing the Institute of International Finance (IIF), a lobbyist group for international banks. At first it was suggested that private holders, including banks, agree to a 60 percent mark-down in the value of Greek bonds. That proposal was advanced as superior to a 100 percent loss from default. Mr Dallara winced at 60 percent but agreed to 50 percent. Perhaps billing the voluntary mark-down as a "haircut" lent it some dignity. According to press accounts, Mr Dallara commented:

> The IIF agrees to work with Greece, euro-area authorities and the IMF to develop a concrete voluntary agreement on the firm basis of a nominal discount of 50 percent on notional Greek debt held by private investors.[7]

President Sarkozy voiced the worries that inspired the agreement: "France wanted to avoid the drama of a Greek default, when you remember the consequences of the failure of Lehman Brothers, and it's done."[8] The agreement also multiplied several-fold the lending capacity of the European Financial Stability Facility. This was the bailout vehicle set up with the first Greek bailout. It was now armed with additional firepower aimed at protecting Spain and Italy from sovereign debt contagion. A third prong of the agreement boosted the capital cushion among the weakest of Europe's largest banks. By 30 June 2012 the banks in thirteen European countries had to come up with 106 billion euros of extra capital. To help raise capital, bank bonds carried government guarantees.

The Greek debt crisis remained an ongoing cause of suspense throughout 2012. Eventually the bond holders had to accept slightly more than a 50 percent write-down. Austerity measures worsened economic conditions. In May 2012 talk was rampant that Greece would leave the eurozone after elections failed to elect a party strong enough to form a coalition government. In June 2012 a narrow victory by a center-right party revived hope that Greece would remain in the eurozone. In August the prime minister, Antonis Samaras, unveiled another round of cost-cutting measures. The coalition government hoped these new cost-cutting measures would persuade eurozone officials to give Greece a two-year extension on its budget targets.

By early November 2012 Greece had seen 39 consecutive months of rising jobless rates. Its parliament was still pushing through more rounds of spending cuts, tax hikes, and labor-market reforms amid public protest and tear gas. Meanwhile Greece's creditors squabbled over the specter of further assistance to Greece. Fears remained of Greece exiting the eurozone.

Toxic mortgages and a pricked housing bubble had little to do with the Greek debt crisis. There was one eye-opening link. Both the subprime crisis and Greece's debt crisis were aided and abetted by Wall Street financial engineering and wizardry.

## Ireland

Ireland was another story. In its case a deflating housing bubble and banking crisis figured prominently. Until 2008 Ireland belonged in the showcase of Europe's success stories. Firms flocked to Ireland to take advantage of low corporate tax rates coupled with a low-cost, well-educated, English-speaking labor force. When that was not enough, government subsidies sweetened the deals. Climbing salaries fueled a decade-long real-estate bubble. Among the fastest-growing industries was banking, aided by fervent demand for property loans.

According to Eurostat Statistics, Ireland in 2007 registered a budget surplus of 0.1 percent of GDP. On average the eurozone reported a modest deficit that year. Before July 2007 the Irish government ten-year bonds paid interest rates below that of comparable German bonds, putting a negative value on the risk premium for Irish bonds. After the Bear Stearns rescue the Irish bond rate stood only 0.3 percent points above the German rate. The Irish "spread" was only 30 basis points. In the wake of Bear Stearns, interest rate spreads widened between bonds issued by various eurozone governments. After the nationalization of Anglo Irish Bank Corporation in January 2009 the Irish spread stood at 300 basis points. The Irish spread soared above 1,000 basis points before retreating to 650 basis points by mid-September 2011.

In the wake of the global financial crisis, Ireland skidded into the deepest slump of all eurozone countries. Ireland's GDP shrank 3 percent in 2008, 7 percent in 2009, and remained flat in 2010 and 2011. Portugal, Spain, and Italy could not match Ireland's economic retrenchment. Ireland also saw the worst of the deflation. Consumer prices fell over 1.5 percent annually in 2009 and 2010. Unemployment climbed from 4.5 percent in 2007 to 13.6 percent in 2010. Other European countries finished 2010 with a higher unemployment rate only because they started with a higher rate. No other eurozone country witnessed a heart-rending threefold increase in the unemployment rate.

To prop up Ireland's banking system, the Irish government shouldered huge bank liabilities, enough to weigh heavily on public finances. Ireland's two largest banks by assets, Allied Irish Banks PLC and Bank of Ireland Group, received 3.5 billion euros apiece from the Irish government. Anglo Irish Bank Corporation, known as the "builder's bank," had open-handedly lent to commercial property developers during Ireland's wild construction boom. In mid-2009 the Irish government injected four billion euros into a recently nationalized Anglo Irish to cover record losses from toxic loans. A year later Anglo Irish received another two billion euro. In 2009 Anglo Irish reported the largest loss in Irish corporate history.

In 2008 the Irish government's budget crossed from the surplus column to the deficit column, and by no small amount. In 2008 the deficit stood at 7.3 percent of GDP, according to Eurostat. The deficit sink hole opened wider, hitting 14.5 percent of GDP in 2009 and a huge 32.4 percent in 2010, ten times the eurozone limit. By October 2010 the Irish government had spent 45 billion euros rescuing banks, an amount equivalent to nearly 30 percent of a year's GDP.[9] As recently as 2007 Ireland's public debt stood at an enviable 25 percent of GDP. Ireland saw that percentage blossom to 44.4 percent in 2008, 65.6 percent in 2009, and 96.2 percent in 2010.

Irish banks lost deposits as fast as the European Central Bank pumped in money. By September 2010 government-guaranteed support of Irish banks equated to 32 percent of GDP, rattling financial markets.[10] Eurozone governments pressured Ireland to seek a bailout rather than watch matters go further downhill. Fear of an Irish default haunted financial markets. Rising yields on Irish bonds deepened the crisis. In November, seven months after Greece received its first bailout, Ireland requested bailout aid from the IMF and European authorities. The European Financial Stability Facility contributed the largest share, supplemented with loans from the European Commission, UK, and Sweden. About one-third came from the IMF. Unlike the second Greek bailout, the Irish bailout required no bond holders to take a "haircut."

As a condition of the bailout the Irish Parliament passed austerity measures aimed at bringing Ireland's budget deficits down relative to GDP. The European Union wanted Ireland's deficit down to 3 percent of GDP by 2014. The austerity measures cut the minimum wage, widened tax brackets, reduced tax credits, cut social-welfare payments, and introduced a levy on property owners. One sore point was Ireland's 12.5 percent corporate income tax. Germany, France, and other eurozone governments felt this low tax gave Irish corporations an unfair advantage. The Irish government held its ground on that issue, but it raised its value-added tax. The austerity measures cut public sector payrolls by 25,000, and the salaries of new public sector workers. While the U.S. debated the extension of expiring tax cuts, Ireland levied taxes for the first time on lower-wage workers.

The austerity measures and bailout failed to quiet investors' nerves. Irish bond yields continued to climb. Austerity budgets hammer economic growth short-term, causing matters to worsen before they improve. U.S. officials warned European governments that severe austerity measures could derail economic recovery. On 29 September 2010 an online *Wall Street Journal* piece opened with the header "U.S. Official Warns Europe on Austerity." In October 2010 the Irish ten-year government bond yield hovered at 6.42 percent.[11] Rates steadily marched upward, reaching 12.45 percent in July 2011. On 12 July Moody's became the first rating agency to downgrade Irish government bonds to junk-bond status. Talk about Greek bond holders taking a "haircut" unnerved financial markets. Moody's feared that holders of Irish bonds might be in for a similar "haircut". There was brief talk of a second Irish bailout. Investor fears about Ireland eased in the second half of 2011. Irish ten-year government bond yields fell, posting 8.1 percent in October 2011. The government's austerity measures remained on track. Toward the end of 2011 the government announced plans to push through tighter austerity measures.

Brutal deflation had a silver lining. It left Ireland's goods more competitive in the global marketplace. Irish exports grew 6.3 percent in 2010, and the IMF projected 6 percent export growth for 2011.

In 2009 Ireland reported a current-account deficit of almost 3 percent of GDP. In 2010 the current-account deficit turned to a widening surplus. The *Wall Street Journal* carried a story, "Lessons of the Irish Comeback."[12] Over the next two years Ireland shared in the difficulties of a global slump, but it remains the leading light among countries that received bailouts. Unlike Greece, Ireland finished 2007 with a budget surplus and a debt burden just 25 percent of GDP. These numbers should have been the clue that betting against Ireland might not turn out so well. Ireland weathered its economic crisis.

## Portugal

Portugal became the third eurozone country bowing to market forces that mercilessly marched it straight to the bailout window. It was another case of shaky public finances but with a different origin. Both Greece and Ireland enjoyed strong economic growth leading up to the crisis. Lax fiscal control brought down Greece, and a mighty hangover from a bursting property bubble tripped up Ireland. Portugal suffered neither housing nor banking crisis. The seeds of Portugal's downfall lay in sputtering growth leading up to the crisis. Portugal's limping GDP growth inched up slightly above 2 percent in 2007 after remaining below 2 percent for the previous six years. That put Portugal's long-term growth rate among the smallest in the euro area. Before China's cheap textiles poured into world markets, Portugal played the role of Europe's sweatshop. Admission of Eastern European countries in 2004 diverted foreign direct investment away from Portugal.

In 2001 Portugal boasted a 4.6 percent unemployment rate. For the next six years the unemployment rate crept up every year. It read 8.9 percent in 2007 before backtracking slightly to 8.5 percent in 2008. Then the needle on the unemployment gauge swung to the double-digit range in 2009. Lumbering worker productivity growth staggered behind wage growth, pushing up labor costs. Portugal's textile industry could not compete with the low prices of Chinese textiles or the high-fashion branded textiles of France and Italy. Between 2005 and 2007 Portugal's current account deficit measured as a percentage of GDP remained in the 10 percent range. It peaked in the 12 percent range for 2008 before sliding back to single-digit territory. Sluggish GDP growth hobbled growth in tax revenue. Portugal did not share Ireland's riotous roller-coaster ride in GDP growth. In 2007 Ireland posed 5.1 percent GDP growth and Portugal 2.3 percent. By 2009 Ireland's 5.1 percent growth had wildly somersaulted to -6.9 percent. Portugal's 2.4 percent growth gently flip-flopped to -2.5 percent.

Portugal never quite rivaled Greece in rickety public finances. Its public debt as a percentage of GDP stood at 68.3 percent in 2007 according to Eurostat. That number climbed at a healthy rate, putting it at 93 percent in 2010. At 3.1 percent of GDP Portugal's budget deficit in 2007 bordered on the 3 percent limit of the eurozone. In 2009 Portugal reported a budget deficit of 10.1 percent of GDP, closer to France's 7.5 percent than to Greece's 15.4 percent or Ireland's 14.3 percent.

Portugal differed from Greece and Ireland in a key respect. Its government by 2010 had off and on been tightening the fiscal screws for nearly a decade, raising value-added taxes, intermittently cutting spending, freezing pay of civil servants, and reforming pensions, including high penalties for early retirement. Most observers missed the sobering thought that fiscal austerity measures only led Portugal to the financial abyss. Portugal's Achilles heel lay in the dependence of its households and businesses on foreign borrowing. Portugal's net foreign debt (what residents owe to foreigners minus what residents own of foreign assets), stood at 96 percent of GDP in 2008.[13] That indebtedness measure made Portugal worse off than Greece. Foreign banks held a good chunk of Portugal's gross debt, an amount totaling 120 percent of GDP.[14] Dependence upon foreign lending left Portugal exposed to gyrations in investor sentiment. High borrowing and slow growth rarely spell a happy ending. In July 2010 Moody's rating agency cut its rating on Portugal's government bonds to A1 from Aa2, a two-notch cut. The rating agency cited Portugal's poor growth prospects, sharply rising ratio of public debt to GDP, and worries that Portugal's labor-market reforms would not bear fruit.

In October 2010 Portugal's government unveiled austerity measures. That month the ten-year government bond paid a 6.05 percent yield. The interest rate steadily climbed as rating agencies broadcast warnings. The government counted on austerity measures to win investor support, but heated defiance in Portugal's parliament left markets unimpressed. In March 2011 the Portuguese parliament willfully cast aside new austerity measures advanced by the government. By April 2011 the interest rate stood at 9.9 percent, well above the German benchmark rate of 3.34 percent for that month.

Not all observers saw these events as the outcome of blind, impersonal market forces. Some saw the cold forces of unfettered capital flexing muscle, securing its dominance. On 12 April the Opinion Pages of the *New York Times* carried an op-ed piece by Robert M. Fishman, a professor of sociology at the University of Notre Dame. This piece painted a dark picture of wicked forces at work:

Portugal had strong economic performance in the 1990s and was managing its recovery from the global recession better than several other countries in Europe, but it has come under unfair and arbitrary pressure from bond traders, speculators and credit rating analysts who, for short-sighted or ideological reasons, have now managed to drive out one democratically elected administration and potentially tie the hands of the next one . . . But in Greece and Ireland the verdict of the markets reflected deep and easily identifiable economic problems. Portugal's crisis is thoroughly different; there was not a genuine underlying crisis. The economic institutions and policies in Portugal that some financial analysts see as hopelessly flawed had achieved notable successes before this Iberian nation of 10 million was subjected to successive waves of attack by bond traders . . . Market contagion and rating downgrades, starting when the magnitude of Greece's difficulties surfaced in early 2010, have become a self-fulfilling prophecy: by raising Portugal's borrowing costs to unsustainable levels, the rating agencies forced it to seek a bailout. The bailout has empowered those "rescuing" Portugal to push for unpopular austerity policies affecting recipients of student loans, retirement pensions, poverty relief, and public salaries of all kinds.[15]

Portugal opened negotiations for a bailout in April 2011. In May 2011 the European Union and the IMF gave the nod to a 115.5 billion

euro bailout package for Portugal. In return the Portuguese government agreed to impose austerity measures aimed at reining in its
budget deficit and reigniting economic growth. Negotiations leading up to the agreement embraced opposition parties. All three of
Portugal's major political parties signed the agreement. Without their
approval the Portuguese government could not be counted on to
keep its side of the bargain. Part of the funds was put at the disposal
of banks to help enlarge capital cushions, but Portugal's large banks
claimed they would not need the help. The austerity measures
included 500 million euro in cuts from annual central government
expenditures, and an elimination of tax deductions. Portugal's
government also pledged to overhaul an inflexible labor market and
Portugal's housing market. Privatization of government-owned
companies entered into the deal, including national airline TAP Air
Portugal and power companies Energias de Portugal SA and Redes
Energeticas Nacionais SGPS SA. The austerity ax spared minimum
wage floors and public-sector jobs.

In June 2011 Portuguese voters ousted Jose Socrates of the
Socialist Party in favor of Pedro Passos Coelho of the Social Demo-
crat Party. The election was billed as the end of leftist rule. The new
leadership was expected to fast-forward privatization plans and
expand Portugal's austerity measures beyond those outlined in its
bailout package. Investors still only saw a straggling economy with
reforms unlikely to hand over quick results. The yield on Portugal's
government bonds kept climbing. In July 2011 Moody's became the
first rating agency to downgrade Portugal's debt to junk status. The
yield on Portugal's bond for that month stood at 12.15 percent. Yield
remained high, registering 11.72 for October 2011.

In September 2011 the autonomous government of the Portuguese island of Madeira disclosed one billion euros in hidden debt.
This disclosure raised credibility issues about Portugal's budget policies. Moody's promptly lowered the island's rating from B3 to B1.
This development forced Portugal's bailed-out government to face
the task of rescuing another debt-ridden government itself.

Throughout 2012 Portugal's government faced rising discontent
fueled by high unemployment, steep taxes, and a shrinking economy. Nevertheless bright spots calmed the nerves of investors. Ex-

ports rose, imports fell, and Portugal enjoyed the support of its official lenders. A debt restructuring or haircut remained unlikely.

## Italy

After the second Greek bailout of October 2011, Italy popped up on investors' radar screens. In October 2010 Italy's government bonds posted a yield of 3.8 percent, well below the 9.57 percent of Greek bonds, the 6.42 percent of Irish bonds, or the 6.05 percent of Portuguese bonds, according to European Central Bank website data. In 2007 Italy's budget deficit equaled 1.5 percent of GDP, well within the eurozone's limit of 3 percent. The deficit grew, but in 2010 it equaled only 4.6 percent of GDP, a rather tiny amount when put beside Ireland's 32 percent of GDP deficit for the same year. Greece for 2010 reported a deficit at 10.5 percent of GDP, and Portugal 9.1 percent. By these numbers Italy belonged in the category of Germany with a 2010 budget deficit of 3.3 percent of GDP.

In the eyes of now tender-footed investors the scary part of Italy's profile lay in its public debt as a percentage of GDP. This statistic was not growing particularly fast compared to other countries, but it started out high. In 2007 Italy's public debt stood at 103.6 percent of GDP, well above debt levels for Ireland and Portugal for that year, but comparable to Greek public debt, according to Eurostat data. Between 2007 and 2010 public debt as a percentage of GDP went from 25 percent to 96.2 percent in Ireland, 68.3 percent to 93 percent in Portugal, 105.4 percent to 142.8 percent in Greece, and 103.6 percent to 119 percent in Italy. Italy corralled the growth of public debt reasonably well given the difficulties all eurozone countries faced. The snag was that it started at a high debt level, over 100 percent of GDP. Because Italy was a much larger economy, the absolute level of debt reached a towering height. In 2010 Greece boasted over twice the public debt of Portugal and Ireland, and Italy boasted over five times the debt of Greece. Italy was both too big to fail and too big to bail out. A large chunk of outstanding Italian government bonds were due to be rolled over in 2012. The size of Italy's debt lifted the eurozone's debt crisis to a shakier level. Italian banks came under pressure not because of toxic real-estate loans, as in Ireland, or because of a contracting domestic economy as in Greece, but because they held large positions in Italian government bonds. Rating agencies downgraded debt of Italian banks.

In July and September 2011 Italy enacted austerity measures, a mix of tax hikes and spending cuts. In a bid to bring its debt burden below 100 percent of GDP, the government also unveiled plans to sell state-owned assets, real estate and stakes in state-owned businesses. These investments paid rates of return below interest rates on Italian government bonds. In September 2011 Standard & Poor's cut Italy's bond rating to A. Early in October Moody's cut it three notches, down to A2, a rating comparable to Standard & Poor's A. In November Italian bond yields crossed into 7 percent territory, a key psychological milestone. Bond yields of 7 percent had become a line in the sand, the point of no return in the cases of Greece, Ireland, and Portugal. So far, every country that crossed that line had staggered to the bailout window.

The Italian government enacted stiffer austerity measures, including raising the retirement age to 67, opening up professions, more privatization, and tougher measures against tax evasion. A long-standing prime minister stepped down. Teachers, airline workers, and public transport workers went on strike. Students took to the streets in noisy protest. Italy's antiquated labor-market institutions both retarded economic growth and added to discontent. Older workers enjoyed contracts that rendered termination difficult. Younger workers had to put up with temporary contracts that conferred no job protection. European authorities, knowing that the only answer lay in faster economic growth, pressured Italy's government to overhaul pensions, slash red tape, and ease labor market restrictions. In December a new prime minister advanced a three-year plan of additional austerity measures. One provision upped the retirement age for women in the private sector from 60 to 66.

In 2012 Italy's economy struggled against austerity measures. Slow growth and continued troubles in Greece pushed up Italy's borrowing costs. In June 2012 eurozone authorities announced a plan to use rescue funds to purchase bonds of governments threatened by high borrowing costs. Expectations that the European Central Bank would buy Italian bonds helped to hold borrowing costs within sustainable levels.

By the end of 2011, the debt crisis had infected the entire euro-zone. Rating agencies that had missed the subprime debacle were taking no more chances. On 5 December 2011 Standard & Poor's issued a warning on fifteen euro countries that signaled a 50 percent chance of downgrade within 90 days. Standard & Poor's hinted that Germany, Belgium, Austria, Finland, Luxembourg, and the Nether-lands were unlikely to see more than a one-notch drop. France and other eurozone countries risked a drop of two notches.

## Spain and Belgium

A few storm clouds in Spain's economic sky were sufficient to alert nervous investors. In July 2011 Moody's put Spain's AS2 rating under review for possible downgrade. Early in October Fitch's rating agency downgraded Spain's debt two notches, to AA-. Later in October Standard & Poor's and Moody's downgraded Spain's government debt. Moody's downgraded it to A1, a two-notch cut, citing Spain's poor growth prospects given slow European and global growth. Banks burdened by sour real-estate loans also weighed in the downgrade.

In November 2011 Spain saw the yield on its ten-year bond touch the 7 percent line in the sand. In 2010 Spain's public debt sat at 60 percent of GDP, well below the levels of Greece, Ireland, Portugal, or Italy. For that matter it was below the levels of France or Germany. Spain had already clamped on austerity measures that squeezed its budget deficit from 11.1 percent of GDP in 2009 down to 9.2 percent in 2010. A half-hearted socialist premier had already cut public-sector wages, overhauled Spain's labor market, and lightened the cost of worker termination. Pension reform lifted the retirement age from 65 to 67. The IMF projected a 6.1 percent of GDP deficit for 2011. The odorous side was that Spain had shared in the global housing bubble. The Spanish economy and banks suffered when the housing bubble popped. The unemployment rate hit 20 percent and recovery from a harsh contraction in 2009–10 remained annoyingly sluggish. In November 2011 Spanish voters elected a new government pledged to a harder line on austerity measures, but without raising taxes. European Union authorities could hardly ask for more.

In June 2012 worries about Spain again surfaced in the eurozone. Once again interest rates on government bonds hit 7 percent. Spanish banks stood in need of bailout. Apparently accounting methods intended to smooth out earning over the business cycle has misled regulators. Spain accepted a bailout package for its banks that would not become part of its sovereign debt. In August 2012 there was some concern that the Spanish government would need a financial bailout. However, hopes that the European Central Bank would step in to purchase Spain's bonds kept interest rates down.

Spain may eventually have to accept a bailout to keep its bonds above junk bond status. A bailout reassures investors, and unemployment remains in the 25 percent range as of October 2012.

Belgium was another eurozone country buffeted by the sovereign debt crisis. In 2010 Belgium's budget deficit equated to 4.1 percent of GDP, normally not a scary number. Its total public debt as a percent of GDP, however, stood at 96 percent, which put it on the nerve-racking high side. In November Standard & Poor's rating agency downgraded Belgium's debt from AA+ to AA. The failure of Belgium's politicians to agree on austerity measures contributed to the downgrade. The economic outlook for Belgium's trading partners shared in the reasons for the downgrade. The interest rate on Belgium bonds never reached the 7 percent level. It moved into the 5 percent range before Belgium's government settled upon a plan to trim deficit spending. Afterwards the interest rate fell back to the 4 percent range.

## The Euro in the Cross-hairs

Sovereign debt crises in the eurozone occurred against the backdrop of the new euro currency. The European Union launched the euro in 1999 at roughly one euro to one U.S. dollar. The euro arrived upon the scene after monetary authorities in advanced countries had waged a twenty-year battle against inflation, assuming that inflation would always be public enemy number one. At first the exchange rate of the euro sank. By mid-2001 it was worth only $0.85. The euro was new and establishing it in the confidence of investors and speculators was a top-drawer eurozone goal. The euro could not establish itself as a serious currency if its value sank. The euro started climbing in value. It reached a high in July 2008 at 1 euro = $1.57. As late as July 2011 the euro stood at $1.42. In November 2011, as the eurozone sovereign debt crisis raged, the euro traded at $1.35. In summary the euro gradually strengthened against the dollar. The strong euro left eurozone goods costlier in other countries and foreign imports cheaper for the eurozone.

While the eurozone stood biased in favor of moving the value of its currency higher, China stood equally biased toward keeping the value of its currency low. These two currency policies complemented each other perfectly. A strong euro and weak yuan held eurozone inflation in check and preserved the euro as a reserve currency rivaling the status of the dollar. Given the magnitude of the eurozone's economic and financial woes, the strength of the euro has puzzled experts. Press accounts quoted Kenneth Rogoff, Harvard professor and former chief economist for the IMF, as saying, "I find today's relatively robust value for the euro somewhat mysterious."[16] True to form, speculators came outfitted with a special nose for scenting situations in which the subterranean forces of economic law are at variance with government pronouncements and policies. They stood eager to make foreign exchange markets a stage for placing bets on how the future of Europe would play out. A Greek debt crisis that radiated to other European countries meant trouble for the euro. In February 2010 a boutique investment bank hosted an "idea dinner" at a private Manhattan townhouse.[17] This gathering of all-star hedge fund managers aired the likely fall of the euro. This meeting would later draw accusations of collusion against the euro. Afterwards hedge funds bought credit-default swaps against the risk of a Greek sovereign default risk. In January 2010 Goldman Sachs's analysts took a group of investors on a field trip to meet with banks in Greece. The group comprised of representatives from a dozen money managers, including Chicago hedge-fund giant Citadel Investment Group, the New York hedge funds Eton Park Capital Management, and Paulson. The Paulson hedge fund was the one that designed a Collateralized Debt Obligation with a high risk of failure. Goldman Sachs sold the security without telling the buyers that the designer of the security was betting it would fail. The euro steadily trended downward in the first half of 2010. It reached a low of $1.20 = 1 euro in June 2010 before turning back up.

One New York firm trying to profit from European sovereign debt paid dearly. MF Global Holdings Ltd drew its strength from futures and commodity trading. In March 2010 a new CEO, Jon Corzine, assumed leadership of the firm. Corzine's resumé boasted service as Governor of New Jersey and Chairman of Goldman Sachs Group Inc. Under new leadership MF moved toward a full-service investment bank akin to Goldman. A more aggressive business strategy included a $6.3 billion bet on European sovereign debt.[18] The bet involved the sovereign debt of Portugal, Italy, Spain, Belgium, and Ireland, countries where yields were high because perceived risk were high. Given the company's capital reserves, exposure to European sovereign debt unsettled regulators, creditors, customers and credit agencies. The company's only hope for survival lay in finding a buyer. As potential buyers scrutinized the books of MF Global, it came to light that $600 million was missing from customer accounts. The discovery pushed MF Global into bankruptcy on 31 October 2011. A large chunk of customer money remained missing. The debacle led to hearings in the U.S. Congress.

Sovereign debt crises stir up broader debilitating problems for macroeconomies in general and banking systems in particular. Banks are harassed from four different angles. Firstly, they hold large amounts of sovereign debt, particularly from the domestic government. A fall in the credit worthiness of these assets weakens the balance sheets of banks. Secondly, sovereign debt bonds are the main collateral banks use to secure wholesale funding. As the perceived risks of sovereign debt widen, the market value of sovereign debt bonds falls. Banks end up with less collateral for raising funds. If rating downgrades are large enough, the bonds of affected sovereign debts may end up unacceptable as collateral. Thirdly, the funding benefits banks derive from government guarantees depends upon the creditworthiness of the government. Policy steps taken to protect banks when markets froze in 2008 counted on creditworthy governments. This can be a large factor in countries like Ireland that committed vast sums to shoring up banks. Fourthly, rating agency downgrades of a country's sovereign debt are often the advance agent for credit downgrades of a country's banks. These four considerations cripple the ability of banks to take a bold stance on meeting the needs of borrowing customers.

Pinning the blame on the credit rating agencies and financial investors veered from the mark. The rating agencies neither sounded the alarm on the subprime crisis, nor were the first to hoist the red flag in Greece. Before the financial crisis central bankers brandished the threat of deflation. In the past deflation invariably foreshadowed high loan default rates. The financial crisis made deflation an even likelier scenario. Just as central bankers ceased prophesying deflation, actual events validated the deflationary scenario. Adding to the financial atmospherics were governments openly adopting deflationary policies to maintain confidence of government bond markets. The global economy's potential for recovery lessened each time another government adopted fiscal austerity policies.

Sovereign debt crisis had more often been linked with developing countries. If sovereign debt markets caught a cold in Europe, they caught pneumonia in Latin America. The 2011 sovereign debt crisis was different. It was centered in the developed world. The secret to this asymmetry was twofold. Part of the story lay in commodity markets. Booming commodity prices favored commodity-exporting developing countries and weakened developed countries that export manufactured goods. While developed countries struggled against debt crises, developing countries rode the crest of a commodity-led wave of prosperity. In developing countries incomes kept up with debt. Another part of the story lay with monetary policy. The European Central Bank was the most inflation-hawkish central bank in the developed world. The euro was the newest currency, a currency still developing a track record. It had more to prove than other leading currencies. It may have had more to gain by surviving the sovereign debt crisis, given that the u.s. dollar lost ground. In December 2011 the European Central Bank's benchmark interest rate stood higher than the benchmark rates of the u.s.'s Federal Reserve System, the Bank of Japan, the Bank of England, or the Swiss National Bank. The European Central Bank raised its benchmark interest rate in July 2008, while central banks in the u.s. and UK wrung their hands over deflation. The Bank of England and the Federal Reserve started cutting rates in 2007. The Bank of Japan's rate was already less than 1 percent in 2007. Amid strong commodity price inflation, it is hardly surprising that the countries fighting hardest to hold the line on inflation suffered the most.

As the crisis deepened the European Central Bank relaxed its hawkish stance and began buying bonds of eurozone countries such as Greece, Portugal, Spain, and Italy. It did just enough to preserve the eurozone. In September 2012, the bank unveiled its boldest step for saving the eurozone.[19] A new plan provided for unlimited purchases of government debt from riskier countries. Before a country could qualify for relief under this plan it had first to apply to Europe's bailout fund. Then other European governments and possibly the IMF could impose austerity measures and economic reforms as a condition of help from the European Central Bank. The strategy seemed to be one of holding borrowing costs down until economies could start benefiting from reform measures.

### Drinking the Austerity Kool-aid

Europe's sovereign debt crisis highlights the tendency for austerity measures to make matters worse. In November 2012 economists at the European Commission issued a grim forecast for 2013.[20] In a semiannual report, these economists slashed expected 2013 growth in the seventeen-nation eurozone from 1 to 0.1 percent. These economists also slashed Germany's growth outlook from 1.7 to 0.7 percent. Germany's unemployment rate has remained at record lows throughout the crisis, but the number of newly unemployed has risen for five straight months. In September 2012 Germany's industrial production slid 1.8 percent from August. Further stagnation in Spain and Italy, coupled with suspense about Greece's future in the eurozone, has taken its toll on the eurozone's main economic driver, Germany.

Countries that ran up large debts in the First and Second World Wars ended up with some inflation before the ratio of debt to GDP was brought down to agreeable levels. The best scenario is an episode of moderate inflation stretched out over a decade or more. Moderate inflation helps with the economic growth and reduces the real value of the debt. France after the First World War and the u.s. after the Second World War are examples of debt-burden reduction with the help of modest inflation over a number of years. Germany's strong distaste for inflation makes it difficult for the eurozone to consider a solution that poses an inflation risk.

In earlier chapters we saw that a long-term trend of falling interest rates led investors to hold riskier assets rather than stand a guaranteed loss in investment income. Low interest rates are a symptom of high levels of savings. When more savings are available than are needed to finance private initiatives, it helps if governments can borrow redundant savings to finance public initiatives. After all, if the income earned in producing goods is not all spent, some goods will go unsold. As long as governments borrow and spend redundant savings, these savings do not act as a drag on economic growth. When governments impose austerity measures and absorb fewer savings, it is that much harder for all savings to find eligible borrowers and end up in the spending stream. Austerity measures wield the same recessionary impact on the macroeconomy as higher savings. Excess savings at very low interest rates lead to anemic growth, putting heavier stress on public finances.

# TWELVE
# The Long Road Back

## The Inexactness of Economics

Not all the blame for the colossal financial debacle of 2008 went to wild greed, creative financing, Wall Street sleight of hand, and exuberant financial engineering. A long phase of prosperity had lulled disinterested and dispassionate scholars in economics and finance into focusing on long-run behavior. They became more concerned that the pressure of short-term problems might push governments into enacting policies that were counterproductive long-term. Fragilities in the economic system received scant attention. The roster of the u.s. Congress included members holding phds in economics who seemed more than content with policies that gave Wall Street free rein. Governments hardly go blameless. Protecting people from antisocial economic strength can be just as important as protecting people from antisocial physical strength. It is time now, however, to put these things behind us and sort out what the future holds after this colossal economic and financial debacle. Here we are not concerned with what sparked the crisis, but what accounts for a sluggish and tortuous recovery.

It might help to remember that economics is an inexact science with the same stern precision one expects in weather forecasting. Therefore within a considerable range people are permitted to believe what they please. Our knowledge of a future is a fragile fringe on the vast frontier of ignorance. The best we can do is stand on the edge of that frontier and hold out a light a little further ahead, maybe catching a glimpse of the nearest low-hanging fruit, and throw a roving spotlight a little further out on an infinitely kaleidoscopic and complex future.

Thrown in with this tendency to miss the macroeconomic perspective is general human fallibility. When governments fail to achieve economic goals and expectations, they rarely accept the real reasons for their failure. Instead they rationalize. While rationalization tranquilizes voters and softens feelings of failure, it does involve a certain amount of self-deception and distortion of reality. For these reasons the chances of misdiagnosis run high.

An optimist would like to think that an economic calamity of this magnitude embodies an economic catharsis of some variety. After this catharsis the economic system bounces back healthier. Just as floods push over dead tree trunks to make room for new growth, perhaps these economic crashes deliver the finishing blow to aging and unproductive features of the economic landscape. Others might see laissez-faire global capitalism cracking like a hampering shell under the obstinate growth of a new economic order.

When economies undergo unusually severe and prolonged slumps, it raises the possibility that more than one thing is wrong, that the slump is due to more than one ailment. This proposition may not always be true, but it is a reasonable starting assumption unless one glaring dysfunction overshadows everything else.

## Blaming Commodity Prices

First let's take into account commodity prices. In the post-Second World War era capitalism saw two decades of subdued growth. One decade was the 1970s, when capitalism mirrored more closely a welfare-state version. The other was the 2000s after a purer form of capitalism had surfaced, one born of a global wave of deregulation, privatization, and public-sector austerity. In each case economies stalled out amid booming commodity prices. Oil prices grew multiple-fold in both episodes. Prices boomed in food, energy, and raw materials. Major shortages of these magnitudes signal that private markets are not exhibiting the foresight needed to maintain economic stability. At this point we can make the observation that the slump of the 1970s under the welfare state version of capitalism was slightly shallower. In the 1960s the reigning economic orthodoxy adopted a catchphrase, "fine tuning." It was the voice of a new age that saw an observable improvement in the stability of economies. Credit for greater economic stability went to new knowledge about how economies functioned. Economies had grown more stable it was hoped because governments had mastered the intelligent and timely application of economic stabilization tools, including tax policy, countercyclical government expenditures, and money supply growth. It was believed that success in stabilizing economies had progressed so far that governments could focus on fine-tuning.

The observation that economies had grown more stable was right, but the diagnosis was almost certainly wrong. Most likely economies simply owed added stability to growth in the sheer size of government relative to the private sector. The government sector is non-cyclical. What cycles it experiences are second-hand and tame reflections of private-sector fluctuations. If the private sector is the economic winds in the sails of the economy, the government sector is the economic ballast. The larger government dampened economic oscillations. It stabilized the larger economy.

The link between the size of government and stability is a secondary point. The main point to consider now is that the booming commodity prices of the 1970s coincided with a ten-year hiatus in economic growth. During the ten-year interim, higher commodity prices gave suppliers an incentive to enlarge supplies and find substitutes. Eventually commodity prices came down in the face of swelling supply. As commodity prices subsided, economic growth accelerated.

If we accept the 1970s and early '80s as a useful parallel, then we expect economic growth to remain sluggish until commodity prices crash. With China ingesting large quantities of commodities, the commodity boom could last a few more years but not forever, probably not even past the current decade. While the dates and longevity are inexact, a commodity boom has a beginning and an end. Prosperity returns at the end.

## Blaming High Savings

It is quite unlikely, however, that the commodity boom encompasses the sum total of everything that is wrong. Recall that Japan entered a phase of sluggish growth after stock and property market bubbles burst. That sluggish growth persisted through the 1990s when commodities sold for relatively low prices. Japan's lethargic growth persisted through low and high commodity prices.

Given the chance that Japan's disease has infected the u.s. and the European Union, the current difficulties are far graver. Recall that Japan saw its stock market crumble, followed by a property market that hit the skids. Japan was the first country to see a central bank benchmark interest rate touch zero. These low interest rates reflect the savings glut that central bankers cited in the years leading up to the global financial crisis. The savings glut has to do with fundamental characteristics of the East Asian economies, including Japan and China. These countries register high savings rates and want to produce more goods than they consume.

Not only is China the second largest economy in the world, but it boasts the highest savings rates of the large economies. Its savings rate keeps growing long after Japan's central bank has slashed its benchmark interest rate to zero. According to Kuijs (2006) China's savings as percentage of GDP stands right at 41.7 percent, above Japan's 25.5 percent and South Korea's 31 percent.[1] China's high savings rate has inspired a body of scholarly research. Carroll, Overland, and Weil (2000) argue that fast-growing East Asian societies save larger shares of income out of saving habits developed in earlier times when income levels sat much lower.[2] Consumption lags behind income growth. Jin, Li, and Wu (2010) argue that in China saving is part of keeping up with the Joneses, that conspicuous saving plays the role of conspicuous consumption in other societies.[3] A similar argument advanced by Wei and Zhang (2009) claims that Chinese parents with sons accumulate savings as a strategy for making their sons more attractive in marriage. Wei and Zhang observe that China's household savings as a share of disposable income nearly doubled from 16 percent in 1990 to 30 percent in 2007.[4] It is often thought that China owes its high savings rate to inadequate pensions and healthcare provisions. According to Wei and Zhang China's household savings rate continue to climb after 2003 despite improvements in pensions and healthcare.

China's consumption expenditures as a percentage of GDP have steadily fallen since 1990. China's consumption expenditure grows at a dizzy pace, but not as dizzy as its GDP growth. When China's GDP growth registers 10 percent its growth in consumption expenditures comes in between 8 and 9 percent. That trend persists at least through 2011.[5] If China follows the pattern of Japan, then its growth in consumption expenditures will eventually accelerate, but it is hard to say when.

For the U.S. to buy more than it produces there must be a country that produces more than it buys. This is where China and its high savings rates enter the picture. If China produces more goods than it wants to buy, then it produces more income than it wants to spend. This extra income is savings above what China needs to finance its own internal investment. The mischief caused by high savings involves a rather complex bit of reasoning but it goes as follows. For the sake of argument let's say there are only two countries, the U.S. and China. Whenever a good is produced, the individual producer has the right to consume the good or sell the good and buy other goods of equal value. The option to consume the good or buy other goods of equal value is the income side of the equation. Therefore when a good is produced, precisely enough income is produced to buy the good or other goods of equal value. In the aggregate the output an economy produces and the income it generates are equal, two separate dimensions of the same phenomenon. This means a country only produces enough income to buy all the goods it produces, and no more. For a country such as the U.S. to buy more goods than it produces, it must borrow. Since the U.S. imports more than it exports, it buys more that it produces. Therefore it borrows from the rest of the world or, in our simplified example, China. Since China exports more than it imports, it produces more goods than it wants to buy. If China generates more income than it wants to spend domestically, it can extend loans to the U.S.

Since China has excess goods and savings, China can put its excess savings to work selling excess goods to the U.S., and providing the financing that enables the U.S. to buy more goods than it produces. One way China provides financing to the U.S. is to purchase U.S. Treasury debt. The U.S. can import more than it exports, and China export more than it imports, as long as the U.S. can absorb the excess goods and savings from China.

In the years leading up to the financial crisis, absorbing the excess savings becomes tricky. The innovative mortgage financing in the u.s. betrays a system overburdened with the need to put excess savings to work. Savings of that order can only find enough borrowers if risk levels go up. Economic growth remains healthy as long as high savings are absorbed by high rates of borrowing from eager and creditworthy borrowers. The key ingredient here is creditworthy borrowers. When credit ratings are downgraded for even time-honored governments such as that of the u.s., it sends a clear signal that the supply of creditworthy borrowers is a weak link. There must be a place to park the savings. Without qualified borrowers, a glut in savings acts as strong headwind against economic growth.

Government deficits help absorb excess savings. High levels of government indebtedness in Japan, the u.s., and the eurozone are another symptom of excess savings. Governments find they must run these deficits to stabilize economies sinking into recession. The global financial crisis jammed up the channels for investing these excess savings from countries such as China. The solution lies in China and perhaps other developing countries grasping that export-led growth has run its course, that it is a strategy they can no longer count on.

Part of the long-term solution lies in high-savings countries, particularly China, developing social security programs and other programs that lessen the need for high savings rates. With inadequate pensions systems and health insurance, low interest rates may even lead to higher rather than lower savings rates. Reforms could soften the need to save for educating children or purchasing a house. House purchases in China are still largely financed out of personal savings. Better access to consumer loans and insurance can give boosts to consumer spending. Bringing down savings may involve redistributing income since high-income earners exhibit higher savings rates. Most likely these countries will voluntarily develop along these lines since they can no longer count on the international financial and trading system to siphon off excess savings and goods.

## Finger of Judgment Pointed at Central Banks

So we have now pinned down two factors holding the global economy back from robust recovery. These two ailments alone render unlikely a speedy rebound from the current economic difficulties. A third ailment has to do with the sovereign debt crisis in the eurozone. Here there is much more room debate.

The truth is countries rarely pay off debts by raising taxes and cutting government spending. The u.s. emerged from the Second World War shouldering debt loads comparable to the most debt-ridden countries in the eurozone. The u.s. recovered from deep indebtedness after a 30-year stretch of economic growth coupled with mild inflation. France took a similar path after the First World War. A long phase of economic growth and moderate inflation is what it takes to get out of debt without major economic dislocation. Safeguarding the value and credibility of the euro is a noble goal. This goal may eventually pay off, but only after a long grinding struggle unless the global economy rebounds quickly and on an order that restores robust growth to the eurozone.

Certainly the European Central Bank has taken steps when necessary to keep the eurozone in tack. In central banking, however, reputation alone bears real consequences. The European Central Bank's hawkish stance against inflation has kept some suspense in the mind of investors. The Bank could never quite remove investor fear that it might hold the monetary reins too tight. In its favor the bank has to keep inflationary expectations from forming, which can also pose no small problems. In the final analysis, inflation is the friend of debtors, and few central banks stand unlikelier to allow an outbreak of inflation than the European Central Bank. Again, we are talking about perceptions as much as reality. If robust economic growth can be restored outside the eurozone, then the eurozone can resolve its debt problem much faster. The hitch is that policy-makers worldwide do not have many arrows left in their policy quivers for spurring economic growth. It is easier now to see why the global economic crisis settled in the eurozone.

The commodity price boom, savings glut, and central bank with a perceived bias toward deflation are factors that act against a spirited rebound. Keep in mind that even a slow and steady rebound is by no means guaranteed. After the subprime crisis of 2008 other countries implemented policies to shield domestic economies from a menacing U.S. recession. Because of these policies, house prices in some countries, such as Australia, Canada, and Sweden, stood higher in 2011 than peak levels before the 2008 crisis. For these countries house prices took a short breather during the crisis and then smartly headed up again. These countries may have spawned new bubbles. If these bubbles burst the global economy may really fall to pieces, landing in a deeper slump. That is the scenario that threatens a major global depression. Countries busying themselves taming bubbles of their own can do little to boost global growth.

In summary, the global economy currently suffers from major structural imbalances, shortages of commodities and excess savings. These imbalances suggest that the U.S. and Europe are caught up in a type of economic contraction that will last a decade or longer. This deep contraction is a rather unwelcome reminder that some issues plaguing capitalism from its earliest beginnings have not gone away. Central banks and monetary policy help by purchasing longer-term and riskier assets, which this debacle has taught them to do. These policies bring down long-term interest rates, which encourage large capital projects and give budget-stressed governments a break. The stimulus the economy receives from these monetary policies, however, must be weighed against the proliferation of austere fiscal policies among governments.

## Giving Marx and Keynes the Last Word

To better assimilate this economic turn of events, it might help to integrate with our reflections and observations the thoughts of capitalism's bitterest critics in past years. Societies can always count on their enemies to find and spotlight faults. Taking advantage of enemies involves making intelligent use of the knowledge they enjoy uncovering and highlighting. In 1848 Karl Marx and Friedrich Engels published the *Manifesto of the Communist Party*. To appreciate the following quote from the *Manifesto*, keep in mind that the "bourgeoisie" refers to the class of capitalists, the owners of the means of production. In words that ring true today, this famous pamphlet on capitalism says:

> The bourgeoisie . . . has been the first to show what man's activity can bring about. It has accomplished wonders far surpassing Egyptian pyramids, Roman aqueducts, and Gothic cathedrals; It has conducted expeditions that put in the shade all former migrations of nations and crusades . . . The bourgeoisie cannot exist without constantly revolutionizing the instruments of production . . . [It] has created more massive and more colossal productive forces than have all preceding generations together . . . bourgeois society . . . has conjured up such gigantic means of production and exchange . . .

From these words the *Manifesto of the Communist Party* might be taken as a hymn sung in praise of capitalism. The vantage point of the new millennium offers even greater evidence of "wonders" attributable to capitalism. What price could be too high to pay for newer "wonders" witnessed after Marx and Engels penned these words? A few other choice morsels lifted from this famous pamphlet may offend our capitalist ears. The words, however, sound a familiar tone amid current discontent with global capitalism:

> Society as a whole is more and more splitting up into two great hostile camps, into two great classes directly facing each other . . . It has converted the physician, the lawyer, the priest, the poet, the man of science, into its paid wage labourers . . . In place of the old local and national seclusion and self-sufficiency we have intercourse in every direction, universal interdependence of nations . . . It compels all nations on pain of extinction to adopt the bourgeois [capitalist] mode of production . . . Independent, or but loosely connected provinces, with separate interests, laws, governments, and systems of taxation, became lumped together into one nation, with one government, one code of laws, one national class interest, one frontier, and one customs tariff. The lower strata of the middleclass . . . sinks gradually into the proletariat . . . partly

because their specialized skill is rendered worthless by new methods of production.[6]

These words were written 170 years ago. If we accept them as an accurate evaluation of the costs and benefits of capitalism, who would not say that the benefits far outweigh the costs? The longer the perspective the more obvious it is that the benefits more than justify the costs. Right now the proponents of global capitalism are suffering from sticker shock at the price attached to the price that capitalism collects for the benefits it bestows. Thinking along the lines of Marx and Engels may acquire a wider following as global capitalism struggles against depression. As individuals grow more affluent in every other aspect of their lives, they may look for an economic system that spares them the whipsawing quakes and somersaults of the capitalist system, as in the past they opted for more leisure and less work.

For study global economic slump that began in 2007–8 is often compared with the previous great slump—the Great Depression of the 1930s. John Maynard Keynes, the most influential and probably wisest economist of the twentieth century, wrote a futuristic essay, "Economic Possibilities of Our Grandchildren." He wrote it in 1930, the beginning of the Great Depression. It sounded a cheerful but thought-stirring note that bears close scrutiny today:

> We are suffering, not from the rheumatics of old age, but from the growing-pains of over-rapid changes, from the painfulness of readjustment between one economic period and another. The increase in technical efficiency has been taking place faster than we can deal with the absorption of labor . . . We are being afflicted with a new disease of which some readers may not yet have heard the name, but of which they will hear a great deal in the years to come—namely, technological unemployment . . . But this is only a temporary phase of maladjustment. All this means in the long run that mankind is solving its economic problem . . . The strenuous purposeful money-makers may carry all of us along with them into the lap of economic abundance . . . we shall endeavor to spread

the bread thin on the butter—to make what work there is still to be done to be as widely shared as possible ... When the accumulation of wealth is no longer of high social importance, there will be great changes in the code of morals. We shall be able to rid ourselves of many of the pseudo-moral principles which have hag-ridden us for two hundred years, by which we have exalted some of the most distasteful of human qualities into the position of the highest virtues. We shall be able to afford to dare to assess the money-motive at its true value ... All kinds of social customs and economic practices, affecting the distribution of wealth and of economic rewards and penalties, which we now maintain at all costs, however distasteful and unjust they may be in themselves, because they are tremendously useful in promoting the accumulation of capital, we shall then be free, at last, to discard.[7]

Keynes was right in saying that the pessimism of the 1930s ignored the new hopes that were also on the horizon. The same is true in 2013.

# REFERENCES

## ONE Overview

1  Will Durant, *The Story of Philosophy* (Garden City, NY, 1927), p. 46.
2  Francis Bacon, *The New Atlantis* (Chicago, 1952), p. 207.
3  Francis Bacon, *Essays* (New York, 1942), p. 102.
4  Milton Friedman, "The Monetary Theory and Policy of Henry Simons," in *The Optimum Quantity of Money and Other Essays*, (Chicago, 1969), pp. 81–93.

## TWO Twilight of the Japanese Miracle

1  Arthur Link, ed., *The Papers of Woodrow Wilson*, vol. VI (Princeton, NJ, 1969), p. 168.
2  Masahiko Takeda and Philip Turner, "The Liberalization of Japan's Financial Markets: Some Major Themes," Bank for International Settlements BIS Economic Papers, no. 34 (1992).
3  Ibid.
4  W. W. Rostow, *The World Economy: History and Prospect* (Austin, TX, 1978), p. 418.
5  Japan/U.S. Foreign Exchange Rate, www.economagic.com, accessed 6 November 2012.
6  Henry George, *Progress and Poverty: An Inquiry into the Cause of Industrial Depressions and of Increase of Want with Increase of Wealth, The Remedy* (New York, 1935) p. 268.
7  Christopher Wood, "Enduring Myth," *Economist*, CCCXVII/7684 (8 December 1990), pp. 9–15.
8  "Gently May do It," *Economist*, CCCXVII/7679 (3 November 1990), pp. 19–21.
9  Kenichi Ohmae, "Business Forum: Tokyo's Soaring Property Prices: If They Fall, So Will Our Stock Markets," *New York Times* (11 October 1987).

10  "Gently May do It," *Economist.*
11  Robert L. Cutts, "Power from the Ground Up: Japan's Land Bubble," *Harvard Business Review*, LXVIII/3(1990), pp. 164–72.
12  Ibid.
13  Elisabeth Bumiller, "The Japanese Art of Buying," *Washington Post* (17 December 1989), p. A3.
14  Ibid.
15  "Demolition Time in Japan's Property Market," *Economist*, CCCXVII/7684 (8 December 1990), pp. 83–4.
16  "Gently May do It," *Economist.*
17  "The Cracks Spread and Widen; The Euro Zone's Debt Crisis," *Economist*, CCCXCV/8680 (1 May 2010), p. 63.
18  G. Eisenstodt, "Wooosh!" *Forbes*, CXLVIII/14 (1991), pp. 113–14.
19  Statistics Bureau, Director-General for Policy Planning of Japan, Tokyo, www.stat.go.jp, accessed 7 November 2012.
20  Eisenstodt, "Wooosh!"
21  IMF, World Economic Outlook Database (October 2012), www.imf.org.
22  "Leaders: Back from the Dead; Japanese Banks," *Economist*, CCCXCVIII/8722 (26 February 2011), p. 13.
23  IMF, World Economic Outlook Database (October 2012), www.imf.org.
24  Ibid.

### THREE  Financial Revolution

1  Sir Nicholas Goodison, "How London Can Remain on Top," FT.*com, Financial Times* (26 October 2006), p. 1.
2  Joe Nocera, "Poking Holes in a Theory on Markets," *New York Times* (5 June 2009), p. 1.
3  Pankaj Jain, "Financial Market Design and the Equity Premium: Electronic Versus Floor Trading," *Journal of Finance*, LX/6 (2005), pp. 2,955–85.
4  "Five Years Since the Big Bang," *Economist* , CCCXXI/7730 (26 October 1991), pp. 23–5.
5  Ibid.
6  Peter Truell and Matthew Winkler, "UK Set Today For 'Big Bang' Amid Questions: Rocky Start Seen as London Moves Toward Uniting Local, Foreign Markets," *Wall Street Journal* (27 October 1986), p. 1.
7  James Sterngold, "The Big Bang that Never Was," *New York Times* (16 May 1993), p. 1.
8  "Bang, Pop, or Sputter?" *Economist*, CCCXLVII/8067 (9 May 1998), special section, pp. 29–31.

9   "MS in Financial Engineering," at http://ieor.columbia.edu, accessed 5 November 2012.

10  Bank of International Settlements, Semiannual OTC Statistics at end-December 2011 (September 2012), www.bis.org.

11  International Swaps and Derivatives Association, "ISDA Market Survey (Annual Only, PDF), 1987–present," www.isda.org/statistics, accessed 9 November 2012.

12  Nelson Schwartz and Julie Creswell, "Who Created this Monster?" *New York Times* (23 March 2008), p. 1.

13  Dawn Kopecki, and Shannon D. Harrington, "Banning 'Naked' Default Swaps May Raise Corporate Funding Cost," *Bloomberg News* (24 July 2009).

14  James B. Ang, "Financial Development, Liberalization and Technological Deepening," *European Economic Review*, LV/5 (2011), pp. 668–701.

15  Michael Shroeder, "CFTC Chairwoman Won"t Halt Study of OTC Derivatives Rules," *Wall Street Journal* (11 June 1998), p. C1.

16  David Barboza, "Chief Regulator of Futures to Step Down," *New York Times* (20 January 1999), p. 1.

17  Ibid.

18  Michael Shroeder, "CFTC Chairman Seeks to Deregulate Trading," *Wall Street Journal* (29 October 1999), p. 1.

19  Stephen Labaton, "Agency's '04 Rule Let Banks Pile Up New Debt," *New York Times* (3 October 2008), p. 1.

20  Ibid.

21  Stephen Labaton, "S.E.C. Concedes Oversight Flaws Fueled Collapse," *New York Times* (26 September 2008), p. 1.

## FOUR  Euphoria in the Housing Market

1   "The Big Mac Index," www.economist.com, accessed 8 November 2012.

2   Karen Talley, "S&P Will Launch Indexes to Track Housing Prices," *Wall Street Journal* (23 March 2006), p. D2.

3   M. Iacoviello and R. Minett, "Financial Liberalization and the Sensitivity of House Prices to Monetary Policy: Theory and Evidence," *Manchester School*, LXXI/1 (2003), pp. 20–34.

4   D. B. Diamond and M. J. Lea, "Chapter 5: United Kingdom," *Journal of Housing Research*," III/1(1994), pp. 115–43.

5   P. Catte, N. Girouard, R. Price, and C. Andre, "Housing Markets, Wealth, and the Business Cycle," Working Paper 394, Organization for Economic Cooperation and Development (Paris, 2004).

6   Organization for Economic Cooperation and Development, *OECD*

*Economic Surveys: 2005* (June 2005), p. 53.

7 "Leaders: Lifting the Roof: Europe's Housing Market," *Economist* 373/8405 (11 December 2004), pp. 12–14.

8 OECD, OECD *Economic Surveys: 2005.*

9 Greg Ip, "Greenspan Again Plays Down Fear Of Housing Bubble," *Wall Street Journal* (20 October 2004), p. A2.

10 Bank for International Settlements, "Property Price Statistics" (October 2012), www.bis.org.

11 Jon E. Hilsenrath and Patrick Barta, "Treasure Hunt: Amid Low Rates, Home Prices Rise Across the Global Village; Armed With a 'Saving Glut,' Investors Chase Returns; Londoners Buy in Bulgaria; Bangkok Market Is Hot—Again," *Wall Street Journal* (16 June 2005), p. A1.

12 Ibid.

13 Troy McMullen, "The Home Front: Private Properties," *Wall Street Journal* (4 March 2005), p. W10.

14 Allison Bisbey Colter, "In Housing's Hottest Markets, Builders Tell Speculators to Cool It," *Wall Street Journal* (22 September 2005), p. B9A.

15 Ruth Simon, "Teaser Rates on Mortgages Approach 0%; As Lending Frenzy Slow, Banks Add Twists to Lure Homeowners; Many of the Deals Have Pitfalls", *Wall Street Journal* (Eastern edition), 15 February 2005, p. D1.

16 Michael Shroeder, "Mortgage Lenders Dismiss Concerns Over Risky Loans," *Wall Street Journal* (30 March 2006), p. D2.

17 Ibid.

18 Ruth Simon, "Mortgage Lenders Loosen Standards," *Wall Street Journal* (26 July 2005), p. D1.

19 Ruth Simon, "New Type of Mortgage Surges in Popularity; Fixed-Rate Interest-Only Loans Offer Lower Initial Payments but Delay Debt Reduction," *Wall Street Journal* (19 April 2006), p. D1.

20 Janet Morrissey, "Housing Bubble Is Seen by Lenders," *Wall Street Journal* (5 April 2006), p. B4.

21 Rich Motoko, "Middleman Now Rich Man in Real Estate Boom," *New York Times* (31 May 2005), p. 1.

22 Ibid.

23 "The Big Bad Bubble," *Economist*, CCCLXXI/8374 (8 May 2004), pp. 53–4.

24 "In Come the Waves," *Economist*, CCCLXXV/8431 (18 June 2005), pp. 66–8.

25 Ibid.

26 Ibid.

27 Bank for International Settlements, "Property Price Statistics"

(October 2012), www.bis.org.

28  *Wall Street Journal*, (Eastern Edition) "Hot Topic: The Subprime Market's Rough Road" (17 February 2007), p. A7.

29  Ruth Simon, "Lenders Get Tougher; Qualifying for a Mortgage Becomes Harder, Even for Applicants with Good Credit, as Banks Probe Deeper into Personal Finances, *Wall Street Journal*, Eastern edition (15 May 2007), p. D1.

30  Robbie Whelan, "Second-Mortgage Misery; Nearly 40% Who Borrowed Against Homes are Under Water, *Wall Street Journal* (online) (7 June 2011).

## FIVE  Perils of Taming Inflation

1  Kenneth Rogoff, "Globalization and Global Disinflation," paper prepared for the Federal Reserve Bank of Kansas City Conference, Jackson Hole, WY, www.imf.org (29 August 2003).

2  Greg Ip, "Greenspan Says U.S. Deflation Threat is Small—Potential Harm is Serious So Central Bank Might Act to Minimize the Jeopardy," *Wall Street Journal* (22 May 2003), p. A2.

3  Brian S. Wesbury, "Mr. Greenspan's Cappuccino," *Wall Street Journal* (31 May 2005), p. A2.

4  Greg Ip and Thomas Sims, "U.S. and Europe Signal That Rates May be Cut Soon—Greenspan and Duisenberg Hope to Boost Economies, Avert Threat of Deflation," *Wall Street Journal* (4 June 2003), p. A1.

5  Ibid.

6  Jeff D. Opdyke, "Are You Ready for Deflation?" *Wall Street Journal* (5 June 2003), p. D1.

7  Bank for International Settlements, "Property Price Statistics" (October 2012), www.bis.org.

8  *Wall Street Journal* (2 April 2004), p. A4.

9  David Wessel, "Capital: The Fed Starts to Show Concern at Signs of Bubble in Housing," *Wall Street Journal* (19 May 2005), p. A1.

10  Ibid.

11  C. A. Goodhart, "Price Stability and Financial Fragility," in *The Central Bank and the Financial System*, ed. C. A. Goodhart (Cambridge, MA, 1995).

12  International Monetary Fund, "Chapter 2: When Bubbles Burst," *World Economic Outlook* (April 2000), pp. 61–94.

13  G. Thomas Sims, "Housing Prices in Euro Zone Worry the ECB," *Wall Street Journal* (4 February 2005), p. A7.

14  Ben S. Bernanke, Vincent R. Reinhart, and Brian P. Sack, "Monetary Policy Alternatives at the Zero Bound: An Empirical Assessment," *Brookings Papers on Economic Activity*, XXXV/2 (2004) pp. 1–100.

15  Alan Greenspan, Federal Reserve System's Semiannual Monetary
    Report to Congress, Testimony Presented Before the Committee on
    Banking, Housing, and Urban Affairs, U.S. Senate, 16 February 2005,
    www.federalreserve.gov.
16  Wesbury, "Mr. Greenspan's Cappuccino."
17  Ruth Simon, "New Type of Mortgage Surges in Popularity,"
    *Wall Street Journal* (19 April 2006), p. D1.
18  Michael Hudson, "Grading Bonds on Inverted Curve,"
    *Wall Street Journal* (8 January 2007), p. C1.
19  Carrick Mollenkamp, Alistair MacDonald, and Joellen Perry,
    "A UK Lender is Latest to Join Mortgage Crisis," *Wall Street Journal*
    (15 September 2007), p. B1.

## SIX  Global Banking and Financial Crisis

1  Jim Stewart, "Shadow Regulation and the Shadow Banking System,"
   *Tax Justice Focus*, IV/2 (2008), pp. 1–3.
2  *Wall Street Journal* (10 August 2007), p. A1.
3  Carrick Mollenkamp, Alistair MacDonald, and Joellen Perry,
   "A UK Lender is Latest to Join Mortgage Crisis," *Wall Street Journal*
   (15 September 2007), p. B1.
4  Chris Hughes, "Confidence in Northern Rock Collapses," *FT.com*,
   *Financial Times* (14 September 2007).
5  Nicholas Dunbar, "Dr Frankenstein of Dusseldorf," August 2007,
   www.nickdunbar.net.
6  Nicholas Dunbar, "The Great German Structured Credit
   Experiment," *Risk*, XVII/2 (2004), pp. 16–19.
7  Louise Story and Gretchen Morgenson, "S.E.C. Accuses Goldman of
   Fraud in Housing Deal," *New York Times* (17 April 2010), p. 1.
8  House of Commons, Treasury Committee, "Banking Crisis: Dealing
   with the Failure of UK Banks," HC416 (London, May 2009).
9  Drew DeSilver, "$7 Billion Give Shaky WaMu Firmer Footing for
   Now," *Seattle Times* (9 April 2008).
10 Damian Paletta and David Enrich, "Crisis Deepens as Big Bank Fails,
   IndyMac Seized in Largest Bust in Two Decades," *Wall Street Journal*
   (12 July 2008), p. A1.
11 Helen Power, "Peter Cummings Stayed Loyal and Brave at the Wrong
   Time," *Times* (13 December 2008).

## SEVEN  The Rebirth of Keynesian Economics

1  Alan Greenspan, Chairman of the Board of Governors of the Federal
   Reserve System, Remarks before the Council on Foreign Relations,

Washington DC (19 November 2002).

2 Alan Greenspan, Chairman of the Board of Governors of the Federal Reserve System, "Economic Flexibility," Remarks to the National Association of Business Economics Annual Meeting, Chicago, IL (via satellite, 27 September 2007).

3 Abba Lerner, *The Economics of Control* (New York, 1944).

4 Alan Blinder, "The Case Against the Case Against Discretionary Fiscal Policy," in *The Macroeconomics of Fiscal Policy*, ed. R. W. Kopcke, Geoffrey M. B. Tootell, and Robert K. Triest (Cambridge, MA, 2006), pp. 25–61.

5 Esteban P. Caldentey and Matias Vernengo, "How Stimulative Has Fiscal Policy Been Around the World?" *Challenge*, LIII/3 (2010), pp. 6–31.

6 Ibid.

7 Carter Doughtery, "Driving Out of Germany, to Pollute Another Day," *New York Times* (7 August 2009).

8 Eswar Prasad and Isaac Sorkin, "Assessing the G-20 Stimulus Plans: A Deeper Look," Brooking Institution, www.brookings.edu (March 2009).

9 Mike Barris and Karen Richardson, "The Buzz: Buffett Warns Insurance Business May Get Tougher; Berkshire Reports Drop of 18% in Quarterly Net; A Swipe at Lenders," *Wall Street Journal* (1 March 2008), p. B3.

## EIGHT **China and India Knock at the Door**

1 Murray Rothbard, "Concepts of the Role of the Intellectual in Social Change Toward Laissez Faire," *Journal of Libertarian Studies*, IX/2 (1990), pp. 43–67.

2 Will Durant, *The Lessons of History* (New York, 1968), p. 61.

3 Ibid., p. 62.

4 This data is taken from the Federal Reserve of St Louis data set in "Trade Weighted U.S. Dollar Index: Major Currencies: Index March 1973 =100," www.economagic.com, accessed 8 November 2011.

5 James Areedy, Neil King, and Mary Kissel, "Behind Yuan Move, Open Debate and Closed Doors," *Wall Street Journal* (25 July 2005), p. A1.

6 Loretta Chao and Jason Leow, "The Home Front: Buying into China's Land Rush," *Wall Street Journal* (18 January 2008), p. W1.

7 Jonathan Cheng, "Buyers' or Sellers' Market? In China Slump Stokes Activity," *Wall Street Journal* (17 December 2008), p. C9.

8 Andrew Batson, "China Housing Market Shows Signs of Life," *Wall Street Journal* (2 April 2009), p. A8.

9  *Wall Street Journal* (14 August 2009), p. A13.
10 Andrew Peaple, "China Takes Hard Road on Housing,"
   *Wall Street Journal* (20 November 2009), p. C10.
11 Esther Fung and Andrew Batson, "China Urban Property Prices
   Rise," *Wall Street Journal* online (14 April 2010).
12 Aaron Back and Joy Shaw, "China Tightens Property Regulations,"
   *Wall Street Journal* (20 April 2010).
13 Aaron Back and Esther Fung, "China Scraps Property Data, Clouding
   view—Accuracy of the Figures was Questioned," *Wall Street Journal*
   (17 February 2011), p. A8.
14 Ajay Shah and Ila Paatnaik, "India's Financial Globalization,"
   IMF Working Paper WP/11/7, Washington, DC (2011).
15 IMF, "World Economic Outlook Database" (October 2012),
   www.imf.org.
16 Devita Saraf and Prathima Manohar, "India's Real Estate Boom is on
   Shaky Ground," *Wall Street Journal* online (7 March 2010).
17 Sara Seddon Kilbinger, "India Faces Housing Slowdown,"
   *Wall Street Journal* (20 February 2008), p. B7.
18 Jackie Range, "Real-Estate Finance: Indian Builders Lower Sights—
   'Affordable,' Not Luxury, Is New Watchword in Housing,"
   *Wall Street Journal* (18 March 2009), p. C11.
19 Saraf and Manohar, "India's Real Estate Boom is on Shaky Ground."

## NINE  Commodity Prices Take Flight

1 World Bank, *Global Economic Prospects—Commodities at the
   Crossroads* (Washington, DC, 2008).
2 John Spence, "A Real Growth Play: Agricultural ETF's,"
   *Wall Street Journal* (15 April 2008), p. C13.
3 IMF, "World Economic Outlook Database" (October 2012),
   www. imf.org.
4 World Bank, *Global Economic Prospects.*
5 See "Producer Price Index: Finished Goods: Capital Equipment:
   Index 1982–84," "CPI-U: U.S. City Average: All Items : 1982–84," "CPI-U:
   U.S. City Average: Durables; 1982–84," www.economagic.com, all
   accessed 23 November 2012.
6 John E. Cairnes, *Essays on Political Economy: Theoretical and Applied*
   [1873] (New York, 1965).
7 Frank D. Graham, *Exchange, Prices, and Production in
   Hyperinflation: Germany, 1920–1923* (Princeton, NJ, 1930).
8 Michael D. Bordo, "The Effects of Monetary Change on Relative
   Commodity Prices and the Role of Long-Term Contracts," *Journal of
   Political Economy*, LXXXVIII/6 (1980), pp. 1,088–109.

9  Frank Browne and David Cronin, "Commodity Prices, Money and Inflation," Working Paper no. 738, European Central Bank (March 2007).

10 Jeffrey Frankel, "The Effect of Monetary Policy on Real Commodity Prices," in *Asset Prices and Monetary Policy*, ed. John Campbell, National Bureau of Economic Research (Chicago, IL, 2008).

11 W. W. Rostow, *The World Economy: History and Prospect* (Austin, TX, 1978).

12 Craig Sugden, "Responding to High Commodity Prices," *Asian Pacific Economic Literature,* XXIII/1(2009), pp. 79–105.

13 Phil Izzo, "U.S. News: Bubble Isn't Big Factor in Inflation," *Wall Street Journal* (9 May 2008), p. A2.

14 Donald Mitchell, "A Note on Rising Food Prices," Policy Research Working Paper 4682, The World Bank Development Prospects Group (July 2008).

15 Russell Gold, Neil King Jr, and Ann Davis, "Oil's Rise to 100: Confluence of Events Drove Crude's Ride from $10.72," *Wall Street Journal* (3 January 2008), p. A6.

16 Gregory Meyer, "Crude Stocks Above $100 on Speculators' Activity," *Wall Street Journal* (21 February 2008), p. C4.

17 Ben Bernanke, "Semiannual Monetary Policy Report to the Congress," testimony given before the Committee on Banking, Housing, and Urban Affairs, 15 July 2008, www.federalreserve.gov.

18 International Monetary Fund, "Chapter 3: Is Inflation Back? Commodity Prices and Inflation," *World Economic Outlook* (October 2008).

19 M. W. Rosegrant, "Biofuels and Grain Prices: Impacts and Policy Responses," testimony for the U.S. Senate Committee on Homeland Security and Governmental Affairs, Washington, DC (7 May 2008).

20 Mitchell, "A Note on Rising Food Prices."

21 Ibid.

22 Ian Salisbury, "Investing in Funds: A Monthly Analysis," *Wall Street Journal* (5 May 2008), p. R1.

23 Susan Buchanan, "Sugar Futures Climb on buying by Producers and Speculators," *Wall Street Journal* (3 November 2005), p. C4.

24 Tom Sellen, "Sugar Prices Hit Contract Highs as Speculators Buy," *Wall Street Journal* (16 November 2005), p. C4.

25 Susan Buchanan, "Sugar Futures Fall as Speculators Exit," *Wall Street Journal* (29 March 2008), p. B6.

26 Susan Buchanan, "Commodities Report: Coffee Soars as Speculators Buy Back Their Short Positions," *Wall Street Journal* (9 September 2003), p. C18.

27 Susan Buchanan, "Commodities Report: Coffee Futures Trickled

Down as Speculators Pocket Profits," *Wall Street Journal* (29 January 2004), p. C6.

28 Carolyn Cui, "Speculators Put Jolt into your Cup of Joe; Managed Funds Main Driver of Coffee Prices," *Wall Street Journal* (1 March 2008), p. B1.

29 International Monetary Fund, Table 1a. Indices of Primary Commodity Prices, 2002–2012, at www.imf.org.

30 "Pope Benedict XVI Denounces Commodities Speculation, Demand Global Response," *Huffington Post* (1 July 2011).

31 International Monetary Fund, *Global Financial Stability Report: Durable Financial Stability—Getting There from Here* (Washington, DC, April 2011).

32 Ben Bernanke, "The U.S. Economic Outlook," speech given to International Monetary Conference, Atlanta, Georgia, 7 June 2011, atwww.federalreserve.gov/newsevents.

33 Scott Patterson and Jamila Trindle, "CFTC Raises Bar on Betting," *Wall Street Journal* (19 October 2011), p. C3.

## TEN The Weakening of the Labor Market

1 International Monetary Fund, "World Economic Outlook Database" (October 2012), www.imf.org.

2 Daron Acemoglu and David Autor, "Skills, Tasks and Technologies: Implications for Employment and Earnings," in *Handbook of Labor Economics, Volume IV*, ed. David Card and Oriey Ashenfelter (Amsterdam, 2010), pp. 1,043–171.

3 Maarten Goos, Alan Manning, and Anna Salomons, "The Polarization of the European Labor Market," *American Economic Review Papers and Proceedings*, XCIX/2 (2009), pp. 58–63.

4 Guy Michaels, Natraj Ashwini, and John Van Reenen, "Has ICT Polarized Skill Demand? Evidence from 11 Countries Over 25 Years," National Bureau of Economic Research, Working Paper No. 16,138 (June 2010).

5 U.S. Department of Labor, Bureau of Labor Statistics website database. Data series PRS85006092, http://data.bls.gov, accessed 7 November 2012.

6 Robert Solow, "We'd Better Watch Out", *New York Times Book Review* (12 July 1987), p. 36.

7 Paul David, "The Dynamo and the Computer: A Historical Perspective on the Modern Productivity Paradox," *American Economic Association Papers and Proceedings*, LXXX/2 (1990), pp. 355–61.

8 D. Aaronson and K. Housinger, "The Impact of Technology on Displacement and Reemployment," *Federal Reserve Bank of Chicago*

*Economic Perspectives* (2nd Quarter, 1999), pp. 14–30.

9 Center of the Study of Living Standards, Ottawa, Ontario, Canada, www.csls.ca, accessed 7 November 2012.

10 Ibid.

11 Ibid.

12 L. Friedberg, "The Impact of Technological Change on Older Workers: Evidence from Data on Computer Use," National Bureau of Economic Research, Working Paper no. 8297 (May 2001).

13 Edward Wolff, "Computerization and Rising Unemployment Duration," *Eastern Economic Journal*, XXXI/4 (2005), pp. 507–36.

## ELEVEN **String of Sovereign Debt Jitters**

1 Charles de Secondat, Baron de Montesquieu, *The Spirit of Laws* [1748], trans. Thomas Nugent (Chicago, IL, 1952), p. 183.

2 Carmen Reinhart and Kenneth S. Rogoff, "From Financial Crisis to Debt Crisis," *American Economic Review*, CI/5 (2011), pp. 1,676–706.

3 White House Web Site, Table 7.1: "Federal Debt at the End of the Year: 1940–2016," www.whitehouse.gov, accessed 9 November 2012.

4 Michael Davies and Tim Ng, "The Rise of Sovereign Credit Risk: Implications for Financial Stability," BIS *Quarterly Review* (September 2011), pp. 59–70.

5 Louise Story, Landon Thomas Jr, and Nelson D. Schwartz, "Wall Street Helped Mask Debt Fueling Europe's Crisis," *New York Times* (14 February 2010), p. A1.

6 Ibid.

7 Stephen Fidler and David Enrich, "EU Forges Greek Bond Deal— Private Investors To Take 50% Hair Cut," *Wall Street Journal* (27 October 2011), p. A1.

8 Ibid.

9 Simon Nixon, "Irish Eyes Are Watering Over Banks," *Wall Street Journal* (1 October 2010), p. C14.

10 Dick Roche, "Did Ireland Need a Bailout? One Year Ago This Week, Dublin's Finances were Being Repaired and the Economy was Recovering. What Went Wrong?" *Wall Street Journal* online (23 November 2011).

11 European Central Bank Statistical Data Warehouse, www.ecb.int, accessed 9 November 2012.

12 *Wall Street Journal* (10 October 2011), p. A17.

13 "The Cracks Spread and Widen; the Euro Zone's Debt Crisis," *Economist*, CCCXCV/8680 (1 May 2010), p. 63.

14 Ibid.

15 Robert Fishman, "Portugal's Unnecessary Bailout," *New York Times*,

op-ed (19 April 2011), p. 24.

16  Mike Dolan, "Analysis—Puzzle over Euro's 'Mysterious' Stability," *Reuters*, www.reuters.com (15 November 2011).

17  Susan Pulliam, Kate Kelly, and Carrick Mollenkamp, "Hedge Funds Pound Euro—Traders Pile On, Using Multiple Big Bets Greek Crisis Will Push Currency Lower," *Wall Street Journal* (26 February 2010), p. A1.

18  Jean Eaglesham, Aaron Cucchetti, and Jacob Bunge, "Regulators Enter the MF Fray," *Wall Street Journal* (3 November 2011), p. C1.

19  Brian Blackstone and Charles Forelle, "Stocks Jump on Europe Action," *Wall Street Journal* (7 September 2012), p. A1.

20  Matthew Dalton, Matina Steris, and Brian Blackstone, "EU Slashes Growth Prospects," *Wall Street Journal* (7 November 2012).

## TWELVE **The Long Road Back**

1  Louis Kuijs, "How Will China's Saving-Investment Evolve," World Bank Policy Research Paper, Working Paper no. 3958, http://papers.ssrn.com/sol3 (2006).

2  Christopher D. Carroll, Jody R. Overland, David N. Weil, "Savings and Growth with Habit Formation," *American Economic Review*, XC/3 (2000), pp. 341–55.

3  Ye Jin, Hongbing Li, and Binzhen Wu, "Income Inequality, Consumption, and Social-status Seeking," *Journal of Comparative Economics*, XXXIX/2 (2011), pp. 191–204.

4  Shang-Jin Wei and Xiaobo Zhang, "The Competitive Savings Motive: Evidence from Rising Sex Ratios and Savings Rates in China," *Journal of Political Economy*, CXIX/3 (2011), pp. 511–64.

5  Steven Barnett, Alla Myrvoda, and Malhar Nabar, "Sino-Spending," *Finance and Development* (September 2012), pp. 28–30.

6  Karl Marx and Friedrich Engels, *Manifesto of the Communist Party* [1848] (Chicago, IL, 1952).

7  John M. Keynes, *The Economic Consequence of Peace* (New York, 1920), p. 20.

# BIBLIOGRAPHY

Aaronson, D., and K. Housinger, "The Impact of Technology on Displacement and Reemployment," *Federal Reserve Bank of Chicago Economic Perspectives* (2nd Quarter, 1999), pp. 14–30

Acemoglu, Daron, and David Autor, "Skills, Tasks and Technologies: Implications for Employment and Earnings," in *Handbook of Labor Economics, Volume IV*, ed. David Card and Oriey Ashenfelter (Amsterdam, 2010), pp. 1,043–171

Ang, James B., "Financial Development, Liberalization and Technological Deepening," *European Economic Review*, LV/5 (2011), pp. 668–701

Areedy, James, Neil King, and Mary Kissel, "Behind Yuan Move, Open Debate and Closed Doors," *Wall Street Journal* (25 July 2005), p. A1

Back, Aaron, and Esther Fung, "China Scraps Property Data, Clouding view—Accuracy of the Figures was Questioned," *Wall Street Journal* (17 February 2011), p. A8

Back, Aaron, and Joy Shaw, "China Tightens Property Regulations," *Wall Street Journal* (20 April 2010), p. C11

Bacon, Francis, *Essays* (New York, 1942)

——, *The New Atlantis* (Chicago, IL, 1952)

"Bang, Pop, or Sputter?" *Economist*, CCCXLVII/8067 (9 May 1998), special section, pp. 29–31

Barboza, David, "Chief Regulator of Futures to Step Down," *New York Times* (20 January 1999), p. 1

Barnett, Steven, Alla Myrvoda, and Malhar Nabar, "Sino-Spending," *Finance and Development* (September 2012), pp. 28–30

Barris, Mike, and Karen Richardson, "The Buzz: Buffett Warns Insurance Business May Get Tougher; Berkshire Reports Drop of 18% in Quarterly Net; A Swipe at Lenders," *Wall Street Journal* (1 March 2008), p. B3

Batson, Andrew, "China Housing Market Shows Signs of Life," *Wall Street Journal* (2 April 2009), p. A8

Bekaert, Geert, and Campbell Harvey, "Foreign Speculators and Emerging Equity Markets," *Journal of Finance*, LV/2 (2000), pp. 565–613

Bernanke, Ben, Vincent R. Reinhart, and Brian P. Sack, "Monetary Policy Alternatives at the Zero Bound: An Empirical Assessment," *Brookings Papers on Economic Activity*, XXX/2 (2004), pp. 1–100

Blackstone, Brian, and Charles Forelle, "Stocks Jump on Europe Action," *Wall Street Journal* (7 September 2012), p. A1

Blinder, Alan, "The Case Against the Case Against Discretionary Fiscal Policy," in *The Macroeconomics of Fiscal Policy*, ed. R. W. Kopcke, Geoffrey M. B. Tootell, and Robert K. Triest (Cambridge, MA, 2006), pp. 25–61

Bordo, Michael D., "The Effects of Monetary Change Relative Commodity Prices and the Role of Long-Term Contracts," *Journal of Political Economy*, XXXVIII/6 (1980), pp. 1,088–109

Browne, Frank, and David Cronin, "Commodity Prices, Money and Inflation," Working Paper no. 738, European Central Bank (March 2007)

Buchanan, Susan, "Commodities Report: Coffee Soars as Speculators Buy Back Their Short Positions," *Wall Street Journal* (9 September 2003), p. C18

——, "Commodities Report: Coffee Futures Trickled Down as Speculators Pocket Profits," *Wall Street Journal* (29 January 2004), p. C6

——, "Sugar Futures Climb on buying by Producers and Speculators," *Wall Street Journal* (3 November 2005) p. C4

——, "Sugar Futures Fall as Speculators Exit," *Wall Street Journal* (29 March 2008), p. B6

Bumiller, Elisabeth, "The Japanese Art of Buying," *Washington Post* (17 December 1989), p. A3

Cairnes, John E., *Essays on Political Economy: Theoretical and Applied* [1873] (New York, 1965)

Caldentey, Esteban P., and Matias Vernengo, "How Stimulative Has Fiscal Policy Been Around the World?" *Challenge*, LIII/3 (2010), pp. 6–31

Carroll, Christopher D., Jody R. Overland, and David N. Weil, "Savings and Growth with Habit Formation," *American Economic Review*, XC/3 (2000), pp. 341–55

Catte, P., N. Girouard, R. Price, and C. Andre, "Housing Markets, Wealth, and the Business Cycle," Working Paper 394, Organization for Economic Cooperation and Development (Paris, 2004)

Chao, Loretta, and Jason Leow, "The Home Front: Buying into China's Land Rush," *Wall Street Journal* (18 January 2008), p. W1

Cheng, Jonathan, "Buyers' or Sellers' Market? In China Slump Stokes Activity," *Wall Street Journal* (17 December 2008), p. C9

Colter, Allison Bisbey, "In Housing's Hottest Markets, Builders Tell Speculators to Cool It," *Wall Street Journal* (22 September 2005), p. B9A

Cui, Carolyn, "Speculators Put Jolt into your Cup of Joe: Managed Funds Main Driver of Coffee Prices," *Wall Street Journal* (1 March 2008), p. B1

Cutts, Robert, "Power from the Ground Up: Japan's Land Bubble," *Harvard Business Review*, LXVIII/3 (1990), pp. 164–72

David, Paul, "The Dynamo and the Computer: A Historical Perspective on the Modern Productivity Paradox," *American Economic Association Papers and Proceedings*, LXXX/2 (1990), pp. 355–61

Davies, Michael, and Tim Ng, "The Rise of Sovereign Credit Risk: Implications for Financial Stability," BIS *Quarterly Review* (September 2011), pp. 59–70

"Demolition Time in Japan's Property Market," *Economist*, CCCXVII/7684 (8 December 1990), pp. 83–4

DeSilver, Drew, "$7 Billion Give Shaky WaMu Firmer Footing for Now," *Seattle Times*, serial online (9 April 2008)

Diamond, D. B., and M. J. Lea, "Chapter 5: United Kingdom," *Journal of Housing Research*, III/1 (1994), pp. 115–43

Dolan, Mike, "Analysis—Puzzle over Euro's 'Mysterious' Stability," *Reuters*, www.reuters.com (15 November 2011)

Doughtery, Carter, "Driving Out of Germany, to Pollute Another Day," *New York Times* (7 August 2009), p. 4

Dunbar, Nicholas, "The Great German Structured Credit Experiment," *Risk*, XVII/2 (2004), pp. 16–19

Durant, Will, *The Story of Philosophy* (Garden City, NY, 1927), p. 46

——, *The Lessons of History* (New York, 1968)

Eisenstodt, G., "Wooosh!" *Forbes*, CXLVIII/14 (23 December 1991), pp. 113–14

"Federal Support for Research and Development," Congressional Budget Office, Congress of the United States, pub. no. 2927 (June 2007)

Fidler, Stephen, and David Enrich, "EU Forges Greek Bond Deal—Private Investors To Take 50% Hair Cut," *Wall Street Journal* (27 October 2011), p. A1

Fishman, Robert, "Portugal's Unnecessary Bailout," *New York Times*, op-ed (19 April 2011), p. 24

"Five Years Since the Big Bang," *Economist*, CCCXXI/7730 (26 October 1991), pp. 23–5

Frankel, Jeffrey, "The Effect of Monetary Policy on Real Commodity Prices," *Asset Prices and Monetary Policy*, ed. John Campbell, National Bureau of Economic Research (Chicago, IL, 2008), pp. 291–327

Friedberg, L., "The Impact of Technological Change on Older Workers: Evidence from Data on Computer Use," National Bureau of Economic Research, Working Paper no. 8297 (May 2001)

Friedman, Milton, "The Monetary Theory and Policy of Henry Simons,"

in *The Optimum Quantity of Money and Other Essays*
(Chicago, IL, 1969), pp. 81–93

Fukao, Mitsuhiro, "Japan's Lost Decade and its Financial System,"
*World Economy*, XXVI /3 (2003), pp. 365–84

Fung, Esther, and Andrew Batson, "China's Urban Property Prices Rise,"
*Wall Street Journal* online (14 April 2010)

"Gently May Do It," *Economist*, CCCXVII/7679 (3 November 1990),
pp. 19–21

George, Henry, *Progress and Poverty: An Inquiry into the Cause of Industrial Depressions and of Increase of Want with Increase of Wealth, The
Remedy* (New York, 1935)

Gold, Russell, Neil King Jr., and Ann Davis, "Oil's Rise to 100: Confluence
of Events Drove Crude's Ride from $10.72," *Wall Street Journal*
(3 January 2008), p. A6

Goodhart, C. A., "Price Stability and Financial Fragility," in *The Central
Bank and the Financial System*, ed. C. A. Goodhart (Cambridge, MA,
1995)

Goodison, Sir Nicholas, "How London Can Remain on Top," FT.com,
*Financial Times* (26 October 2006), p. 1

Goos, Maarten, Alan Manning, and Anna Salomons, "The Polarization of
the European Labor Market," *American Economic Review Papers and
Proceedings*, XCIX/2 (2009), pp. 58–63

Graham, Frank D., *Exchange, Prices, and Production in Hyperinflation:
Germany, 1920–1923* (Princeton, NJ, 1930)

Greenspan, Alan, Chairman of the Board of Governors of the Federal
Reserve System, Remarks before the Council on Foreign Relations,
Washington, DC (19 November 2002)

——, Federal Reserve System's Semiannual Monetary Policy Report to
the Congress, testimony presented before the Committee on Banking,
Housing, and Urban Affairs, U.S. Senate, 16 February 2005,
www.federalreserve.gov

——, "Economic Flexibility," Remarks to the National Association of
Business Economics Annual Meeting, Chicago, Illinois (via satellite)
(27 September 2007)

Grossman, Sanford, and Joseph Stiglitz, "On the Impossibility of
Informationally Efficient Markets," *American Economic Review*, LXX/3
(1980), pp. 393–409

Hilsenrath, Jon E., and Patrick Barta, "Treasure Hunt: Amid Low Rates,
Home Prices Rise Across the Global Village; Armed With a 'Saving
Glut,' Investors Chase Returns; Londoners Buy in Bulgaria; Bangkok
Market Is Hot—Again," *Wall Street Journal* (16 June 2005), p. A1

"Hot Topic: The Subprime Market's Rough Road," *Wall Street Journal*
(17 February 2007), p. A7

House of Commons, Treasury Committee, "Banking Crisis: Dealing with the Failure of UK Banks," HC416 (London, May 2009)

Hudson, Michael, "Grading Bonds on Inverted Curve," *Wall Street Journal* (8 January 2007), p. C1

Hughes, Chris, "Confidence in Northern Rock Collapses," FT.com, *Financial Times* (14 September 2007)

Iacoviello, M. and R. Minett, "Financial Liberalization and the Sensitivity of House Prices to Monetary Policy: Theory and Evidence," *Manchester School*, LXXI /1 (2003), pp. 20–34

"Income the Waves," *Economist*, CCCLXXV/8431 (18 June 2005), pp. 66–8

International Monetary Fund, *Global Financial Stability Report: Durable Financial Stability—Getting There from Here* (Washington, DC, April 2011)

International Monetary Fund, "Chapter 2: When Bubbles Burst," *World Economic Outlook* (April 2003)

International Monetary Fund, "Chapter 3: Is Inflation Back? Commodity Prices and Inflation," *World Economic Outlook* (October 2008)

Ip, Greg, "Greenspan Again Plays Down Fear Of Housing Bubble," *Wall Street Journal* (20 October 2004), p. A2

——, "Greenspan Says U.S. Deflation Threat is Small—Potential Harm is Serious so Central Bank Might Act to Minimize the Jeopardy," *Wall Street Journal* (22 May 2003), p. A2

——, and G. Thomas Sims, "U.S. and Europe Signal That Rates May be Cut Soon—Greenspan and Duisenberg Hope to Boost Economies, Avert Threat of Deflation," *Wall Street Journal* (4 June 2003), p. A1

Izzo, Phil, "U.S. News: Bubble Isn't Big Factor in Inflation," *Wall Street Journal* (9 May 2008), p. A2

Jain, Pankaj, "Financial Market Design and the Equity Premium: Electronic Versus Floor Trading," *Journal of Finance*, LX/6 (2005), pp. 2,955–85

Jin, Ye, Hongbing Li, and Binzhen Wu, "Income Inequality, Consumption, and Social-status Seeking," *Journal of Comparative Economics*, XXXIX/2 (2011), pp. 191–204

Keynes, John M., *The Economic Consequence of Peace* (New York, 1920)

——, "Economic Possibilities for Our Grandchildren," in *Essays in Persuasion* (London, 1933), pp. 358–73

Kilbinger, Sara Seddon, "India Faces Housing Slowdown," *Wall Street Journal* (20 February 2008), p. B7

Kopecki, Dawn, and Shannon D. Harrington, "Banning 'Naked' Default Swaps May Raise Corporate Funding Cost," *Bloomberg News* (24 July 2009)

Kuijs, Louis, "How Will China's Saving-Investment Evolve," World Bank Policy Research Paper, Working Paper no. 3958, http://papers.ssrn.com/sol3 (2006)

Labaton, Stephen, "S.E.C. Concedes Oversight Flaws Fueled Collapse," *New York Times* (27 September 2008), p. 1

——, "Agency's '04 Rule Let Banks Pile Up New Debt," *New York Times* (3 October 2008), p. 1

"Leaders: Back from the Dead; Japanese Banks," *Economist*, CCCXCVIII/8722 (26 February 2011), p. 13

Lerner, Abba, *The Economics of Control* (New York, 1944)

Link, Arthur, ed., *The Papers of Woodrow Wilson*, vol. VI (Princeton, NJ, 1969)

McMullen, Troy, "The Home Front: Private Properties," *Wall Street Journal* (4 March 2005), p. W10

Marx, Karl, and Friedrich Engels, *Manifesto of the Communist Party* [1848] (Chicago, IL, 1952)

Meyer, Gregory, "Crude Stocks Above $100 on Speculators' Activity," *Wall Street Journal* (21 February 2008), p. C4

——, "'The Mother of All Bubbles'? Oil's Record Run Baffles Bears," *Wall Street Journal* (21 February 2008), p. C4

Michaels, Guy, Ashwini Natraj, and John Van Reenen, "Has ICT Polarized Skill Demand from Eleven Countries over 25 years," National Bureau of Economic Research, Working Paper no. 16138 (June 2010)

Mitchell, Donald, "A Note on Rising Food Prices," Policy Research Working Paper 4682, The World Bank Development Prospects Group (July 2008)

Mollenkamp, Carrick, Alistair MacDonald, and Joellen Perry, "A UK Lender is Latest to Join Mortgage Crisis," *Wall Street Journal* (15 September 2007), p. B1

Montesquieu, Charles de Secondat, Baron de, *The Spirit of Laws* [1748], trans. Thomas Nugent (Chicago, IL, 1952)

Morrissey, Janet, "Housing Bubble Is Seen by Lenders," *Wall Street Journal* (5 April 2006), p. B4

Nixon, Simon, "Irish Eyes Are Watering Over Banks," *Wall Street Journal* (1 October 2010), p. C14

Nocera, Joe, "Poking Holes in a Theory on Markets," *New York Times* (5 June 2009), p. 1

Ohmae, Kenichi, "Business Forum: Tokyo's Soaring Property Prices: If They Fall, So Will Our Stock Markets," *New York Times* (11 October 1987), p. 3

Opdyke, Jeff D., "Are You Ready for Deflation?" *Wall Street Journal* (5 June 2003), p. D1

Organization for Economic Cooperation and Development, OECD *Economic Surveys: 2005* (June 2005)

Paletta, Damian, and David Enrich, "Crisis Deepens as Big Bank Fails,

IndyMac Seized in Largest Bust in Two Decades," *Wall Street Journal* (12 July 2008), p. A1

Patterson, Scott, and Jamila Trindle, "CFTC Raises Bar on Betting," *Wall Street Journal* (19 October 2011), p. C3

"Pope Benedict XVI Denounces Commodities Speculation, Demand Global Response," *Huffington Post* (1 July 2011)

Power, Helen, "Peter Cummings Stayed Loyal and Brave at the Wrong Time," *Times* (13 December 2008)

Prasad, Eswar, and Isaac Sorkin, "Assessing the G-20 Stimulus Plans: A Deeper Look," Brooking Institution, www.brookings.edu (March 2009)

Pulliam, Susan, Kate Kelly, and Carrick Mollenkamp, "Hedge Funds Pound Euro—Traders Pile On, Using Multiple Big Bets Greek Crisis Will Push Currency Lower," *Wall Street Journal* (25 February 2010), p. A1

Range, Jackie, "Real-Estate Finance: Indian Builders Lower Sights— 'Affordable,' Not Luxury, Is New Watchword in Housing," *Wall Street Journal* (18 March 2009), p. C11

Reinhart, Carmen, and Kenneth S. Rogoff, "From Financial Crisis to Debt Crisis," *American Economic Review*, C1/5 ( 2011), pp. 1,676–706

Renaud, Bertrand, and Kim Khung-Hwan, "The Global Housing Price Boom and Its Aftermath," *Housing Finance International* (December 2007), pp. 3–15

Rich, Motoko, "Middleman Now Rich Man in Real Estate Boon," *New York Times* (31 May 2005), p. 1

Riley, Clint, "Investors' Puzzle: Banks and the Flat Yield Curve," *Wall Street Journal* (30 January 2006), p. C1

Roche, Dick, "Did Ireland Need a Bailout? One Year Ago This Week, Dublin's Finances were being Repaired and the Economy was Recovering. What Went Wrong?" *Wall Street Journal* online (23 November 2011)

Rogoff, Kenneth, "Globalization and Global Disinflation," paper prepared for the Federal Reserve Bank of Kansas City Conference, Jackson Hole, WY, www.imf.org (29 August 2003)

Rosegrant, M. W., *Biofuels and Grain Prices: Impacts and Policy Responses*, testimony for the U.S. Senate Committee on Homeland Security and Governmental Affairs, Washington, DC (7 May 2008)

Rostow, W. W., *The World Economy: History and Prospect* (Austin, TX, 1978)

Rothbard, Murray, "Concepts of the Role of the Intellectual in Social Change Toward Laissez Faire," *Journal of Libertarian Studies*, IX/2 (1990), pp. 43–67

Salisbury, Ian, "Investing in Funds: A Monthly Analysis,"

*Wall Street Journal* (5 May 2008), p. R1

Saraf, Devita, and Prathima Manohar, "India's Real Estate Boom is on Shaky Ground," *Wall Street Journal* online (7 March 2010)

Schwartz, Nelson, and Julie Creswell, "Who Created this Monster?" *New York Times* (23 March 2008), p. 1

Sellen, Tom, "Sugar Prices Hit Contract Highs as Speculators Buy," *Wall Street Journal*, (16 November 2005), p. C4

Shah, Ajay, and Ila Paatnaik, "India's Financial Globalization," IMF Working Paper WP/11/7, Washington, DC (2011)

Shroeder, Michael, "CFTC Chairwoman Won't Halt Study of OTC Derivatives Rules," *Wall Street Journal* (11 June 1998), p. C1

——, "CFTC Chairman Seeks to Deregulate Trading," *Wall Street Journal* (29 October 1999), p. 1

——, "Mortgage Lenders Dismiss Concerns Over Risky Loans," *Wall Street Journal* (30 March 2006), p. D2

Simon, Ruth, "Teaser Rates on Mortgages Approach 0%," *Wall Street Journal* (15 February 2005), p. D1

——, "New Type of Mortgage Surges in Popularity," *Wall Street Journal* (19 April 2005), p. D1

——, "Mortgage Lenders Loosen Standards," *Wall Street Journal* (26 July 2005), p. D1

——, "Lenders Get Tougher," *Wall Street Journal* (15 May 2007), p. D1

Sims, G. Thomas, "Housing Prices in Euro Zone Worry the ECB," *Wall Street Journal* (4 February 2005), p. A7

Solow, Robert, "We'd Better Watch Out", *New York Times Book Review* (12 July 1987), p. 36

Spence, John, "A Real Growth Play: Agricultural ETF's," *Wall Street Journal* (15 April 2008), p. C13

Statistics Bureau, Director-General for Policy Planning of Japan, Tokyo, Japan, www.stat.go.jp, accessed 7 November 2012

Sterngold, James, "The Big Bang that Never Was," *New York Times* (16 May 1993), p. 1

Stewart, Jim, "Shadow Regulation and the Shadow Banking System," *Tax Justice Focus*, IV/2 (2008), pp. 1–3

Story, Louise, and Gretchen Morgenson, "S.E.C. Accuses Goldman of Fraud in Housing Deal," *New York Times* (17 April 2010), p. 1

——, Landon Thomas Jr, and Nelson D. Schwartz, "Wall Street Helped Mask Debt Fueling Europe's Crisis," *New York Times* (14 February 2010), p. A1

Sugden, Craig, "Responding to High Commodity Prices," *Asian Pacific Economic Literature*, XXIII/1 (2009), pp. 79–105

Takeda, Masahiko, and Philip Turner, "The Liberalization of Japan's Financial Markets: Some Major Themes," Bank for International

Settlements BIS Economic Papers, no. 34 (1992)

Talley, Karen, "S&P Will Launch Indexes to Track Housing Prices," *Wall Street Journal* (23 March 2006), p. D2

"The Cracks Spread and Widen; the Euro Zone's Debt Crisis," *Economist*, CCCXCV/8680 (1 May 2010), p. 63

Truell, Peter, and Matthew Winkler, "UK Set Today For 'Big Bang' Amid Questions: Rocky Start Seen as London Moves Toward Uniting Local, Foreign Markets," *Wall Street Journal* (27 October 1986), p. 1

Wei, Shang-Jin, and Xiaobo Zhang, "The Competitive Savings Motive: Evidence from Rising Sex Ratios and Savings Rates in China," *Journal of Political Economy*, CXIX/3 (2011), pp. 511–64

Wesbury, Brian S., "Mr. Greenspan's Cappuccino," *Wall Street Journal* (31 May 2005), p. A2

Wessel, David, "Capital: The Fed Starts to Show Concern at Signs of Bubble in Housing," *Wall Street Journal* (19 May 2005), p. A1

Wolff, Edward, "Computerization and Rising Unemployment Duration," *Eastern Economic Journal*, XXXI/4 (2005), pp. 507–36

Wood, Christopher, "Enduring Myth," *Economist*, CCCXVII/7684 (8 December 1990), pp. 9–15

World Bank, *Global Economic Prospects—Commodities at the Crossroads* (Washington, DC, 2008)

# ACKNOWLEDGMENTS

The contents of this book are considerably enriched by conversations with my son, Kris Allen, who follows economic and financial news daily, and keeps his father inspired to continue the study of economics. Also, researching this book substantially benefited from the excellent resources available through Lamar University's Mary and John Gray Library.

# INDEX